THE BURGLAR'S DOG

THE BURGLAR'S DOG

ALTERNATIVE GUIDE TO DRINKING IN NEWCASTLE UPON TYNE

by Mark Jones

tonto press

www.tontopress.com
www.theburglarsdog.co.uk

ISBN 0-9552183-4-9
978-0-9552183-4-7

A catalogue record for this book is available from the
British Library

Cover illustration by Garen Ewing
Interior images by Mark Jones

Based on the website www.theburglarsdog.co.uk

The opinions expressed in this book are those of the author
and do not necessarily reflect the views of the publisher

Printed & bound in Great Britain by Cox & Wyman Ltd

Tonto Press
Blaydon on Tyne
United Kingdom
www.tontopress.com

Thanks

This book is indebted to Burglar's Dog co-founder John Egdell. Website designer, technical advisor, unstoppable publicity machine; he is all of these things and more, and his presence rifts through these pages like last night's kebab.

Special love and thanks are long overdue to Karen Benfold, without whose patience, understanding, dedication and extra long lie-ins, none of this bellyaching would ever have been written up.

Thanks also to Paul Brown and Stuart Wheatman at Tonto Press, and to the following: Parveen Ali, Naveed Aslam, Rachel Baxter, Lorna Bell, Ian Bell, John Deary, Kathleen Devlin, Anita Duffy, Michael Egdell, Julia Graham, John Gray, James Grey, Anna Griffin, Darren Hubbard, Beverly Hurst, Marie Jones, Jonathan Linklater, Wayne Mason, Kelly Mounsey, Ray Nesbitt, Paddy Parker, Laura Peart, Anne Potter, Jennie Redmond, Paul Sharkey, Joanne Stuart, Richard Warren, Allan Weir, and to everyone who has contributed to The Burglar's Dog website over the years.

The Burglar's Dog is based on an original swift half by Jones and Egdell.

Contents

Introduction

Newcastle upon Tyne is regularly voted as the best place in the country for a night out. With its world-famous Bigg Market, its plethora of relaxed lounge bars and its thriving gay scene, Newcastle guarantees a warm welcome for all and a tremendous evening's entertainment. There's a drinking venue to suit every taste, from boisterous and fun-loving, to quiet and contemplative and, young or old, large or small, you're certain to have the time of your life. Open any guide to Britain and you'll see it there at the top of the page: Newcastle is the place to be.

Cobblers. Why? Because – frankly that whole idea is a sham. It's a clichéd, cynical, tourist board lie, like Paris as a city of romance, or the Golden Viennese Heart. We've all been sneered at by the surly French, and you need no more than half an hour in Vienna to fully understand how Hitler could only have been Austrian. But as long as 'Newcastle! Party City!' looks good on paper the media will churn it out and stupid people will swallow it. Aye, Newcastle is a party city, but it's a party that's been gatecrashed by absolute idiots; someone's puking in your fishtank, there's a couple fornicating on your kitchen sink, and what that dirty beggar is doing upstairs with your mother's knicker drawer you really don't want to know. People flock to Newcastle for one reason, and one reason only: they think that if Bigg Market lasses are daft enough to wear next to nothing when it's minus five then they're daft enough to chew on their dirty cocks if they tell them it's a Peperami. And don't try to tell me otherwise. Are our pubs as they stand really part of a great Geordie tradition? Are our tacky chain bars so much better than the tacky chain bars elsewhere? Like hell are they. It's the dubious promise of a quick scuttle down an alleyway that hauls in the tourists, and that's crystal clear.

Have you ever wondered exactly why every publication from every other city in the country is so keen to promote Newcastle's drinking circuits above their own bars and pubs? It's because they want you, you drunken oaf, to come and wreck our city with your appalling behaviour and leave their carefully tended Britain in Bloom town squares in one piece. Did you know that Newcastle's council has the largest budget in the European Union for street cleaning services? No, of course you didn't, because it's not true. But that doesn't matter. The facts about drinking in Newcastle are really quite simple: you're going to get served swill, you're going to be soundly ripped off and, at the end of the night, someone is going to try to kick your teeth out.

The Burglar's Dog aims to stick a whopping great monkey wrench in the works. We refuse to perpetuate the myth of the happy, smiling city, and when someone tells us what a snook is, you can be sure we'll be cocking it. If you're expecting to read things like, 'The walls are blue and the carpet is brown and a DJ spins most nights. Happy hours 5-8', then this probably isn't the book for you. The Burglar's Dog has no time for any of that nonsense. There will be no glossy featurettes and no eight-page spreads of underdressed inebriates pulling stupid faces.

We will simply say it as we see it. The fun pubs are our worst nightmare, the student hovels make us wince, and those indistinguishable, extortionate luxebars for berks with more vanity products than IQ points are going to get what's coming to them. We are pig-sick of reading the same stock phrases pulled from the ridiculous hat of style-mag journalism, and we won't be using any of that guff in our reviews. Chilled, smooth, designer, swanky, sumptuous; utter rot, all of it. We will not try to convince you that it's somehow chic to dribble your overpriced pint onto laminate flooring, no matter what those liars insist. We will not attempt to sell you mediocrity packaged as sophistication. And we fully understand how disappointed you're going to be when you realise that having a black napkin under your drink doesn't necessarily turn you into a VIP.

I can hear what you're saying. What about the bars themselves? Won't they be a tad perturbed by your irascible comments? It makes absolutely no difference to them, believe us. They'll still be packed to the rafters every night regardless of whatever cantankerous pasting this book has dished out, and I'm sure they could give a splattery cack about what some sanctimonious old bastard thinks about their establishments. Besides, there is no favouritism at The Burglar's Dog. None of the bars reviewed in this book have been singled out for abuse, so it's no good them getting the lip on because we've insulted their business; we've taken extra care and attention to slag off the whole bloody lot of them. It's a level playing field. If we've hammered one, then we've hammered its competitors, too. We'd like to make that abundantly clear.

You're probably expecting a disclaimer somewhere down the line, and this is it. Obviously we didn't spend-all-night-every-night for a week in each of Newcastle's pubs to give a balanced view: objectivity is someone else's job. Nor did we have a drink in every bar the day before this book was sent to the printers, hurriedly typing up the reviews through a 140-pint hangover to meet the deadline. With the best will in the world and even with the lightning turnaround of modern publishing, things will have changed, usually and deliberately for the worse. This won't be here, that won't be there, and they'll have shifted that other thing out from behind the piano. But the atmosphere, the ethos and, most importantly, the people will never change. You still won't be able to get past the pinstriped, braying buffoon at the bar, and that twitching bag of bones in the fake sports gear will still be by the bandit. She'll still be looking at you like you're dirt, and he'll still be waiting outside to glass you.

But don't let us put you off. Just because we hate almost every pub in Newcastle and are all too aware that our tolerance of the rest is based on tearful nostalgia for an age that never existed; just because we have a range of personal issues that would have Sigmund Freud crying off with stress; and just because, clearly, there is something wrong with us, there's no reason why YOU shouldn't have the wondrous time that seems to pass us by every weekend. And every working day. And every Bank Holiday Monday.

Our reviews are all just opinion and observation. And stuff we've made up. In sticking our jaundiced heads above the parapet, we've opened ourselves to just as much ridicule as the bars we've lampooned. And ask yourself this: who is the bigger fool? The penniless critic or the publican with the yacht?

We like to think you'll find something you recognise in our interminable rants, even if it's only a crudely sketched caricature of yourself. We also hope you'll find some of this stuff amusing, as one man's heartbreak is another man's comedy hour. And we know all there is to know about heartbreak.

But we think it's only fair to warn you before you start reading: there might be one or two cuss words.

1

Quayside

'The rejuvenated Quayside is the flagship of the neighbouring areas of Newcastle and Gateshead. With a wealth of historical buildings, spectacular views, and the river's famous old crossings contrasting with the mechanical and design marvel of the "blinking eye" Millennium Bridge, this is a place to make any local proud. The redevelopment of this once run-down area has seen the emergence of the magnificent Sage building and the nearby Baltic gallery for contemporary art, plus a whole host of restaurants and cafes.' – Norman Undercroft, Historian.

Akenside Traders
The Side, NE1 1PQ
'It's really packed, so it must be good'

Every single office night out from my work for the last 2,000 years has followed the same depressing route. Bar 42, The Lodge, The Akenside and Buffalo Joe's. Honestly. And since I detest every one of my colleagues, their friends and all members of their families past, present and future, my appearance record makes Michael Owen look like an ever-present, so it'd be fairly safe to say that the Akenside is not one of my favourite haunts. Oh, I dunno, call me a dripping wet blart if you like, but I do quite like being able to breathe when I'm supping my pint. The thing about this place is that people, being naturally as thick as the thickest pig's thickest shit, see it from the outside and think, 'It's really packed, so it must be good', but fail to understand exactly why there's a queue six deep all the way along the bar: because the service is fucking terrible. Me, I just take one look at the number of parched, angry punters, desperately waving tenners and getting redder and redder in the face, and head straight back down to the door. I'm not alone. There's something I've noticed in the distant past, standing alongside idiot middle management while they try to pull rank with the doormen about the age of the office junior. (You can call that a show of solidarity; I call it 'I'm not fucking going in there if she's getting out of it.') And what I've noticed is this: imagine you're plodging on the beach at Whitley Bay, and you spy a used Durex floating on the brine. The waves bring it in, and the waves take it back out, but even if you splash further along the sand, the fucker keeps coming at you. No, it won't bite you or give you a jellyfish sting, but it's still deeply unpleasant and you'd prefer if it kept the hell away from you. In their tides of exasperation and departure, each of the Akenside's customers is that rubber johnny. Of course, abusing the flotsam and jetsam of the clientele is just a way of getting me off the hook when it comes to describing the mass of idiots at the bar, although plankton is a word that springs to mind. With this being a pub review book, I'd imagine you're expecting to find a comprehensive description of the décor at some point. It isn't going to happen, I'm afraid, but – over the crush and buried behind the promotions posters – I think I could make out a vague shipping theme, hence the tiresome nautical references in this piece. I'm going to say it straight: I hate this place and everything it represents. I've got nothing but bad memories of terrible nights out amongst imbeciles and of ricking my ankle on those stupid fucking steps. And if you've ever seen me here, looking close to suicide, I can guarantee I was either pissed senseless, or at knifepoint. Or both.

For: Cheap beer and plenty of frottage potential.
Against: Doesn't matter where you stand, there's always someone grunting at you to move.

*I want to get this out of the way as soon as possible, even if the
Akenside doesn't serve it: how is Foster's 'head tap' legal? How
come trading standards haven't jumped on their case yet? How
can they get away with saying, 'Well, your pint's shite and we're
sorry about that but, to make you think you're getting a better
quality product, we're gonna stick this dollop of foam on the top
so it looks more authentic'? It's criminal, it really is.*

Blue
Mansion House Chambers, Quayside, NE1 3RE
'A particularly savage divorce'

Formerly Julies 2 night club - the one that got bollocked for sticking an ugly sign on an historical Quayside building - this place has
reopened with longer hours and more emphasis on the bar side of
things while still keeping the club angle for later on. Don't ask
me for a review of the club part; I'm too old to bother, I refuse
to embarrass anyone with my dancing, and - as all my previous
forays into clubbing have ended in tears - it's best for all concerned if I avoid it altogether. Consequently, I can't tell you anything about whether the much-rumoured presence of Premiership
footballers in that bit is actually true. What I can say is that, up
to about nine bells of an evening, the bar part is absolutely
swarming with middle-aged blokes in pastel shirts, all of them
looking pained and defeated and clearly coming to terms with a
particularly savage divorce. I hope they're not looking for love in
here, since, judging by the clip of the women we saw sprawled
around, they'd just be making the same, stupid, yes-dear mistakes as they did last time. And what the fuck are those old boil-
ers doing, anyway? Sit up straight, you lazy, fat puddings. See
when travel companies buy buses with seats facing each other,
yet are surprised when people put their damned feet all over the

upholstery? The seating layout in the window in Blue is going to leave them wondering how all their lovely - blue - stools are covered in mud and chewing gum and gravel and dog shit at the end of the night. They'll learn. Switching seats to the VIP / champagne area - where people with no grasp of reality can pay £205 for a bottle of Cristal fizzy wine - I can see the reflections in the mirrored bar of a carpet more suited to covering a corpse sliding down a quarry side, and the spotlit chandelier that keeps changing colour, from blue to blue, and then all the way back to blue again. The wallpaper is black and flowery, the booths red and leathery, the seating around the white plastic tables is fuck-knows-what-ery, and it's all starting to hurt my eyes. I am not having a good time. I doubt whether I'll ever set foot in here again, but I'll tell you this: it's not because of the people, the staff or the atmosphere. It's not even because of the prices. My problem is the decor. I've seen it all before, and I can carbon date it. I want to state this quite clearly here: I've lived through one 1980s already. And it was fucking shite.

For: The shining silver bazaar curtain at the back...
Against: ...hides the bogs, which, in the age of the designer toilet installation, looked to me just like a swimming pool changing room, complete with wall-to-wall foot pool. I'm going to take it as read that something was bust in there, unless getting pissy water all over your best kecks is some sort of new Quayside trend.

It's one thing second guessing your target customers - we do it often enough with the sweary cobblers we bung together for our punters - but a bar pandering to the extent that they've called a cocktail a 'Newcastle United' is just plain tragic.

Bob Trollop

Sandhill, NE1 1PG
'Everyone knows that beagles are the heavy smokers'

'Vegetarian Pub of the Year', says the sign on the window. Fine, I've got no problem with that, but explain this to me: on the wall in here they've got a picture of a terrier smoking a pipe, so do you think they're saying it's alright to leave the poor animals riddled with lung cancer as long as you don't actually eat them? Besides, they're miles off the mark with that terrier: everyone knows that beagles are the heavy smokers. The main theme of Bob Trollop seems to be the ramshackle 19th Century boozer experience, and they've done it pretty well, even if they did have a head start in this row of National Trust 'keep it tatty, the tourists love it' buildings. The place has low-beamed ceilings that look like they're falling apart and is stuffed with chandeliers, horse brass and knackered old clocks, setting it at least an inch apart from the designer-scruffiness of the fake-Irish bars in town. On top of that, the beaten-copper tables and rickety chairs seem to have been just thrown together instead of picked from a catalogue, although I'm a little concerned about the arse-ache seating: had haemorrhoids not been invented in 1862? The pub is split into two areas with the bar in between and you need to go out into the alleyway and try not to fall over the milk churns if you want to change rooms. The bit at the front has huge windows looking over the Guild Hall, Tyne Bridge and general Quayside carnage, but that unfortunately means that you'll have to put up with pissed-up passers-by laughing at your couscous and courgette casserole if you're stuffing your face, while the back room is more dark and depressing. One thing to watch, though, is that Bob Trollop shares its bogs with the Red House next door, so try to remember which way you went after you've emptied your bladder, or you'll end up red-faced and bewildered and in the wrong pub. I've done it dozens of times and I'm warning you out of genuine love and affection. So, Bob Trollop, then. Nowt remarkable overall, but nothing to start stamping my booties about. Depends what you're after. If you fancy slumming it with the beards and cardigans and deniers of the basic realities of the food chain, then get in early on, but if you think vegetarians are deviants who should be beaten and starved and tortured with sausage butties, go a bit later when the more typical Quayside crowd arrives.

For: The beer and food in here are excellent. No, really.
Against: The back room stunk of puke on our visit. Also: no, really.

Not that you'd know it from my ashen face, my appalling mood swings, my disciplinable sickness record and my pan-blocking turds, but I'm a vegetarian too. Twelve whole years without animal flesh passing my lips. And, FUCK ME, I'm hungry. I could eat a scabby horse and go back for seconds.

Bonded Warehouse
9-17 Broad Chare, NE1 3DQ
'A worthwhile tourist trip'

Located in an old Quayside building, the Bonded Warehouse has miraculously managed to make genuine historical detail look like a tacky theme bar. With stone walls and an old wooden floor, and with the weight of tradition behind it, this place just couldn't fail, yet has still pulled off a spectacular disaster. Blame it on the pictures and signs picked at random from the 'almost authentic' page in the catalogue; point to the neglect that's left their carpeted area looking like fresh tarmac; pin it on the punters if you like, but the Bonded Warehouse is - even for the Quayside - one to avoid. A crash-landing strip for whatever that bloody hotel up the road is called, this bar is a starting point for visitors to the city whose idea of a worthwhile tourist trip is to fall out of their rooms, get absolutely hammered in the first pub they come across, bellow about how they plan to go 'fucking mental, let's go fucking mental, la-la-la' before passing out and pissing their pants. There's a stag party sprawled in the window, a student bickerfest up by the pool table and, next to me at the bar, some thick pig in devil's horns is telling her equally porcine mate how lovely James Blunt's voice is. That's not a voice, you dumb floozy; it's the sound of someone wiping a bogey down your double-glazing. What the hell am I doing here? My pint has a head like Angel Delight, my peanuts are stale and everywhere I look there's a berk thumping a table. My migraine's kicking in, my teeth are clenched and my rage is bursting through. And this is at six bells on a Saturday evening; what am I going to be like in an hour when the DJ's pumping and the joint is jumping? They're what? They're frigging searchlights? That's it, I'm off.

For: Not long before the review visit, the Bonded Warehouse caught fire and was subsequently deemed fit only for demolition. I was overjoyed...

Against: ...until I found out they meant the actual Bonded Warehouse at the other end of the Quayside, and not this crappy bar of the same name.

High on the wall as you first go in - face the bar and look up and left - is by far the worst picture of Alan Shearer I've ever seen, and I'm including the works of the under-fives here. Imagine the way he'd look after a hemiplegic stroke and you'd be almost there. What the fuck did he do to deserve that?

Buffalo Joe's

Pipewellgate, Gateshead, NE8 2BJ
'Oozing post-coitally'

Pornography's a great leveller. No matter what the personality, background or interests of the wide-eyed adult industry starlet, each one will end up in exactly the same position: butt naked, on her knees, giving an inane, thumbs-up grin to the camera, with semen dripping off her chin. And while not everyone is lucky enough to have their back doors kicked in for money and the evidence posted on the internet, Buffalo Joe's provides a similar yet only slightly less degrading experience for Newcastle's young ladies. Every giggling wench with an eye for 'fun' and a clutch bag full of fivers finishes the night in here, caged and humiliated and wearing a fucking sparkly pink cowboy hat. Mandatory 'mystery' destination on every Comic Sans, clip-art-champagne-bottle office night out poster ('10.30pm - 2.00am Wherever???!!'), Buffalo Joe's has long been one of the most depressing bars in what the geniuses at the neighbouring councils would like you to call NewcastleGateshead, and its mornings-after the prime instigator of calls to the Samaritans. See it for yourself. Witness gang after gang of frustrated fools oozing post-coitally along the Quayside to this 'amazing Western fun theme bar' to piss the pittance they've earned over a hot photocopier up the nearest fake-saloon wall. See barmen dressed as Native Americans in lieu of getting a fucking proper job, groping soggy-knickered puddings in the cage until they're splashing around in batter. Watch the nightly snake pit of writhing, bottle clutching idiots chucking themselves around to a filling-loosening kick drum and muse on how much of a pity it is that we - and not Hitler - won the bloody war. Take it from me; the hanged man at the top of the stairs got the best deal. In his place I'd have run to the scaffold and thrown my head in the noose, anything to get away from this awful, awful bar. And if I ever hear that you've bought one of those stupid bastard hats, I'm going to punch you squarely in the face until my knuckles break. Have a nice day, y'all.

For: It's cruel and inhumane, but you can always join in the pointing and laughing and the poking with sticks by clicking on the image gallery on www.buffalojoes.co.uk.
Against: I hate people being young. I hate people going out. I hate people getting drunk. And I hate people having a good time. There: I've said it.

And while I'm on the subject of pornography, I'd like to ask this: how is it that there are thousands upon thousands of people only too eager to perform naked for goggle-eyed masturbators, yet there's a maximum of three people doing the voiceovers for all porn films ever? Surely it's not that bad a job. I used to work for

*a well-known utility company - whose name I won't mention be-
cause the cunts aren't getting any free publicity out of me - and
my daily routine consisted of telling people 'Hello? No, sorry,
that's British Gas. Goodbye.' I'd have gladly chucked that in to
read out a script saying 'Fuck yeah! Fuck yeah! Oh fuck yeah! It's
so good! Fuck yeah!' for eight hours a day. I could do it in German, too. No problem.*

Casa

58 Sandhill, NE1 3RG
'An inch deep in birdshit'

Back when we hadn't strayed much from the old man's dives and
the indie rock bars we were genuinely amazed to find that a pub
could have 'just off-white or oh-so-tastefully-cool blue walls,
blonde wood furniture and stripped flooring', and were flabber-
gasted that they could charge the earth for normal brand lager.
What a bunch of crackpots we must have been. Now, years later,
we're a lot wiser, a lot more cynical and a hell of a lot skinter. It
is, to put it bluntly, a parcel of poop. The laminate flooring is
looking battered, the pastel walls sickly, the staff rightly pissed
off, and the protruding glass box at the back - the one with the
views along the river - is an inch deep in bird shit. There's a
crestfallen look about the place, yet they're still charging the
same ludicrous prices, clearly hoping that the fickleness of fashion will put them back at the top of the league one day. No
chance. Even the fancy-Dan food seems to have disappeared,
along with any sort of charm, not to mention most of the customers. Yeah, we know they've changed the original artworks on the
walls and had the decorators in a couple of times, but it still just
looks like some pretentious home interior from a Sunday supple-
ment, and not somewhere anyone would actually want to spend a
great deal of time. To be honest, we thought - judging from the
fact that the place was in darkness at eight bells on a Friday night
- that it'd gone bust or was closed for refurbishment, and we only
nipped in for a swift one a week later to check. And apart from us

and some old codger with Alzheimer's, the only other punters in the entire bar were some bellowing moose and her co-cacklers on a hen night, and they'd clearly have sat in a bucket of shite as long as the doorman had let them all in it without a fight. What do we normally put at the end of reviews like this? Avoid? We see you already have.

For: Still happy with the greenhouse effect on a sunny afternoon.
Against: When it finally goes tits up through neglect, we'll have to trudge down here and review its replacement.

Original artwork, though. Pile of wank, most of it. And I used to be its biggest fan until the following happened: when I was about to be made redundant from my last job, I got a part-time position at a well-known art and craft retailer to make ends meet. Miserable fuckers the lot of them, right from day one, with their hand-made this and their limited edition that. So, to take away some of the pain of the daily grind, I made some stickers for their six quid wedding cards, the ones with the little cellophane wrappers that stop the public from getting their grubby fingers all over the bits of tissue and bent fuse wire. You know what the stickers said? 'The message inside this card reads: Please Don't Breed.' And you know what they did? They fucking sacked me. On the spot. Absolutely astonishing.

Chase
10-15 Sandhill, NE1 3JE
'Hitler's mother behind the counter'

'Turn of the century' is a phrase that used to imply a certain charm when it came to pubs. If pushed, I tend to think of some dainty Parisian cafe bar, possibly in the Marais, with handwritten signs, a clanking till, and maybe Hitler's mother behind the counter. However, with the change from 1900s to 2000s, the fin de the last fucking siècle produced pubs that look just like Chase. Once described by some idiot on a website - well, me - as a pretty good bar, Chase is now looking battered, chipped, scuffed and bruised, and all the stuff that gave it a bunk-up above the crowds has disappeared; the fish tanks on the way to the toilets have gone, and once you get there the barbed wire bog seats have also vanished. In our original website review for Chase we told the (true) tale of how legendary DJ Carl Cox was once ordered outside on pain of a kicking by the hardest man in Gateshead, partly for acting the champagne superstar, but mainly for trying to cop off with the bloke's girlfriend. That's not the sort of thing you'd witness now: not the pointing and shoving, but the celebrity presence. Let's face it; you'd be pushed to even see a Big Brother evictee in here these days. What you will see - as you will in every single Quayside bar on every single weekend - is a raging tidal flow of hen and stag parties, depositing broken glass and plucked feathers on their way out. Oh man, I really used to like this place, back in the days when it first opened and was crawling with surreally beautiful minxes who wouldn't so much as hockle on this fat, ugly bastard for less than a rollover jackpot. And sitting here years later, I can't even joyously make sarcastic mental notes for later use, since the very thing I hoped they'd ditch - the seating that looks like a lilo but is as comfortable as a cast iron radiator - is the one item they've seen fit to keep. Very disappointing.

For: The enclosed outdoor terrace with the patio heaters; global warming be damned.
Against: Coming in through the back way, from the eastern end of the Quayside, you have to avoid all the seagull shite under the Tyne Bridge. Those beaky bastards have no shame.

Call it coincidence if you like, but I've had more mentalist episodes after drinking in Chase than in anywhere else in town. Last time, I got home very drunk and even more maudlin after some trivial misunderstanding, and I decided to sulk away my worries with some late-night melancholy music. Stumbling around in the dark, I stuck the headphones on and sat down with a whisky and the remote control. Thing is, I couldn't for the life of me work out why the music sounded so muffled no matter how much I pissed about with the settings, and it was only when I realised that the extra percussion was the neighbours braying on the windows that I understood what I'd done. Turns out that, instead of the headphone jack, I'd somehow managed to plug my shoelaces into the stereo. I'll be laying off the cocktails in future, I think.

The Cooperage

32 The Close, NE1 3RQ
'Salvaged from a shipwreck'

Looking for some quality beer in a ramshackle 17th Century alehouse, and one that's haunted to boot? The Cooperage is the place to go. Or at least it used to be. With its tumbledown tilt and its splintered exterior, it's long been a wonder how the place is still standing. I read many years ago on a sign in the pub that the timbers used to build the Cooperage were salvaged from a shipwreck, and that was certainly true of most of the grizzled old bastards who got in there. Thanks to the joys of listed status, this knackered old building will always be the same from the outside, but - and here's the real pisser - the inside seems to me to be suffering from a slow, creeping death. It's almost like they've been prescribed a dose of deliberate neglect so they can get the designers in to inflict a 'much-needed' refit and leave it looking polished and contemporary and utterly bereft of soul, like some million quid church conversion in one of those ghastly weekend pullouts. That's our prognosis, anyway. At the minute, on the ground floor there's still the dusty dungeon of the main bar, plus a smaller separate room to the left that holds some sort of old-time-daytime cafe, hence the chained-up fridge with the pop in it. But that's where the tradition ends, along with our enthusiasm for the place. Upstairs - catering for the kids, and the only part of the building that seems to be getting any attention - is a night-club-stroke-venue, with the dividing line between traditional pub clatter and floor-thumping disco bollocks being firmly marked by an 'amusing' sex-aids machine next to the bogs by the stairs. And that dividing line really sums up the Cooperage's problem: surrounded by the likes of Jimmyz, Casa, Blue and Chase, plus that wretched superclub Sea over the way, the pub seems to be struggling to appeal to the average meathead Quayside drinkers without farting in the face of its old die-hards. And even though I'd rather drink my own jizz after a fortnight eating nowt but creamy Philadelphia than even ask for a half of Pedigree, it's a shame that the stoic real ale-ness has been replaced by Blue WKD and other assorted bitchpiss. But then we've always known jack about market forces.

For: It hasn't been purpled or laminated.
Against: Yet.

The Cooperage's ghost is that of Henry Hardwick, 16th Century cooper who, after failing to escape from pressgangers, was nailed to the back door of the Cooperage, had his eyes gouged out and his testicles severed. His spectre has been seen walking along Newcastle Quayside, with eyes just bloody sockets. Wait a minute? A bloke, on the Quayside, face covered in blood and holding his groin? And you're telling me that's a GHOST? I think someone's been pulling your pisser.

Crown Posada
31 The Side, NE1 3JE
'Shoddy'

If you ever look at an official guide to Newcastle, and check under 'bars', you're guaranteed to find the Crown Posada being hailed as a fine example of a Northern pub. That's a bit strange, really, because - at a time when the rest of Newcastle is stocking up on the alcopops and the imported premium draught - it's anything but. For a start, you'll not find many Geordies in here, unless they've been dragged in on a work's night out by the office bore. What you will find, though, are legions of guidebook-clutching foreign tourists, gazing in awe at the surroundings. And with good reason; it's not very often you find a pub round here with stained glass windows and a cravat-wearing landlord, let alone one with an old record player spinning Billie Holiday 78s (that's ancient vinyl, by the way, mp3 kids). There's no shoddy drinks promotion posters clogging up the walls, no hen night atrocities, and time seems to have stopped here when 'DJ' meant Jimmy Savile and Tony Blackburn. We've thought long and hard about this: is this the most pretentious bar in the town, or does the fact that it has remained untouched for so long make it the very opposite of pretentiousness? We like their style, either way. How many other bars in this city are prepared to stick so rigidly to wartime opening hours? Name us another pub in town that understands that all you need to refurbish a bar is a pot of paint and a wipe down with a damp cloth. This is a bar we like so much, we're not going to complain about the snug at the front always being full of bloody students. Even the beer, for bog standard Carling, is pretty good. Most people come for the real ales, which are supposed to be at their best here; I wouldn't know about that, but then I've always been suspicious of people who think that drinking warm, flat vinegar makes them an intellectual.

For: The guides are right. It is a damn fine pub.
Against: This place is a magnet for cigar smokers. Deviants, the lot of them. Anyone who enjoys the smell of cigar smoke is only a step away from enjoying the tangy taste of their own turds as far as we're concerned.

If I do have a complaint about the place, it's that it's too damn narrow - you get two lard-arses at the bar and you're stuck there all day. Not necessarily a bad thing, come to think of it.

Egypt Cottage
117 City Road, NE1 2AN
'I'm pig sick'

While I'm too young to claim to have ever been in the audience for *The Tube*, I could, if you asked me, tell you exactly where I was when Jools Holland called me - personally - a groovy fucker. Seeing the Egypt Cottage on the telly during *The Tube*'s star-in-the-bar interviews always made me feel like it was something legendary, and when my balls finally dropped it was one of the first pubs I wanted to drink in. Class, it was: authentic no-messing pub atmosphere, good jukebox and a decent pint. I will confess, however, that laziness and peer pressure forced me into other venues over the years; well, that plus the fact that I'd heard it had become a, quote, *poncy wine bar*. Strolling up from a sunny Quayside Sunday the other day, we decided to face our fears and check it out. Sad to say, the oldest licensed premises in Newcastle has now become just another DJ-centric bar, with what they tell me is smooth and deep house beats meets bongomania. I haven't got a fucking clue what that entails, to tell the truth. Nor does the warm-up-bar-for-Foundation concept make much sense to me. Is that what used to be the Riverside, then? Hang on...(does research)...now Shindig I AM aware of, mainly 'cause I'm pig sick of seeing their bloody flyers strewn over every pavement of a Saturday night. So, aye, it's two floors of the very latest design, all rag-rolled red and gold, with Sphinx statues and Nefertiti tables, plus huge fan-shaped leather seats in the back room. The lights seem to be made out of samosas and the haphazard MDF fittings with their particularly prominent screws just plead with you to take the whole lot out and make them put it back the way it used to be. I'm reading here that they put live music on as well as the DJ shite, so perhaps it's not all untold misery in the noise department. Unless you include the bloody buskers nights, that is. What's my problem, then? The Egypt Cottage isn't even that bad: the beer's alright and the people seem pleasant enough. I just find it really depressing to see history replaced by yet more bandwagon jumping, but maybe what I see as cynical cashing-in is just the taste of a generation I have no connection with, and I'm a sad, past-it, four-eyed, greying arsehole. Maybe there's not much call for Dickensian taverns these days. Never mind groovy: I feel like an ancient fucker more than anything. Next birthday I'll be 85.

For: The photos on the walls of the place when it was good.

Against: Becoming a miserable old bastard and being the last one to realise.

If you really want to get me started, ask me about the Rose & Crown that used to be across the road from the Egypt Cottage: now there was a class boozer, with spit 'n' sawdust and big picture windows looking right down the Tyne. And what's there now? A bloody car park, that's what.

Exchange
Premier Travel Inn, Lombard Street, NE1 3AE
'Polite and welcoming'

Do I have to do this one? Why? As far as I'm concerned this place doesn't even count, since it's just a hotel bar, and not even a separate one like Martha's at the Vermont. Let's make it quite clear from the start: you will see no locals here, only visitors (I mean fucking stag and hen parties really, but I'm trying to be polite and welcoming) who think the Quayside IS Newcastle. This bar serves no other purpose than a meeting point for pack upon pack of hotel residents, knocking back eight pints and an Apple Sourz while they wait for the slowcoaches. And I can understand the wait. I can see why the party boys need so long to get ready. It takes a lot of time and effort to splash around a bit of Hugo Boss and choose which of their shirts to pull on. Should it be the plain white one, the same as worn by half the group, or the checked white one, as sported by all the fucking rest? Sometimes I think they might as well not bother leaving the hotel, and instead just grab one of the cafeteria-style chairs over by the windows, from where they'll get a commanding view of all that NewcastleGateshead (8,9,10... and relax) apparently has to offer, namely the Sage, the bridges, and that goddamn Tuxedo Princess moored opposite. This way they could save themselves the trouble of being spat at by the indigenous population AND conserve energy for banging on every door on every floor from midnight until the cock crows. Seen from my position well away from the action, this bar is something special to behold. With the sickly colour palette of a tortured artist in the months leading up to suicide, the greys, tans, and pale wood produce a disquieting effect unrivalled in any other bar in town, while the ornate ceiling seems to lower in parallel with the froth on my pint. And I'm watching in amazement as some fucking caveman pits his wits against the quiz machine, unaware that he'd be better matched in taking on the plantpots. 'Ey oop, Torrr-neh!' he yells to his mate, 'What's t'Queen's first name, eh?' Of course, every cloud has a silver lining; even a lollystick in a dog turd has a joke on it. And this bar's saving grace is the theme corner set to the left of the main entrance. This marvellous installation aims to take you away from the look of the national chain reception area and into the realm of the family-run establishment. The lobby they've modelled this on seems to be those of London's hotel trade, where any room cheaper than £200 a night is going to be in some grotty annexe; bring your own door and mind the rodents. And so skilfully is it rendered, so exact in every detail, that it even looks like they've employed some toothless old skank to play the role of bag lady, slumped on the gnawed settee and with a face that suggests she's emptying her bladder between the cushions. Look, I know it's not claiming to be anything grand, and I know it's our own fault for expecting better, but there's only one way to deal with this place, and that's to pretend it doesn't exist. Just tell people it's the staff canteen of the Slug & Lettuce in the same block and pray they believe you. And knock them out if they don't.

For: Quality rooms from only £63 per night.
Against: Think who'll be booked in next door.

You've got to admire the optimism of the Premier Travel Inn, helpfully pointing out the local art galleries, opera house and countryside trails for the benefit of their guests, in the hope that one day - if only for that day - the tanked-up cretins will find something more cultural to do than seeing which travels furthest from the third floor windows; Foster's piss or Corona puke. Clue: the secret's in the lime.

Fever

Akenside Hill, NE1 3XP
'Think, man, think'

For crying out loud, how are you supposed to review a pub that leaves no lasting impression? Fever is a big room with walls and doors and a counter where drunk people are served with alcohol. Really, that's about it. Formerly The Newcastle Arms, The Pump House, Muse and now Fever, I've never been able to string together more than three sentences by way of an accurate appraisal. The beer's alright, the cocktails cheap enough to swill down your throat before you have to taste them, the decor makes cut-price look palatial and the punters are run-of-the-mill Quayside goers. Christ, I am really struggling here. Think, man, think. This place seems to follow the bizarre party-bar pattern of being absolutely heaving or howlingly desolate with no comfortable grey area in between; and either way it's not much cop. There's certainly nowt that would entice me in here if it wasn't for the fact that I NEED to write this garbage up for the sake of completeness. The music's an eclectic mix of shite and fucking shite, all served up in that mic-gobbling 'Yeeees indeedy, that's the sound of...' style so beloved of pot-bellied, amateur-hour DJs the world over, and if there is any sort of interesting theme to this bar then I'm damned if I can see it. They've got geometric patterns on the walls, a stack of circular mirrors at the far end behind some zebra skin stools, more terrible modern art than could ever be deemed necessary, plus a mirror-tiled ceiling that looks like it might be easy to repair, if nothing else. And those tiles might provide the clue to why there's never any effort put into doing this place up; why bother if it's just going to get wrecked by stag and hen nights anyway? Is this long enough yet? It's not? Balls. You'll be wanting more ranting, then. I never thought I'd ever type these words, but Fever is as entertaining as the stag do that's in it. And more astounding than that, I'm going to say that the last time I was in I found myself chuckling at the antics of a gang of lads-off-the-leash, even if I was laughing at the fucking pillocks rather than with them. In fancy dress poor enough to have the hire shop going, 'Who's this supposed to be again?' and throwing shapes to leave even the hardcore Quayside crowd looking mortified, the dancing turned to pogoing turned to somersaulting, like Lomana Lua Lua on tartrazine after nabbing a roll-over jackpot. Call me cruel, condescending, toffee nosed or biscuit-arsed, but there's always a joy to be had in watching people debase themselves completely, to the point where they could get no lower, short of shitting in a bucket and wearing it as a crown. Think how much they've pissed away on their big night out. Add it all up: the costumes, the hotel, the train fare and the ale. The dry-cleaning, the bail, the solicitor and the back-quack. And balance it against what they've got to show for it: a thumping head, a regrettable tattoo, an embarrassing itch and a Boots CD of blurred snaps to remind them of their stupidity. 'Here's one of me... pulling a face! There's Dave... showing us his beer! Where's that? Who the hell's she? And why the fuck do we do it..?'

For: The quintessential Bigg Market bar.
Against: Except it's, like, on the Quayside.

Inevitably the fancy dress party moved on, and was replaced by a more typical crowd. It was at that point that I was subjected to my worst pub nightmare: everyone buggers off and leaves me to get the round in while they nip to the bogs, and I get lumbered with two huge hen night parties in the same bar. And what does the DJ try in his desperation to drum up some atmosphere? He gets them to out-squeal each other. What a fucking idiot. The doctors say I may recover some of the hearing in my left ear, but the right one is beyond help. Thanks for that, you porky bastard.

Flynn's

63 Quayside, NE1 3DE
'It was your fault they elbowed you in the kisser'

Like a trip to the clap clinic, we've been putting off revisiting Flynn's for years and, now that we've been in for another squint, we realise our hesitation was fully justified. Hurrying in for a swift one purely to get out of a sudden downpour, we quickly saw why Flynn's has acquired a reputation as a bar you either hate unreservedly or visit just to take the piss out of it; there's no way on earth you could actually like it, unless you were educationally subnormal and a nasty little git an' all. The exterior of this place seems to change every fortnight (along with the name of the damn place - see the Flynn's / Slice Bar / Flynn's again debacle for proof), but no matter how they dress it up, it's still one of the rottenest bars on the Quayside. I notice that the latest paint job states that they're calling it a 'bar diner' these days: I didn't see any menus lying about, but whatever they rustle up, I'd still rather go scrabbling around the bins with the rats than ever eat my bait in here. Why? For a kick off, I'm buggered backwards if I'm standing about eating my grub, since there are about three seats in the whole bar, and even those are brutally pockmarked with tab burns. Secondly, Flynn's has a policy of pumping out '80s cheesy pop sounds from the moment it opens. And on top of that, the place is falling apart, hamstrung by the last corner-cutting spruce-up they attempted unravelling at the seams. There's tatty laminate flooring and the usual depressing modern colour scheme, with only a collage by the door of what seems to be Frankenstein's monster and random bits of cleavage to give it any character of its own. Fuck alone knows what they were thinking when they bunged that up. And while I'm aware that the layout of three levels and low ceilings is due to the pub's location in an old Quayside building, the whole experience reminded me of being stuck on one of those cut-price party boats down the Tyne, where there's nowt but steep stairs, terrible music and contemptible berks you can't seem to escape from. On a brighter note, there was nothing wrong with the beer, except that it seemed pretty expensive to me since Flynn's is such a battered dump. I'd expected to pay Wetherspoon's prices for my standard pint, and not get shafted by a luxebar premium; maybe they'd got word that that imbecile with the freaky eyebrows and his stumpy bird were in town with their smug matching notebooks and decided to charge us triple out of general spite. Unlikely, I know, but if writing bollocks like that is enough to pad out this so-called review, then I'm a happy man. I suppose that just leaves the punters to gripe about: from the dawn of time until Armageddon shatters the last bottle of Smirnoff Ice, Flynn's will attract knuckleheads and hinnies, spastic dancing and yelling and knocking you sideways in their lobotomised over-exuberance. And you will smile and apologise and wipe their sticky cocktails off your best shirt, because, clearly, it was your fault they elbowed you in the kisser. It really is rough. Aye, it might have been friendly enough at five bells when we forced ourselves to go and review the place, but I'd be damned if I'd go any later. In fact I'll be damned if I go again.

For: Nice view of the Sage and the Tyne bridges.
Against: It truly is shocking. Imagine a punishment cell with a view and you're almost there.

I tried looking up some of the history of Flynn's - or at least of the building that houses it - on the internet. Bugger all there, I'm afraid. What I did find out, though, is that Flynn's is a notorious pick-up joint for pathetic, middle-aged men preying on underage, underdressed teenage drinkers. Fuck, I wish I'd realised that at the time.

Jimmyz
48-52 Sandhill, NE1 3JF
'(sic)'

I've been studying journalism lately. I have. Well, I've been reading the Chronicle while I'm having my dinner, but it amounts to much the same thing. What I've become most aware of while I'm stuffing my fat face is the concept of give-'em-enough-rope, of letting people reveal themselves to be idiots by just standing back and allowing them have their say. From that dumb bint from Byker who pissed away a million quid of Lottery winnings and couldn't fathom why her new 'snob' neighbours would object to a millionaire trying to cadge a cup of sugar, to the boneheads try-

33

ing to claim compensation (and a replacement pair of underkegs for the ones they shat) from some bar that 'made' them drink thirty pints in happy hour, it's all there in black and white. Turn the page through 180 degrees and you'll see the words 'you stupid bastard; you stupid tart' written between every line. It's a fascinating approach and it's one I'm going to take for Jimmyz Bar, liberally quoting from the blurb on their promotional website to give you the review straight from the horse's slobbering mouth. Here, in their own officially-sanctioned purple prose is what they think you want: Oppulence (sic), decadence and seduction. Style, cocktails and dreams. Conspiratorial corners. Chandaliers (sic). Champages (sic)... ah, fuck it. This feels really unkind, like refusing to help a single mother off the bus with her buggy. The truth is that Jimmyz was always, and still remains, a farcically expensive, desperately crass Quayside bar catering to bozos looking to fight with - or gold-digging sexual predators in sparkly tops aiming to fuck - overpaid, immoral, more-red-cards-than-brain-cells Premiership footballers. Bloody hell: that was a clunky sentence, wasn't it? But if you like bordello reds, laminate flooring and damn-your-eyes wallpaper, and you don't give a sloppy shit how much it costs, then maybe Jimmyz is the bar for you. Perhaps you consider 1940s photos of people necking on to be seductive and glamorous. It takes all sorts, I fully understand. When will people realise, though: there is no glamour in Newcastle, and there never will be. It is not a luxury destination, and people who have the cash to throw about in here pretending that it is should have their bank accounts raided and the money given to charitable causes. Jimmyz is the bar equivalent of a cocaine habit, a way of wasting money trying to kid yourself that you're not worthless shite, and if you drink there you're a fool. It's as simple as that.

For: Their idea that a happy hour game - press the silver button and look at a screen, basically - could somehow be 'decadent' fills me with mirth.
Against: We missed the happy hour and got absolutely shafted.

In typical newspaper style, I'm going to tuck away the apology at the bottom of the page, hoping your mind will have been set in its ways by the screaming headlines of the initial report. You know what I mean. Page 1 of Sunday edition says 'Evil Teacher Tortures Kids'; hidden away on page 17 of Tuesday's late night final, long after windows have been put through and tyres slashed you get 'We're sorry. We meant to say that he only gave a B instead of an A+' Where am I going with this? Oh aye, apparently it's a lot cheaper through the week and a vast improvement on the pre-refit state. I'm just bitter that I'm skint and always will be.

Martha's

The Side, NE1 8TD
'A happy finish off the Pope'

Pinching the service questionnaire from one of the booths in Martha's, the drab little bar of the Vermont Hotel, I notice from the website it directs me to, that this pub is a 'popular meeting place for the over 20s'. Well, aye, technically that's correct, but when they say over 20s, I can tell you without fear of contradiction they really mean the over 40s. And, by crikey, it's desperate. Martha's is an ideal blind date venue for love's second and third-chancers, each with a buttonhole of woe and dragging matching Samsonite emotional baggage along by its dodgy handle. 'H-how will I recognise you?', they'll nervously stammer beforehand. 'I'll be the blancmange in the corner, gawping at the myriad photos of the heroes of my heyday, all bunged on the wall in no real order except where they fit round the aircon vents.' Fucking hell, man: those photos are a joke. What are they getting at? Are they the sort of people they wish would turn up to give this place a bit of class? Ha! I've got more chance of getting a happy finish off the Pope - the last one, the dead one - than these bastards have of seeing Natalie Imbruglia in here. Why would any respectable celebrity patronise this horrible bar, whose only concession to the turn of the millennium was to ditch the embarrassing Blues

Brothers dummies, the ones that looked like they'd been swiped from a high street amusement arcade? Has George Michael got a thing about distempered walls? Is Björk big on conservatory windows? Will Sharleen Spiteri's next CD have a pervading atmosphere of defeat and reflections on wasted life inspired by a night spent weeping in here? Of course not. They wouldn't come here in a million years, not even if there was a wad of beer vouchers alongside the complimentary After Eight on their hotel room pillow. And I can't even hand out plus points for the courtyard outside, since it's right under the railway viaduct. You're sitting on a summer's eve, chilling in the breeze and snorking up the smells of the Quayside's restaurants, and what happens? A train thunders over, the seagulls start flapping and shitting with fear, and their dribbling, fishy poop falls straight into your pint. Doesn't sound like my ideal night out.

For: It wasn't - when we visited - as ferociously expensive as we'd found it on all the other times we'd been conned into going. However, joining up the dots on the drinks menus, there seems to be a black hole for Saturday night peak time prices, where we suspect even a plain pint of Foster's will be £POA.
Against: The mezzanine level. If you dive at the correct angle, and propel yourself with the right force, you'll snap your neck the instant you land and it'll all be over. The fucking mezzanine was locked.

Celebrities? Trains? I remember once standing on the platform of Central Station and seeing this specky little fart that I vaguely recognised. Finally it dawned on me where I knew him from, so I said to our lass, 'Look - subtly - over my shoulder. Is that Paul McKenna over there?' Sure was: a quick peek at his tour schedule in the paper proved it. A couple of minutes later, though, the baldy bastard walks up behind me and mutters to the back of my head, 'Yeah. I am.' What an arrogant wanker. The thing that struck me as odd was this: if he's such a mindbender and king of the paranormal, why did he have to come and tell me I was right? Why couldn't the weasel have just stayed where he was and sent the news over by telepathy? Something funny going on there.

Offshore 44

40 Sandhill, NE1 3JF
'Rammed like Fudges in a fat girl's face'

Offshore 44 is a bar that looks like it can't decide what it wants to be. Is it a timber framed old grunter pub playing on its genuinely historical Quayside tradition, with nautical pictures and ropes around the bar and furniture? Or is it a thumping, wailing, shuddering fun bar for the newly paid and short of responsibility? I'll tell you what I think it is, and that's a fu...hang on a minute. How many times have I been in here? Dozens. Yet this is the first time I've noticed that it's supposed to look like a ship? Now why is that? Is it because, stripped through vanity of my jam-jar geps, I'm Mr Magoo before the trip to Ultralase? It's possible, aye. But it's more likely that it's because Offshore has always been rammed like Fudges in a fat girl's face every single time I've been piped aboard. With what sort of punters? I don't know, man. There's just a jumble of limbs, with the odd spaghetti-strap here and a bought-ripped jeans leg there. And, floating over it all, are horns and hair dye, wigs and willies, all the tell-tale signs of the stag and hen crowd marking off every bar along the quay like dogs pissing up the lamp posts. It's brimming, it's mobbed, it's overflowing, and it's packed. Any time after Second Dog Watch - that's 8pm to you - you can guarantee it. But why the hell it's so popular I'll never understand. Does anyone actually get the chance to drink in here, let alone get smashed and party? I doubt it, since if they're not pushing for the bogs, then they're pushing to get out. And if they're pushing to the courtyard, it's not the bloody burgers from the summer weekend barbecues they're after, it's just the heavenly scent of the cool night air. Christ, I thought I was going to die in there.

For: The thought that there's a pool table in the front room, and of the forty-a-side teams playing winner-stays-on.

Against: Here man. Watch where you're gannin', you fucking tit.

There is a ghost in this pub, and it resides by the bottom of the staircase to the upper bar. I know ghosts are meant to be frightening, but this spook's party piece just amuses me no end. Stand by the bandit or under the Offshore mosaic and watch it: In pile the screeching factory girls, and out comes the spectral tripwire. Thump, thump, thumpity-thump; another bulking great hippo falls flat on her jowls up the steps, blue cocktail slopping one way and decorum dribbling the other. Never fails, in all the times I've been here. Long live the undead.

Pitcher & Piano

108 The Quayside, NE1 3DX
'Worth the effort'

Architectural marvel and overpriced tourist hotspot, the Pitcher & Piano is like an IKEA store set in a greenhouse, but without the good bits of either. One of the first real movers and shakers in the dolling up of the Quayside - and handily right next to the Millennium Bridge - this place has been pulling in the cultural visitors to sunny Newcastle and fleecing them good and proper for a while now. And I still don't much care for it. Can't quite put my finger on why, though. Maybe it's the advertising focus group punters, all designer distressed clothing, twenty-minute tans and not a complete personality between them. Perhaps it's the depressing sight of the scruffy urchins outside, trudging through the broken glass and trying to scrounge tabs off all and sundry. Or maybe it's just the fact that there are now dozens of similar places in Newcastle where you can pay so much for so little, that it's hardly worth the effort of dragging yourself all the way along here. Plus, I've always found the beer to be nigh on undrinkable, the staff contemptible, and the experience of taking in all the redeveloped views from the beer terrace such a crushing disappointment. I've been in for food and it's always been burnt or tepid. I've tried meeting them halfway by dressing like one of those fucking 'metrosexuals', and still been ignored at the bar. I've even asked - politely - for one of their expensive cocktails and got a full jug of orange juice squirted 'accidentally' in my face without so much as an apology, unless pouting and snorting are the new sorry. Man, this place blows. I hate it, to be honest. Even if I was scratching around for a positive slant, I'd have to say something along the lines of, if there's something decent on at the Baltic over the bridge, you could pop in here afterwards for a swift piss and an even swifter half. But if your bladder was up to it, you'd be a fool to choose it over the likes of the Tyne or the Free Trade.

For: If you hotwired a Navy gunboat, this place would make an excellent target.
Against: Men's facial grooming products - moisturisers, conditioners, cleansers and toners - make it so much harder to land a decent punch.

If there's ever some big event on the Quayside and you think, 'Let's go to the Pitcher and Piano and watch it from the balcony', then forget it: the uppity twats from the BBC will have commandeered the place. Mind you, if Lara Rostron from the local news is up there - TV's foxiest werepig - they'll need more than bouncers to keep me out.

Quayside
35 The Close, NE1 3RN
'Tripping up the joggers'

Although The Quayside is set in a 16th Century medieval warehouse, being one of the bars of the JD Wetherspoon Lloyds No.1 brand it caters to the more discerning, upmarket bland chain bar clientele rather than the traditional, rustic bland chain bar customers of its parent company. A face-slapping racket of thumping tunes, with beach parties out in the cobbled courtyard - or under the umbrellas, if wet - the bar is a popular destination for the unavoidable stag, hen and office parties, and there's not a night goes by without the appearance of a rotund executive done up (like a fucking kipper, I'd say) as Ali G or some other celebrity from the fancy dress shop's sale rail. Sightseers and lovers of industrial heritage among you may care to note that the raised level gives you a perfect view over the Tyne to the delights of the Ovoline Lubricants factory. Tremendous. No, really. And entertainment for the bored and agitated comes in electronic form, with as many flashing buttons as you can press before you're down to your pocket fluff, plus the usual range of plasma screens, minority sports channels seemingly password-locked into place. But that's all immaterial. The main real reason to come here - and jostle with the bastards who just fail to realise it was your idea first and that you alone should have the best seat available - is the beer garden facing the river. Aye, to you it might just be a load of concrete slabs and a few picnic tables, but to us it's the French Riviera, a gorgeous waterside retreat to laze away the hours until the sun sets over Scotswood, then sneaks round the back before the toerags have had a chance to pinch its wallet. And, bless them, the management seem to have no absolutely no problem with you taking your beer out of the confines of the pub area, strolling down the quayside and tripping up the joggers. No bollocks about designated zones or plastic glasses here; just a bit of trust for the customer. And comprehensive insurance cover.

For: It's a Wetherspoon pub. Therefore it's cheap.
Against: Your fantastic view of the Tyne's bridges will be marred - until 2058, if they encounter any more unexpected hiccups - by the flapping great white tarpaulins along the High Level Bridge. Why can't they employ some bored graffiti artists to make a reasonable stab at spraypainting on an image of what's supposed to be underneath? And if a few of the fuckers fall to their doom in the process, that's just unfortunate.

Those lovely lads roaring past on their jet-skis are great, aren't they? Parading their wealth and their knobbly knees on a Sunday

*evening when you're having a couple of sunset jars. Of course
we're rooting for them. Of course we wish them all the best.
That's why we laugh like a gurgling drain and throw celebratory
rocks at them when they fall arse over tit and get a gob-full of
Tyne water. Smugness: karma will intervene.*

Quilted Camel

36 Sandhill, Quayside, NE1 3JF
'Buggy-pushing scratters'

Possibly our least favourite and most infrequently visited pub on
the Quayside, The Quilted Camel has had an extensive refit since
the last time we braved a review and has become, as you'd expect from somewhere subtitled 'Honeyrooms', a tarts' bar. With
a dubious Gothic fetish theme, the place has clearly been redes-
igned to appeal to thick, buggy-pushing scratters who've finally
twigged that they'll never, ever be a princess, but still want to
live out some sort of hackneyed fairytale, even if it's just over a
sickly cocktail on their night off from the kids. It's that sort of
fantasy. I've got no idea when the refit was done, so I don't know
whether they're copying Perdu in the city centre or the other way
round, but there are certainly similarities, what with the beaded
dividers, the retro-space-age chrome fittings, the colour scheme
that ranges from the darkest purple all the way up to black, and
the general murk. There's an ever-changing lighting scheme, so
subtle and useless that still gets overpowered by the candles
flickering to the beat of Backstreet Boys classics and, if that's
still too bright for you then, at the back, they've got a pitch
black room with a pitch black carpeted bed. It confused the fuck
out of me, that thing: I must've looked like I was doing the can-
can while I was edging round it, alternately kicking thin air and
some sort of invisible solid mass, and all the while trying to balance four pints and a bag of late-night shopping. I tried the bed
thing myself, just for gimmickry's sake, once I'd worked out what
it was. And I really wished I hadn't; my self-disgust at rolling
about in the dandruff and scabs and hockle and spilt drink of the

average Quayside drinker who'd been there before me left me feeling more than a little disturbed, and it took a 45-minute shower when I got home just to scrub off the fucking filth. True story. And once we'd sacked off the bed thing and gone hunting for seats, we got a better look at the rest of the decor, especially the big, I dunno, fucking castle or something behind the main bar, made out of earwax. There's a roaring lion's head fire up the far end, glitter balls down the other, Medusa masks here and there, and every available surface is daubed in what appears to be their corporate logo, some sort of inkblot test. And if you visualise all that lot and add pictures of exotic strippers - as opposed to For Your Eyes Only dollops - and other scenes of associated debauchery you'll have an exact mental image of the Quilted Camel: an expensively-refurbished, pretendy-lavish, overcrowded, terrible bar for dunces. I trust I don't need to tell you to give it a miss.

For: If there's ever a pub that'll make you abandon the humiliating Quayside-crawling work night out and piss off home long before the inevitable slide along to Buffalo Joe's, then it's this one.
Against: Burlesque Glamour. What the fucking hell is Burlesque Glamour?

Seriously, though: that bed thing. For about a week afterwards I was plagued by zits and boils and rashes and itches, right around the back of my neck where I'd been lying on their scatter cushions. You can call it psychosomatic if you want; I call it deeply disturbing.

The Red House

32 Sandhill, NE1 3JF
'Life slowly ticking away'

The Red House isn't exactly the former home of celebrated local trollop Bessie Surtees, role model for Newcastle's female Quayside-goers, but it's in the same block and that's close enough for us. Equally a haunt for whistling pensioners and chirruping hens, from the outside the Red House looks like a tiny, rustic boozer, but once you get inside you find a million different rooms, corridors and bricked-up dead ends; I'm ashamed to admit that I've never yet managed to get from the snug to the front door without cocking it up somewhere down the line. The building is from Jacobean times - whenever they were - so I reckon we can safely say that the cellar effect in the back few rooms is genuine, and with its dark wood and orange lighting, the overall atmosphere is one of relaxing gloominess without the perilous descent into depressing. This, you'll agree, makes it better for a slow afternoon session than a night out with the lads. I just wonder what the designers were playing at the last time they gave this place a refit, since I have no frigging idea what the hell the theme is supposed to be in here. It's like they started on a few rough sketches and then never quite got their lazy, overpaid arses in gear for long enough to carry any of them through. I can imagine them sat round a meeting room table on a Friday afternoon, with the stopwatch eating away at their client's budget. 'Red House, yeah? Like, red, like, Russian, yeah? Like, a balalaika? Like, in a glass case?' Meanwhile some other tit is going, 'A cellar? Doesn't that just say 'railway carriage theme' to you?' Typically, nothing is finished and little gets done, and they just bugger off to the pub, or chop out a line, or draw dicks on each other's heads and charge it to the account, or do whatever else designers that I've just invented do on an afternoon. Getting away from all this stupid prattle and down the factual stuff about the damned bar, as I suppose I must at some point, the beer in here is pretty good, and the food - from the same kitchen as Bob Trollop next door, I understand - is decent enough, though I've felt my life slowly ticking away waiting for my Sunday dinner when I've been out with the folks. To be honest, I don't get in here that often, which is a pity because I quite like the place. If you're down on the Quayside and you prefer listening to the sound of your own heartbeat to the din of a DJ, then I'd thoroughly recommend it. But don't blame me if it all kicks off later.

For: It isn't the Quilted Camel.

Against: I've taken to carrying a ball of string with me, like him (or was it her?) out of that story where there's, like, this maze and this gadgie with a bull's head or something. Exactly like that, aye.

Bessie Surtees was the daughter of a wealthy merchant who lived on the Quayside in Newcastle in the eighteenth century. When she fell in love with a coal merchant's son, the match was frowned upon, so the headstrong Bessie climbed out of a first floor window and eloped to Scotland. An eyewitness was later heard to exclaim to reporters from the local Scrofula Times, 'She could have put her fucking bloomers on before she backed down that ladder. Jesus wept! It was like a thatched roof.'

The Slug & Lettuce

Exchange Buildings, Quayside, NE1 3DW
'The last thing anybody needs'

A while ago, the Slug & Lettuce chain took over the premises sullied by those jokers who owned the Parisa pseudo-brand, and in the process quietly restored a little of the dignity to the place. I said a little, mind you. If you're heading back along the Quayside from the Baltic or wherever, and think the Pitcher & Piano is too far up its own arsehole and Flynn's too full of harlots and headbangers, then this is the perfect place for an accidental Sunday afternoon bellyful, chilling amid the muted pastel shades. Perfect, that is, as long as you can get one of the floppy sofas to park your arse on; otherwise it's a pretentious rip-off full of absolute tools. The beer's canny enough, and while it may be a little on the pricey side, at least it's not in the same league as the wine: fourteen quid for a bottle of supermarket red? They're having a laugh, right? The food's a bit steep, too, and I fail to see how serving an itty-bitty burger on a fucking massive plate constitutes value for money, but what the hell do I know about the catering trade? Piss all, that's what. Shall I tell you what the worst thing is about the place? I've been, like, half a dozen times and I still couldn't describe the inside in any great detail. I could try harping on about the split-levels and the extensive seating, but I'd just end up sounding like some sort of sodding estate agent, and that's the last thing anybody needs. Actually, scrap that: I've just had a butcher's at their website in an attempt to pad this out a bit, and I see that under 'events', the Slug & Lettuce chain are holding 'Speed Dating' nights, obviously for the lonely and psychotic. Now THAT is the last thing anybody needs.

For: I noticed on the wall next to my comfy settee that they're starting to do live acoustic sessions on Thursday nights, and while that'll probably be simpering Norah Jones wannabes instead of new-Nick-Drakes, having another live venue - and one with functioning toilets - can only be a good thing.
Against: Back to that website again: could you trust a bar that has 'slurp swill slurp swill' as its headline graphic? They're charging you the earth for a pint, and all they can do is rip the piss out of it, and you. That's just insulting.

This place is still effectively Parisa. And, tasty though those pints were, I always felt that if you went there and enjoyed it then slowly, surely, and almost imperceptibly, you were becoming a wanker.

Stereo

Sandgate, NE1 4AG
'Utopian drinking experience'

When Stereo first opened, I stated quite boldly that the pub had been ruined, and that its only saving grace - a Perspex bubble chair hanging from a chain - would be broken within the month. Clambering up the stairs for a sneaky revisit, we find that 'ruined' doesn't even come close to describing what has happened here: in the past few years this place has been absolutely destroyed, and that flaming bubble chair is now the only thing left intact. Every seat has been slashed, every surface battered, every footstool hoofed about and, as with most derelict buildings, some fucker has snuck along during the night and pasted up fly-posters everywhere. The paint's peeling, decking planks are scuffed to buggery, and everything you accidentally touch has the sticky film of last night's happy hour. How has a pub been allowed to disintegrate so completely in such a short period of time? This to me is the perfect example of what happens when you're a clever shite and you think you know best, and every greedy get with even the slightest interest in updating a pub should be dragged in here by the ear, forced on pain of death to observe what is wrong, and be told, with no room for misunderstanding, that THIS is what their folly will amount to. Buff my bollocks and call me Barry, but the state of this place nowadays has me nostalgic for even the chain bar nonentity of the Fog & Firkin that it was previously, never mind the utopian drinking experience of the Barley Mow before that. There really is fuck all left to see in here, and the only good thing about the whole bar is the view of what's outside, the rejuvenated quayside. And believe me - as long as you're brave enough to wipe the smears off the sliding glass doors first - you'll spend a long time looking at it. You'll need something to justify the ridiculous price of your lacklustre pint, anyway. This can't be right. There must be something I'm missing. Maybe the ruination was part of the plan all along. Could the theme here actually be some sort of post-apocalyptic fallout zone, set shortly after the MDF wars? Maybe to complete their vision, the futuristic shell of the pub needed the natural, organic collapse of its interior. It's all fitting into place. Look at those knobs out there, on the ledge of the bit that used to be the town's best beer garden before some jerk glassed it over. Look at them standing at the barbecue, like tramps round a brazier in a desolate wasteland. Maybe they're all in on the prank, and I'm the only sad bastard who doesn't get it. I certainly hope so, because the alternative is unthinkable.

For: Hey! At least we can't say it's bland anymore!
Against: Indie superclub Stonelove - responsible for every last one of those fly-posters - may possibly have the best music of any club in the land, but for using the word 'Djography' on their web-

site, they should be kneed in the groin from now until Christmas.
Unless you're reading this on Christmas Eve, in which case we'll
say Halloween.

*I picked up a flyer on the way out, advertising the Stereo Sunday
Market, with stalls including vintage photography, records, jew-
ellery and textiles. Add to that 'fixtures & fittings, pint glasses,
competent bar staff, and self-respect' and everything suddenly
becomes clear.*

thirty 3i8ht

Exchange Buildings, Quayside, NE1 3DE
'Look at me! I'm a tourist tit!'

Like weeds strangling down a delicate rose, the ravages of time
and the whims of the drinking public will often destroy a thing of
rare beauty. And so it is with this bar. Once the sleekest of the
sleek and the wankiest of the wanky, with minimal design so
studied that they had bloody kumquats placed for maximum colour scheme effect, thirty 3i8ht has suffered punctured pretensions over the years and, in trying to ingratiate itself with dumb-
fuck Quayside customers, is now no stranger to the humiliating
climbdown. You can even see it from the outside, where they've
had to stick up a sign reading 'Bar 38' for people too remedial-
level to work out what the hell 'thirty 3i8ht' was meant to say.
Inside is no better. The basic shell of the place remains, along
with the fake portholes in the walls and the wavy benches, but all
the eclectic arty stuff, like the mobiles - that's mobiles as in
Alexander Calder and not Nokia (look the bastard up) - and what-
not has long since vanished. And the atmosphere has changed
from a luxury venue into a fading student pub. Not good. Other
elements missing in action? The front room lit from the floor tiles
up is now buried beneath a slouch of scatter cushions, while the
daft leather igloo thing in the corner is painted in back-of-garage
green and bereft of the projections of blue skies and fluffy clouds
that once graced it and the foreheads of the beautiful ones in-

side. And now who's sitting in it, that slashed, scarred, filthy relic from a bygone age? Why, that'll be the out-of-towners, of course. It's a dead giveaway: anyone dim enough to park their arse in there these days might as well wear a T-shirt - retro stencilled by the Duffer of St George, mind - saying, 'Look at me! I'm a tourist tit!' Even the indestructible designer bogs are looking scuffed and defeated; if I'd thought on and applied for some ludicrous research grant when the bar first opened, I could have documented the exact effects of Foster's piss on shiny stainless steel. Missed opportunity there, I reckon. Look, I'll be honest with you; I was no real fan of the manifesto beforehand, and Christ knows we've slagged off enough bars for doing what thirty 3i8ht did first, but it just seems so disappointing that they've buckled under. Let's face it, if you're going to act the cunt, then at least have the courage and the decency to stick to your guns.

For: Set between Fever and Exchange, it shines like a diamond.
Against: Our original review was a triumph of smart-arsery, full of intricate wordplay and scathing social commentary, peppered with references to Catalonian art movements and liberal quotations from Orwell. Shame you'll never see it...

It would have been a breeze to do that research project, though. I'd have - quite literally - pissed £300,000 of taxpayers' money up the nearest wall before handing in my thesis of six words to front-page headline scorn. Those six words? 'Del Boy falling through the bar'. Well, fuck man; it's the answer to most indepth studies these days. I fail to see why I should miss out on my slice of the pie.

The Waterline

96 East Quayside, NE1 3DH
'Cackle, and cackle, and cackle again'

Once a gloomy pub burdened with a tacky shipping theme, the Waterline is now one of the finest spicy wedges restaurant-bars in the whole area between the Law Courts and City Road. An abundance of creams and whites and neutral tones, not to mention a large glass awning projecting onto the East Quayside, have given the bar a spirit-drainingly dull look and, thanks to the massive wood burning pizza oven at the back, every day of the year is like a fucking inferno. The Waterline is very popular with tourists and Quayside strollers who fancy an average pint in an average bar to go with the average contemporary art they've just pretended to understand in the Baltic over the river whilst really only going there to play in the lifts. We know this to be true, because it's exactly what we've done on the rare occasions we've been here. And our lack of attendance - together with the complete absence of anything noteworthy to mock in the decor - is the reason why I'm going to spend the rest of this review expanding on something I half-noticed when the missus was prattling on in my ear. There's an annexe in an older part of the pub off to the right that holds a pool table and, if my eyes don't deceive me, a semi-private party, which is to say a gang of meat-headed lads in co-ordinating catalogue casual clothing, hollering like fuck and casting the odd lecherous glance in the direction of the occupants of the pub's left-hand side. This, as you can probably imagine, means hen party weekenders, stopping by and meeting up, suitcase in tow, on their way to the Travelodge out the back. 'Eeh!' they're all saying, 'Your hair's ever so slightly different from the last time I saw you! Isn't it amazing?!' Then they cackle, and cackle, and cackle again, until one of them ruins the mood and the whole weekend by saying something worthwhile. Only kidding: there's been nothing interesting said on any hen party since Eve went out for a few cocktails with the snake and thought, Stuff this talk about the meaning of original sin; I just want to blather on about the new colour scheme in the Garden of Eden. And about the size of Adam's knob. Hee hee hee! Look at the L-plate on me fig leaf! Ah, you can't knock them for wanting to get away for a while though, can you? Which right-thinking gentleman isn't secretly jealous of the perfect girlie weekend? Don't we all long for a pampering, a few chatty beers and then fourteen hours in casualty waiting to get the bits of Bacardi Breezer bottle removed from the back of our heads? Of course we do. And if that means our entire day is spent saying, I says she says I says she says eeh I says she says never in the world I says she says I says she says I says she says eeeh, just before bursting into tears, then that's the price we'll pay.

For: If you can grab a seat outside on a warm summer evening with the sun setting behind the Tyne Bridge then you'll be laughing.

Against: The fucking stretch limos cruising past, with their shrieking occupants and their trails of spilt alcopops leaking from the bottoms of the doors. Why do people STILL think these things are a 'good laugh'?

Our lass - who is a berk at the best of times - suggests that I ought to give special mention to the little bloke who sits out the back with the tub of spuds, painstakingly carving them into twister fries. I believe my decree nisi should be in the post this very week.

The Wig & Pen

17 Broad Chare, NE1 3DQ
'Nell McAndrew in hotpants, flogging kisses for a fiver'

'You've just beaten the rush,' said the barman, an obvious master of irony. This was about the thirty-fifth time we'd been down here trying to do a review when the pub hit full swing, and still the place was deserted; it's no exaggeration to say that when we arrived at half eight on a Saturday night we were the only punters in there. And with a grimace of shame, the barman tried to tell us that the reason the pub is always so empty is that it's just a bit too far off the beaten track for the majority of Quayside go-ers. He's right. It's a whole twenty feet away from the perennially heaving Bonded Warehouse and stuck forlornly on the direct route between the cheap chain hotel and the tourist sights, so no wonder it doesn't get much trade. The decor in here is more like a local pub than the cheap, flashy tat you normally see on the

Quayside, with a theme clearly done in acknowledgement of bar's position next to the Law Courts. There's that Scales of Justice woman above the door saying, 'Watch me balancing trick! Tell us I'm mint, or I'll slash ye! Hang on: where've ye gone?' There's als... she's wearing a fucking blindfold, man, you dunderhead. There's also a range of gavels and judges' wigs in glass cases, although the pretty charver boys hand-selected to gobble out their punishment under m'lud's bench were nowhere to be seen. In a pathetic attempt to break the uneasy silence, we headed for the pool table, which acts as entertainment for both punters and staff, the barmen being so bored they were reduced to watching us clack the balls around like blind amputees. I swear they had a little tear of gratitude in their eyes that somebody, if just for a quick one, had shown enough charity to step through their doors. It's clear their totaliser needs Nell McAndrew in hotpants, flogging kisses for a fiver, but if all they get is Jeremy Beadle, late, and drunk, with the taxi meter running, then that'll have to do. To be fair, the place started to fill up after we arrived, though a head count of twelve on a Saturday night, including those two sobbing behind the bar, is hardly enough to plan early retirement in the south of France. Oh, look, damn it, I feel really sorry for the Wig, so please, forget having a good time, forget your natural aversion to students and pensioners, and nip in for a pint, if only to put a smile on the cheeky-chappie faces of the staff. And then, for fuck's sake, never set foot in the dismal bloody dump again.

For: Plenty of time and space for reflection, and comfortable chairs on which to muse awhile.
Against: You find yourself wondering things like this: if Jeremy Beadle lost his little hand in a swordfight with, say, that Justice woman, and they gave him a prosthetic one, would it be standard size, or would he get one the same as the stump he'd been used to?

I realise it'll be old news by the time you read this, so I'm probably going to look a bit of a breast, but if I don't jackhammer down my rage about this, then my lid, my cork and my gasket will be in places and states they should never rightfully be.

THE BURGLAR'S DOG

Flicking through the Ceefax on the day of writing, I see that some fucking bright spark has proposed that the victim's family should have a say in the sentencing of murderers. Belt my head square with a shovel and call me Richard Littlejohn, but what sort of justice system can there possibly be if the length of a prison term is determined by the yardstick of tearful hysterics? How can it possibly be a realistic idea to say to the poor relatives, 'Top marks for the quiet dignity at what must be a terrible time, but frankly we were hoping for a little more gnashing and wailing from you, so I'm afraid we'll have to let the killer go'? Why not just get Channel 4 to show 'String Him Up!' for the duration of the trial, with Davina McCall whispering AND SHOUTING her way through the tiny details of the slaying, and maybe throw it open to text message voters to evict the families who don't look quite heartbroken enough? Please tell me - like I won't already know the answer by now - that I read it all wrong. Say it ain't so.

2

The Burglar's Dog Stag & Hen Party Special

People from all over the nation send us e-mails. They say, 'Dear The Burglar's Dog. We are having a stag weekend and plan to visit your town like a biblical plague of locusts, destroy it, and then move on, but we're much too lazy to read all the words that you have so lovingly written. Please tell us everything we need to know about your city so that we can ignore what you say, and busy ourselves with shrink-wrapping our naked mate to a lamp-post and punching passers-by out cold. Oh, and any chance you could pull the birds for us too, and maybe get them moist since we're too bloody stupid and ugly?' It's not just thick blokes, either: myriad are the times we've been promised, 'Hee hee hee! We'll buy you a pint! Thanks hun!' by giggling, smiley-using bimbos for telling them where they can meet 'lush lads' who are just as dim as they are.

And why not? Party organisers have so much on their plates with sorting out Elvis costumes, devil's horns and comedy marital aids that there's very little time left to work out where the hell they're actually going to go. But it is with a gladsome heart that we reply to our correspondents - time and time again - with itineraries and facts, even though there's zero chance of them being followed. Happy-to-help-have-a-nice-day-please-call-again, that's us. After all, stag and hen nights provide a welcome boost to our city's economy, giving many, many hours of overtime to street cleaners, emergency glaziers and community police. And where would our ethnic restaurant and takeaway proprietors be without their weekly helping of ribald racism from pissed-up, kilt-wearing tourists?

Oh, we really love seeing stags and hens doing their stuff, we do. Don't know about you, but every time we see one of those smashing groups of people, we always think, hmm, they look like an affable bunch, think I'll go and talk to them and see what they've got to say about life. Never will you hear these words pass our lips: 'Oh for fuck's sake, not another bunch of tedious cunts. Who would marry that glakey fucker, like? Hope they burn the twat alive.' And those racy little nametags on hen nights! They crease us up! Let's hear it for Anorexic Angela, Burdened-with-six-kids-by-seven-fathers Brenda, Cum-on-my-curtains Caroline, Desperate-to-diet Debs, Egotistical-oestrogen-deprived Yvonne, Fuck-me-in-the-lavatory-I'm-not-getting-it-at-home Fiona, Gargantuan-gunted Glenda... we love 'em to bits, every last pig-squealing one of 'em.

But hey, just because we're honest, upstanding, respectful local citizens, it doesn't mean that they can't come to our city and let their hair down a little. There's no law against interlopers acting like complete tits, wearing stupid outfits and vomiting in our roads. Yet. And let's not forget all those shitty little print-Ur-own T-shirt merchants whose very livelihoods are dependent on slapping fuzzy photos of semi-naked holiday drunkards on ill-fitting, pauper-weight garments for such glamorous occasions. Imagine their fall in turnover if the words 'Billy Bollocks On Tour 2006' were never again seen - in fucking Comic Sans font - in the city's streets, bars and holding cells. Hats off to these champions of industry: they're what makes Britain Great.

So, definitively, once and for all, the Burglar's Dog aims to give the low-down on the stag and hen scene in Newcastle. We'll tell you the places to go to keep out of our faces, the pubs that have a devastation-repair kitty factored into their operating budgets, and the bars where, clearly, Sodom and Gomorrah still thrive. Plus, we'll tell you what's HOT and what's NOT, using the very latest research from our terminally angry reporters.

STYLE AND DEPORTMENT

Acting in the correct manner is important to you, isn't it? You want to be seen wearing only the latest trends, don't you? After all, you wouldn't want to stick out like a sore thumb and have people think that you're an unruly, drunken, manners-of-a-sow travesty of human flesh, would you? These are the things that are currently - and will be forever thus - hot and not in the stag and hen party world. Get them right and we might not kill you; get them wrong and you'll be nailed to a plank and floated up the Tyne.

Hot
Decorum
Warm hands of friendship
Keeping the fuck out of our sight
What the Irish call 'the craic'
Respect for the moral standards of the local population
Only laughing at things that are actually amusing
Sensible shoes
Dignity
Checking in at the hotel before you start drinking
The ability to say 'Why aye, man' without sounding Welsh or Pakistani
Realising you're an complete and utter pain in the arsehole

...and Not
Bacchanalia
Unsolicited displays of genitalia
Being in any way visible
Screaming like a brutally-buggered baboon within our collective earshot
Banging the town bike over a bin
Cackling at your own 'jokes'
Ball and chain combinations
Drag

Leaving your suitcases all over the floor in O'Neill's
Being Scottish. Or Cockney. Or a country bumpkin
Thinking you're in any way cool, funny or original

WHERE TO DRINK
When it comes to the matter of ideal drinking circuits, there is
but one question to ask yourself: Do you want to hang around
with fuckwits, or do you want to hang around with fuckwits wearing Burberry hats? Newcastle has two main areas catering to the
likes of you: The Bigg Market (hats on), home of the football hooligan, the underage drinker and the habitual criminal; and The
Quayside (hats off), where the clothes are more expensive, the
'flap' a little more 'class', but the IQ no higher. These are the
places to be seen in your stupid Mickey Mouse ears or your spew-
spattered gorilla suit. These are the places where anything goes
and where dignity is just a shit song by Deacon Blue on Century
FM's '80s Hour. And these are the places where we absolutely
insist you go.

Sure, there are other neighbourhoods in town, but you,
really, really don't want to go to them. They're full of lemon-
sucking miseries like us, who have ambitions no loftier than a
nice few pints and decent conversation, and would never dare to
scale the dizzy heights of drunken indecent exposure or pizza-
clutching doorway fellatio. Some people just don't know what
'fun' is. Not like you crazy kids.

Cast your mind back to chapter 1 in this book and flick forward to chapter 12: these two sections feature all the bars we
think you should visit. In fact, we insist you do. In each carefully
selected locale mentioned, we guarantee a surly, grudging welcome, queues a mile long and beer within a nanosecond of its
sell-by date. They're loud, they're expensive, and they're far and
away the fightingest bars in the Northern Hemisphere. Choose
wisely.

And for last orders? Let's be honest here: like salmon returning to their native rivers to breed, so do party 'goers' head inexorably for Buffalo Joe's on the Gateshead side of the Swing Bridge
looking for love, friendship, and maybe tops and fingers. Fact:

you will end up there. Fact: you will buy a fucking glittery cow-boy hat. Fact: we will hate you, unreservedly.

WHERE TO STAY

What are we, like: the frigging tourist board? How should we know? Why in the name of Jaheseus Christ would we pay good money to stay in a hotel when we live less than three miles away from the city centre? If it's any help, we hear that the Jury's Inn is quite popular with 'visiting groups'. They apparently have a bit of a downer on loose morals, though: a mutual friend of ours was barred from taking his new lady friend to his room simply because she was an obvious last-orders-on-the-dancefloor case. Yeah, go on; try the Jury's. And make sure you go for a few pints in one of the numerous bars between there and the city centre, too. Those customers with tight T-shirts and handlebar 'taches are guaran-teed to give you the warmest of welcomes, especially if you start spouting your inbred homophobic bollocks the minute you walk through the door.

Or, you could try the Premier Lodge in the centre of town: it's not too far to crawl back to your room from the clubs with a shattered pint pot sticking out of your neck. And the area around it already stinks to high heaven of piss and puke, so you need have no qualms about making it worse with your appalling con-duct.

Where else is there? Oh aye, there's the Malmaison and the Copthorne at opposite ends of the Quayside, if you're feeling particularly flushed, and there's another Premier Lodge in the middle, across the river from that big slugalike Sage building, plus a Travelodge behind the law courts. And bearing in mind bad pub-licity is better than no publicity, I suppose we'd better rope in the Royal Station Hotel next to the, uh, station, and the Quality Hotel off the top of the Bigg Market.

Anywhere else, you're saying? I dunno, man. Have you never heard of the internet?

No matter which friendly establishment you choose as your resting place, we're sure that you'll find the utmost comfort in which to shave each others eyebrows off and take 'amusing' pho-tos of the saggy genitals of the first of the group to pass out. Remember: it's especially hilarious if you chuck one of your mates, bollock-naked, into the corridor and let them holler vengeful threats into the wee small hours. Other guests will shake you firmly by the hand in the morning after hearing such wizard japes. Just before kicking your head in.

We hope you have found our guide to stag and hen parties in Newcastle upon Tyne useful. If you have any further queries, please do not hesitate to ask some other fucker before you bother us. And, as a friendly word of warning, we would like to make this crystal clear:

If you have used the word 'doo' instead of 'do' on any promotional literature, e-mail, or fckng sms txt msg for your event, we will hunt you down with dogs, and tar and feather each and every one of your party, their relatives, and their nodding acquaintances. And then we'll really fucking kick off.

Finally, we wish the lucky couple all the very best for their impending nuptials. We'll give it six months before she starts banging the window cleaner.

Central Station

'Fanning out from John Dobson's 1850 station edifice, the Central Station area is home to some of the city's most architecturally important buildings, and is flanked at each side by a magnificent cathedral; to the west, St Mary's with its statue of Newcastle's own Cardinal Basil Hume, and over to the east the cathedral of St Nicholas, the 15th century lantern tower of which is one of the best known landmarks of the city. The eastern side is also home to the castle built by Henry II between 1168-1178. One of the finest surviving examples of a castle keep in the country, it is this from which Newcastle takes its name.' – Norman Undercroft, Historian.

@Home
36-38 Mosley Street, NE1 1DL
'Bloody hole'

It's a simple fact that by the time street slang arrives in the mouths of advertisers hoping to appeal to kids, that same slang has long since ceased to be anything other than a distant memory to those very same kids. Similarly, though I could have sworn that the use of the '@' symbol was dead and buried to even the most trend-lagging technophobe, it seems that NOW is the time to bring it into the world of the licensed premises. But why, though? Why? Any ideas? Seeing as how the use of that symbol has put this bar alphabetically at the top of this section, and this review might be the first selection of the casual browser expecting to see a serious review of decor and wine lists and happy hours and crap like that, I thought for this one I'd at least try to do this properly. Break 'em in gently, if you like. The word that keeps coming into my head for @Home is 'tasteful'. And that's 'tasteful' with a gentle nod, a furrowed brow, and one eye sort of half shut. Can you picture the expression and hear the rising 'mmMM' sound coming from my throat? The thing is, though, where you'd expect there to be a further something to quantify that, there's just a huge bloody hole in my vocabulary. But I'm going to try. You get elegant decoration, you get stunning light fittings, and you get stone tabletops that guarantee you a lap full of shards when you slam your glass down a little too firmly. You get the choice of social club prices for half the week, and nightclub ones for the rest of the time. You get natural wood and earthy tones. And so subtle are the muted greys and browns of the colour palette, so calming and yet so vibrant, that it took our airhead lass a millisecond to suggest I painted our dining room just like that. Dumb broad. In fact, the subtlety and general lack of any hullabaloo whatsoever could be this place's downfall: I didn't even realise it was a bar at first, suspecting from the other side of the road that this was just another dodgy furniture shop. Much as I'd like to applaud their belief that their services are exclusively tailored to the cognoscenti and the crème-de-la-crème of Newcastle's drinking circuit, I'm afraid that it'll be a matter of months before their minimalist facade becomes plastered with Red Bull cocktail posters like the rest of the city's bars, and not much longer 'til Titty Tuesdays make a regular appearance. You get nowhere catering to snobs like me in this town. Like I said at the start: simple fact.

For: There is no back door, so matins, evensong and all the other happening events at the Cathedral over the way won't be interrupted by some pointless thumping Ibiza mix of '80s cheese every time someone leaves the bar.

Against: @Home, though. @-frigging-Home. How long until the first bar in the town with a text message name, or a bloody ;) emoticon after it? Actually, ALEWRX up on Newgate Street was almost a text message pub name, albeit one that meant fuck all to anyone, and that bit the dust with positively comical haste. So, aye, if anyone wants to invest their capital in a 'cash-in' business that's doomed from day one, then bring it on, I say. I could do with a laugh.

Perception problems. Went downstairs, bursting for a slash, found two doors with no words on. What would you reckon would be the Gents? The triangle or the rectangle? You worked it out yet? Those bastards. I swear that in the time between me getting it drastically wrong and ending up red-faced in the Ladies, and my female companions coming back, like, 'Eh? Are you blind?' the staff had been downstairs with the Araldite and stuck some circles above the shapes to make them look like (hey!) a man and a woman. And I won't be told otherwise.

Agora

1 The Side, NE1 1PR
'Get them to strip it all out again'

Here, I'll tell you what: it's not very often we've been astonished - literally astonished - by a bar. There's a much-remade film called *Brewster's Millions*. In the dire 1985 Richard Pryor version, as a condition of his inheritance, he has to piss thirty million dollars against the wall in a month and have bugger all to show for it. The idea is that he'll be so sick of spending cash, he'll not waste the three hundred million he's due to get. This actually happened to me. One of Pryor's japes is to hire the best interior designer in the land to do up his 'pad' and then, when the last scatter cushion has been placed on the last chaise longue, get them to strip it all out again. Walking into Agora reminded me of that scene. You want to see the place, man. It's fucking palatial. But surely someone's having a laugh, and it'll go back to being the stinking swamp that was Zoots Bar, right? Just take a look at the ridiculously opulent chandeliers, the glass tables and the potted plants that are bigger than my garden. Check out the armchairs and the carefully restored 1920s mirrors from when this place was known as The Empress. And that piano on the stage in the window isn't just there for show, kiddo. The thing I remember most from the review visit was harking back to how the place was beforehand and shaking my head, like it was all a dream. Actually it might have been: I'm sure my beer tasted like wine gums. How man, I still can't believe it. Aye, it had its bad points: pretty expensive drinks, some twat playing bongos, and the fact that we were in three days after it opened meant there were more staff than customers. But screw it; even though they've obviously spent more than they could ever hope to recoup, ambition on such a ludicrous scale has to be applauded. I just hope they succeed in pulling in the punters from the second mortgage bars - the likes of Tokyo and @Home – because if they get overrun by the usual Bigg Market scummers that pass this way, the place will be a bomb site by Easter.

For: I like the Stalinist way that Agora's publicity blurb keeps going on about The Empress, as if Zoots never existed.
Against: The notoriously humming bogs have been given a sprucing up - well, the Gents have, anyway - but our lass says the Ladies were just as vile as ever.

You thought we were going to make some smug, lazy comment about 'agora' and 'phobia', didn't you? Shame on you. The flyer that we pinched heads all those quips off at the pass by explaining that an agora was the large, open public square of any ancient city, hence fear of open spaces is agoraphobia. You never got a history lesson from Zoots, you know. Actually, that's a lie: the manager of that dump once chased us up the road and lectured us on image rights and brand history, just for taking a photo of the front of the building. He seemed to think it was our fault his pub was rotten and he was haemorrhaging cash by the

*second. The fact that his beer tasted like he was drying the pint
pots with lame cocker spaniels obviously didn't occur to him.*

Apartment

28 Collingwood Street, NE1 1JF
'As unthinkable as the Queen having a shite'

Normally we like to let the dust settle after a new pub's opening,
but this place had my piss boiling immediately with its claim to
be Newcastle's first private members bar, and its charge of - wait
for it - TWO HUNDRED QUID A YEAR for membership and access to
the VIP room. There's two ways of looking at that VIP thing: either you, the punter, are the star, which is highly unlikely since
anyone who pays 200 notes to have their own area in a bar is obviously a cock; or they're trying to entice you to part with your
cash on the premise that you'll SEE some VIPs there. Well bollocks to that - if the best they can rustle up for their 'star studded' opening night is Tony Hadley and Boney M then they can piss
off. (Holly Valance would have turned up, too, but the bone-idle
bitch was taking her time doing my dishes.) As for the decor, like
you care, the photo that we ripped out of the Chronicle's name-
and-shame advertisement feature showed us everything we'd
never hoped for in a bar: murky browns, muted oran... and what
in the name of Christ is a 'LUXEBAR' anyway? I'm reading the
blurb that goes with the list of firms responsible for the bar design, and it seems to be implying that the highlights of its innova-
tive features are chairs. And sofas. Apartment is also laying claim
to the fact that playing funk, jazz and soulful Latin House makes
it some sort of trendsetter. My crusty arse, does it. You can get
that shit anywhere, and they don't charge you a week's rent just
to walk through the bastard door. I don't care about the beer
quality, or the happy hours, or even the freshness of the toilet
facilities. I care about not having the piss taken out of me by
knobheads like this, and I care about the systematic erosion of
the English language. It's fine for Baltic to have no 'the', since
that's an art gallery and having them conform to the same rules

as the rest of us is as unthinkable as the Queen having a shite, but THE Apartment is a tuppence-ha'penny boozer, and a boozer just off the Bigg Market at that. Where do they get off with their pretentious crap? Finally, what was it Groucho Marx said about not wanting to join any club that would have him as a member? Oh, aye, he said, 'Apartment? Wankers. Fuck 'em.' And I, for one, can't argue with that.

For: It says here that you can become a 'privilege member' for the princely sum of zero per year, making a mockery of the small fortune paid upfront by the idiots who think they're Charlie Potatoes.
Against: Anything connected with the bar's existence from its idiot conception to its crestfallen closure in eight months time.

Of COURSE the fees we're ranting about are just for the roped off bits, and of COURSE it actually costs nowt for rank and file scum like us to get in. And while it is a pile of laughable toss, it's no worse than, say, Barluga, or any of the other haircut bars trailing in its wake.

The Attic
25-27 Mosley Street, NE1 1YF
'The goody bag of a particularly inept paedophile'

I remember we went in to The Attic when it first opened, were rightly appalled, and swore blind never to return, preferring instead to scowl at it from the other side of the road whenever we're in the vicinity. But, like kids in a horror film checking out the old barn, curiosity forced us in for a revisit to mark and mock the changes. Once notorious for their groundbreaking sloping bar, the one that deposited expensive drinks onto expensive trainers, they've seen sense, backed down, and replaced it with the kind of traditional, level, SAFE counter that's done alehouses proud since beer was invented. That, as far as I can tell, is the only positive thing to have happened over the years. Everything else seems to have taken a turn for the worse and thrown away the bloody map. Glancing around I get the feeling - and I may be wrong, but fingers, toes and testes crossed - that the bottom has fallen out of the luxury bar market. Let's fucking hope so. That would explain why everything I can see in this place seems to have been done on the cheap, from the grubby-looking pictures knocked up on a photocopier with a knackered toner to the bar-gain-bin frames on the walls; just frames, nowt in them. There's plastic ferns dressed in Christmas lights, tables made out of old cornflake packets and sticky-backed plastic, and spray-painted sticks in pots. Even their feature wall of tiles - from a distance like something they've pinched from Notre Dame - reveals itself on closer inspection to be made out of tacky plastic too. And fuck me 'til I fart and follow through, their colour scheme is abysmal. What the hell are they supposed to be? Candy stripes? The only time you'd get candy that depressing is in the goody bag of a par-ticularly inept paedophile, one who's stocked up on Werther's Originals, Mintoes and a couple of Caramacs to tempt the kids to see his puppies. And if that isn't enough to make you turn tail and leave before you've even ordered, then look at the state of that carpet; it was criminal when it was still on the loom, never mind mashed and trampled with years of dog ends, drink and hockle. Don't bother taking the spiral staircase in the corner, either: it just leads to more of the same gloomy shite upstairs, but with curtains nailed haphazardly to the ceiling and a few lonely mirror balls. Unsurprisingly, the Attic is still a cocktail bar, but one with the notion that the clown doing the stirring is the attraction, rather than the drink they're making, so you can still see the inevitable 'practice session' if you get in early enough, plus suffer the surcharge passed on to you for what the twats slop down your their bloody shirts when they do it for real. I'm sorry; I still hate this bar and everyone who drinks in it. I have never been impressed by their questionable claims of greatness or their list of VIP visitors, and I'm certainly not going to be told that a bar is in any way luxurious - despite all the attempts at tarting it up - when the first thing I see when I walk through the door is the fucking goods lift staring dejectedly from the other side of the room.

For: One of the Windsor kids hauled his royal arse in here once. Not sure if it was the baldy one or the ginger one but, either way, it's the kiss of death for credibility.

Against: As far as I can tell, there's only one set of (non-disabled) bogs, and they're down in the basement. So if you're supping upstairs, it's round and round the spiral staircase, through the lower bar and down another flight before you can relieve yourself. I'd guess you'd be gasping for breath by that point, but I'd advise against it, since the whole toilet level still reeks of mould and decay after all this time.

I never understand fashion at the best of times, but what the hell is going on with the kids' haircuts these days? Sticking up at the back, wonky at the sides, huge chunks missing from the fringe, and it's exactly what they fucking well asked for! Look at them as they leave the salon, grinning like Harold Shipman at a tea dance and tipping the stylist a tenner. Eighteen months ago, if they'd walked out of the hairdressers looking like that they'd have cried for a month and phoned Mr Justice. Gullible turds.

The Bodega
125 Westgate Road, NE1 4AG
'It only leads to the crappers'

It's a sad indictment of bar culture that a place we would have ridiculed for being a pub-themed theme-pub when it was last refurbished should now be one of the best low-key boozers in Newcastle. There's something about the Bodega that tickles our plums, even if it's absolutely chock-full of all the stuff we normally start howling in protest about, like broken instruments, job-lots of Olde Worlde pictures, framed cigarette cards and other random tat. Formerly the music hall for the Tyne Theatre next door, the pub has kept the best features, like the two huge art nouveau stained glass domes in the ceiling, and has even semi-convincingly mocked up a sign saying Music Hall, though these days it only leads to the crappers. The grubby wallpaper looks splendidly awful, the booths heroically uncomfortable and the furniture lacking in at least one of the necessary vitamins. I like things like that, me. You get a mixed bag of punters in here: you'd expect either theatre luvvies or the kind of scumbag who hangs around the city walls at the bottom of Westgate Road supping cheap cider from plastic bottles, but the pub is respectably full of, well, normal people. I've noticed a few students as well, but you can't have everything. The beer's pretty good in here, too: it seems to get given an award by CAMRA every other month, and those self-righteous bastards are notoriously difficult to please. In a nutshell, I'd make this one of my regular haunts if I didn't get sidetracked by Tilleys every time I come this way.

For: Last time I went to Edinburgh, mooching through the old town in the fog, I got charged a fiver for a single shot of a 'special' whisky. Bloody robbers; the Bodega served me the same stuff for a quid and a half.
Against: First pint, I nearly broke my neck falling over the brass ornament on the floor at the end of the bar. Second pint, I clacked my ankle off the one at the other end. Turns out one was Punch and the other was Judy. Hobbled by both of the fuckers. What are the chances of that?

The ring road just up the hill from the Bodega has been christened St James' Boulevard by the council. Boulevard? Ha ha ha. Six lanes of traffic snarls and a few spindly trees and they think it's Hollywood.

The Bridge Hotel
Castle Garth, NE1 1RQ
'Chair-gnawing awfulness'

Owned by Sir John Fitzgerald Ltd and far more of a flagship than the snooze and dribble-fest of the bar on Grey Street that bears the company name, The Bridge Hotel is easily one of the finest old pubs in Newcastle. In fact, the only thing I don't like about it is how really, really difficult it is to find something I don't like about it. Overlooking the castle keep and helpfully located right next to a bridge - the High Level, the one that'll be wrapped in swaddling for the next twenty years while they work out what the bloody hell's wrong with it - this is a pub like they used to be made, with leather lounge seating, snugs at the front, wood panelling and bookshelves and stuff. And while the stained glass pictures of bridges and historic scenes dotted about are hardly going to have York Minster bricking it, they're still good enough for this whingeing twat. I'd say The Bridge is a bar for all seasons, if I didn't think I'd get walloped for writing such hackneyed bollocks. Look at it this way: would you, amid the relentless trudge of winter, head for a snooty lounge bar to sit and freeze in the glow of designer candles puttering ineffectually to the beat of some gitboy's white label collection? Or would you snuggle down in here next to the three-bar fire that's hot enough to fuse your britches to your shins? It's a tough choice, I know. Summer means it's time to tiptoe down the back stairs to the beer terrace between the old city walls, where there's views to the riverside and across the water, with the legendary - to dickless film buffs who don't have to look at it every day - Gateshead multi-storey car park rotting in the distance. And all year round, upstairs has the function room with its photos of jazz greats and its planky stage, usually featuring acoustic-something-or-other. Pull up a stool or perch on the windowsill, and see for yourself the canyon between belief and talent, between the greatness of the concept and the chair-gnawing awfulness of reality. But you can't grumble, even if you're guaranteed that, whichever night you choose to go, the one act you could ever tolerate played their final show there the day before. And taking the bar as a whole, you can't really complain about any of it, unless you're desperate to pull or bursting to gyrate like an undead kebab to the latest sounds of maxed-up Corsa land. If that's what you're after you can get it down the hill or back in the Bigg Market. And you can also, make no bones about it, fuck off. I'm not going to deny that everyone in here is a fart, a bore, a fogey and a scruff. But I mean that in a good way. The Bridge is class.

For: Even the crappiest of crappy lagers can usually be relied upon to taste halfway pleasant and not leave you feeling inferior to the snobs sipping single malts or gargling and sluicing on Oggle's Green Cockrot.

Against: Here's the one thing that gets on my nerves: the terrace and the bogs are on the same level, but to get between them you have to go up the stairs to the main level, and then down again to empty your back.

This is how unlucky I am: when I was standing outside like a tit in a trance trying to get the photo for the Dog website, the function room was crammed with loud-shirted lads roaring at some sort of spectacle. A photographer's life is a cursed life: you see the world through a tiny viewfinder, and by the time you've got the frigging camera to focus you've missed most of the event you wanted to record. And so it was that I caught sight of the disappearing bare shoulder of the young stripper who was up there with them, just as they'd realised I was there and dropped their kecks for a full moon. Goddamn it.

Centurion

Newcastle Central Station, NE1 5DG
'Humphrey Bogart'

Picture the scene: it's 7pm on a cold winter's night; you're waiting for your one true love to arrive back in town and meet you in the newly-opened bar in the station's lovingly-restored Grade I listed first class passenger lounge. You're excited, hopeful, apprehensive even, but, slumped in the armchair facing the bar, you try to give off an air of studied nonchalance, scanning the newspaper supplements while sipping nervously at your drink, glancing occasionally at the arrivals board on the screen above the counter, and at the grandeur of the historic Burmantoft tiling. The gentle flicker of the flaming lanterns soothes your soul, while the strains of Barber's Adagio recall the fireside evenings spent in warm embraces. Suddenly the door opens, your beloved enters and, instead of a Humphrey Bogart tear-stained reunion, she drops her case on your foot, starts complaining about the spot on her chin and the breast-feeding bitch at her table who hectored her all the way home, while some glakey bastard hollers, 'SHUT THE FUCKING DOOR, IT'S FREEZING IN HERE, MAN.' Then it hits you: this place, like your hopes, like your very life, is a sham. You're in a train station bar with backpackers leering through the door, the flames aren't real, the beer is overpriced and the target customers - YOU - are complete wankers. I mean, look at you, man. What sort of a fucking fool do you feel like now? You sit there, with your toffee nose in the air, like there's a 30 year-old malt in your hand and not a scabby pint of Foster's, waiting for the Flying Scotsman to come back into service. So you pinned all your hopes on some black and white matinee dream, did you? You wanted *Brief Encounter*, but instead you got *What the Butler Saw* with all the mucky bits cut out. Am I right? Go on, you simpering mug. Give her a kiss like you're at least halfway happy to see her; grab her case like the gentleman you'll never be, and haul your sorry carcass to the taxi queue in shame. You cad.

For: I say, darling. Would you mind awfully if I slipped you a length?

Against: (slap) You bounder! How dare you?! And tell me, sir: Is that your cologne or the faint-yet-unmistakable aroma of man-piss wafting through the bar?

The cad in the review was me, in case you couldn't tell. I've always wanted a train station scene that didn't involve Glaswegian drunks or the smell of Burger King, and, behind your post-ironic exterior, so have you. Nostalgia is the new rock 'n' roll, I'm telling you. And that's why I prefer to write about that instead of thinking about the abomination that I have since found Centurion to be. Take it from me, even the good-bad bits of the original design are history. The fake flames have disappeared, along with the sumptuous café-bar atmosphere and most of the tasteful comfy chairs. In their place is a neglected, echoing shed, with tacky lighting effects clashing with the tiling, and a range of pouffe seating that's only one step up from the bags on a left-

luggage floor. It's crystal clear what's going through the minds
of the management: they're cursing the very idea of listed build-
ings and the restrictions they put on DJ sets. And it's plain to see
they've got as much love for those tiles as they would for a gin-
ger stepchild.

Clear
Pudding Chare, NE1 1JE
'Safe from the bad man'

Brought to us by the people behind the Telegraph, Clear is the
poor relation, the delinquent little brother, the kid in the calli-
pers in every possible way. Just take a look at the place, if your
peepers can stand it. The Telegraph - obviously first to the trough
- took the soothing shades from the family paint box and left the
runt of the litter with the rest to slap around in his clumsy, juvenile manner. And when Mummy came back from the shops and
saw the mess that the brat had made in trying to copy his big
brother, she wasn't very happy. But there'll be no smacked bottoms today, because a child that matches purple walls with a
bilious green doorway and artwork is clearly a special needs child
who requires understanding and tolerance. The Telegraph is an
adult now, a working man, and he has the skills of a time-served
joiner; little shitboy here, meanwhile, should hang his head in
shame at the balls he made of those radiator cupboards when he
found Daddy's tools at the back of the garage. If the Tele can
have a grown-up rooftop beer garden, then junior is going to have
his own, out in the yard and safe from the bad man. He's going to
put up fairy lights and have metal tables to clang. And when he's
bored with the clanging, he's going to go inside and make more
noise; he's going to be like his brother the DJ, except he doesn't
want to have guuuuuurls talking to him and kissing him and saying
they'll put his doo-dah in their mouths if he plays their favourite
song. Instead he's just going to press as many buttons as he can
until he gets told off and starts to cry. You had enough of this
junior theme yet? Are you going to beg us to drop it? Look, the

only reason we've persisted with it is that it ties in neatly with the bar's main customer base, namely barely pubescent girls and angry youths, taking out their frustration at society's ills and their hormonal slavery by slashing the seats and wrecking the booths. Clear - for reasons we have yet to fully understand - is a haven for kids. It is, and that's something we can say confidently without fear of legal action, mainly because they're the ones always up before the beak and in the papers, getting in bother for serving underage drinkers. Beats me why it even gets that far, since I can't see how the damned staff can fail to notice the ages of the punters. Clear never seems full or even break-even busy. It's not like there's ever a crush or a heads-down-and-pour pandemonium at the bar. There's just a steady trickle of shifty teens wasting their pocket money trying to keep the place afloat. Do you go there? No. Me neither. Can't see this one making it to a ripe old age.

For: The entire front wall is made of glass, so you can see exactly what you're letting yourself in for.
Against: That 'For' means I owe the 'end a sentence with a preposition' tin another quid.

I ended the review talking about the lack of customers. The first time we visited Clear finally underlined why you should never trust officially sanctioned photos. We were just sitting there on a Monday evening when we heard all this hollering and 'supervision' going on. Christ, we thought, it can't be some Team Leader bossing around her army of headset-wearing phone monkeys after-hours, can it? Hell no. Rent-a-crowd, I'm telling you, shipped in by the management to make the place look busy for the Chronicle's promo launch photos. Straights. And you know what happened next? Once the snapper had done his business, they just slammed down their courtesy lime and sodas and pissed off. Ungrateful fucking hoors.

Coco.V

Bewick House, Forth Lane, NE1 5EF
'Recklessly unnecessary'

My bus used to stop outside Coco.V every morning, but since the
routes changed following the High Level Bridge fiasco - not to
mention the endless demolition projects around the Station – over
time this place reverted in my imagination from schmoov bar
back to the dull office block it was before. I couldn't give even a
weak Wednesday wank about Coco.V these days, heading straight
for the Forth every time I've walked this way, but returning for
the review I found that it's more or less still laid out as the designers intended. Here's the buzzwords from the old Coco.V website: Leather and Soul. Cappuccinos to Cocktails. Relaxing
Rhythms. Warm Vibes. And here's what you really get: Dansak-
diarrhoea walls and lights that look like a hanging basket of used
condoms. (Well, mine, anyway: the rest of you can just fill each
of a dozen blobs with a glass and a half of full-cream milk and
hang the fuckers on a hook.) There's a handful of booths with Ali-
Baba curtains, handy for trapping the flies and the nicotine smog,
and a zebra skin carpet near the doorway that is nothing but
recklessly unnecessary. Digging further into the decor, I see Moroccan lamps hanging in the windows, hidden nooks decked out
like Arabian tents and, obviously for a 'laugh', plastic palm trees.
This, I would have to conclude, is a souk bar theme, dangerously
similar to the one that caused the ruin of Po Na Na. Do people
never learn? A few pints in on the last time we were here we noticed a couple of blokes dragging out a big box into one of the
raised areas. I'd hoped it was a magic show - maybe saw the
barmaid in half, or something like that - but it turned out to be
another fucking no-mark DJ plying his pitiful trade to a handful of
uninterested early-evening punters. I think I've realised why superstar DJs are such a hit in places like this: it's because for
ninety percent of the time self-appointed 'cultural high' bars play
stuff that sounds like Curiosity Killed the Cat demos, and anything
with half a tune is seen as a godsend. Fucking hell, man, the
howls of a hyena shitting barbed wire suppositories would be

preferable to the dismal 'b-duh-duh-tish-tish' background noise they spin in this place. And this is what the kids today aspire to? Never mind National Service, they should bring back chimney sweeping.

For: It's not too bad in the early evening, basking in the dying rays of the sun with a happy hour pint or two.
Against: Later on, this place will attract wankers like a Gateshead girl's g-string gets, uh, some sort of fly beginning with 'g'. Fucking hell, this alliteration business is hard work. Greenfly! That's the bastards!

I never pay that much attention to toilet fixtures and fittings - maybe because I'd rather wipe my hands on the wife in a fraudulent display of affection than wash my mitts in the sinks - but above the taps in the bogs here are illuminated adverts that turn into mirrors when you approach them. How miraculous is that? And what's this? A machine that dispenses both condoms and breath fresheners for the bar's amorous and hopeful? If only there was an extra slot where they could stick in a £2 coin and get a fucking personality too, they'd be laughing.

Destination

Royal Station Hotel, Neville Street, NE1 5EW
'The world's shabbiest breakfast bar'

I think I know what my problem is with this place. The way I feel about Destination is pretty much the same as the way I felt about Cheryl Tweedy before she opened her mouth. From a distance, first impressions pointed to everything I'd ever wanted; my heart was racing, and I was thinking 'Yes. Yes! Tremendous'. Then the reality whacked me round the back of the napper with a rolled up Chronicle; Cheryl's a fucking charver dimwit encased in the face and body of an angel, and Destination's exterior hides a core of true evil. Well, maybe that's a bit strong, but it reflects my disenchantment: there's something about being promised greatness and delivered mediocrity that pains you much more than expecting and getting shite. Situated downstairs in what used to be the world's shabbiest breakfast bar, of the Royal Station Hotel, Destination is yet another all-flash-no-soul experience, complete with the spirit-sapping colour scheme and other crap we've all come to expect from a modern bar. And although it has a wealth of history to draw on, Destination looks to have tried its gut-busting best to sully anything that might have been good about the period features. The original ceiling tiling has been lovingly exposed and then inexplicably obscured by highly unoriginal air conditioning pipes, the carvings on the pillars painted in a shade of mauve that infringes my human rights, and the walls clad in what looks like scratched plastic. Purple plastic, naturally. The carpet on the upper level will have dictionary committees redefining the word 'hideous', the signal for the expensive plasma screens renders every image like a sketch in cheap coloured pencils, and the divider across the room looks exactly like the bar by the window in Delboy's Peckham flat. Judging by the punters when we were in, I'd say this place is popular with hen night first-pubbers, straight off the train and down the stairs, fidgeting in the window before the rest of the girls turn up with the devil's horns and amusing marital aids, and casually eyeing up the knob-heads at the bar. That bar is nowhere you'd want to loiter for long. Maybe the staff are so sick of dealing with the stream of cocky clothes horses and feral she-cats that they've introduced a policy of making even the pint buying unpleasant: the barman and I concluded the deal with minimal interaction and a display of mutual contempt. On paper there's only one thing that makes Destination just about bearable, and that's the beer terrace outside, but even that crumbles when put to the test; you go out expecting a pleasant outdoor pint with a quick peek up a passing skirt, but instead you just get fag ends and gravel hoofed into your face. And fresh air? Forget it. Better get a taste for the taxi fumes as the greasy, fat heart attack candidates slowly fuse themselves to their seats while they idle in the queue alongside the hotel. Look at the state of me. Look at the expression on my face. Post-work on a Friday, in the sunshine, pint in hand, and I still feel unhappy? That takes some doing.

For: Empty.
Against: The DJ in the corner or in a booth I can accept. The DJ set up on a podium in the middle of the dancefloor, like they're going to wheel the prick around on a forklift, is a different kettle of cod altogether.

The Royal Station Hotel is often host to wedding fairs, at which stressed-out brides-to-be can 'Ooh!' and 'Aah!' at all the ways they can be ripped off on their special day. We were talking about the whole wedding fiasco the other day and I was having problems understanding why, no matter what the bride's hairstyle is for the rest of the courtship, come the big day she has to adopt the regulation wedding barnet. Whether she normally sports tumbling curls, a sleek modern crop, or even a bloody afro, on the happiest day of her life she'll have her hair scraped back in such a fashion that there's a force of 500 Newtons per square inch of scalp. Finally it dawned on me that these poor women don't do it to look good, but because it's the only way they'll be able to keep their rictus grin through eight hundred photos, the best man's speech and a brutal family punch-up. Now I understand. Could YOU look happy watching ten grand being frittered away so people you don't like can wear daft hats and go 'Eeh!'?

Dog & Parrot

52 Clayton Street West, NE1 4EX
'George fucking Formby'

Now back to the Dog & Parrot after all those years of being saddled with the stupid name of the Tut and Shive, this place remains popular with what's left of Newcastle's punk scene. There's not an hour goes by without some middle-aged, potbellied old soak propping up the bar in his Discharge leather jacket, having to convince himself at least once per pint that punk's not dead because, if it was, he'd look a right fucking fool with his tattooed leopard-skin head. Don't get me wrong; I've got nothing against a bit of fancy dress, but if these berks must adopt a look that's just a jump to the left of the Rocky Horror Picture Show, then it makes sense to be able to wash it off the next morning. Bless. For all its outside hints at Traditional Bar, on the inside the Dog & Parrot looks like nothing so much as a purpose-built dump, with old doors clagged to the ceiling, grimy paint-work and all manner of tatty crap on the walls. This is a good thing. There's a fire in the corner, a pool table on the upper level and, on a blackboard above the bar, there's this month's list of wave-chasing live acts. I haven't seen a band upstairs for a while, but it looks to me - judging from the gig stills they show on the plasma screens downstairs - as though the stage walls have gone from plain black to a backdrop of rock posters featuring the sort of legends they wish had cut their performing teeth in places like this. That's clearly a joke: never mind The Who and Led Zeppelin, George fucking Formby would have had problems with the D&P's farcically huffy sound limiter. But that's nitpicking based, probably, on hearsay and misheard sour grapes from people in bands that needed the plug pulling on them as a mercy killing. Looking back at our old reviews, I remember we gave this place a right old skinhead moonstomping when it was the Tut & Shive. But we've mellowed with age. As long as you're prepared to genuflect to Green Day every twenty minutes and don't mind looking at some knacker with a bolt through his nose while you're supping your pint, then there's plenty to recommend.

For: The big roaring fire and the retro rock on the jukebox.
Against: I still have nightmares about the upstairs bogs, where pissing your pants was a more hygienic option than wading about in the dark, ankle-deep in human waste and tripping face-first over the mop and into the trough.

I like to people-watch - or, more accurately, leer - in extreme bars like this. I find it most amusing to see the very moment at which it dawns upon the emerging babe in the ripped fishnets that her galumphing teens are giving way to shapely womanhood. Look deep into her over-painted eyes and you'll see the realisation writ large. It says: 'Nirvana fucking, like, rock. Punk is here

77

to...hey wait! The puppy fat's disappearing! Hang on: what the hell am I doing in here with these uggers?'

Fleet Street

14 Pudding Chare, NE1 1UE
'Ah, bless them'

It's hard to see how anyone without a vested interest in this place could possibly sing its praises. You know when a child comes home from school clutching a sheet of paper with several daubs of primary colours on it and proudly announces, 'It's YOU, Daddy!'? And though Daddy's lips say, 'Well done! That's really good!', his inner monologue informs him, 'Weeping Jesus on the cross, I have spawned the devil'. It's a bit like that. I mean, ah, bless them, they've really had a good go at the refit, and they've obviously tried their best, but it's still about as drab and unappealing as it was before. Were we to be charitable we'd mark it down as a poor man's Popolo, done on a budget of less than a tenner, but if honesty was the order of the day, we'd have to say there's only a broken tile's difference between here and the bogs in the Head Of Steam. Maybe there's something about having to pass all the boarded up derelict restaurants on my way from the centre of town that breaks my spirit before I even get through the door, but I still can't find too much to praise in this place. As expected, the refit amounts to the usual bandwagon-clambering pastel shades, with DIY makeover show tongue and groove affixed here and there, and minimalist designer tables that are six inches lower than the bloody chairs. I'm no fan of the black and white prints of local scenes they've got all over the walls, I must admit, but what I will say in Fleet Street's defence is that I did like the display up the staircase of photos of local characters, journalists and regulars; it certainly makes a change from Marilyn Monroe or cod-African artworks. And maybe that's the answer, the thing that'd stop me from being such a sour bastard towards this bar and its faults as I see them. Maybe if they stopped trying to second guess what the rest of the town's going to do, scrapped all pretence of being a fashion bar like the ones down the road and round the corner, waved two fingers at the fucking lot of it and went back to being the Printer's Pie I'd finally be happy. Where's the shame in being a plain old pub? Does everywhere have to be a 'lounge' these days? I'd much rather sit and have a decent pint in a place that had a bit of personality than subsidise another failing luxebar.

For: The big windows at the front open in summer.
Against: Those windows open out onto a minging back lane with the grunts from the Chronicle despatch leering at you all afternoon.

The standard of the Chronicle's journalism has really gone downhill lately; amongst the usual slipshod clangers last week there was a bit inviting people to a 'pubic' meeting. I'm always blathering on about misused apostrophes on the website, partly because I'm borderline autistic, but mostly because it really gets up my bloody hooter the way that the English language is going to hell in a Humvee and nobody seems to give a shite. Get this, right: there's a fireplace shop along my way, where some bungler has made a sign for the front that says 'Fire's' instead of 'Fires'. A lazy slip of the brush I could accept - provided they sent me a letter of apology, of course - but this sign is in relief, so someone has obviously gone to the trouble of making a separate apostrophe, plus three extra pegs to hang it on. I was along there on Tuesday night, only a little bit drunk, trying to whack it off with a stick to do the shopkeeper and, indeed, the whole town a favour by correcting the sign maker's punctuation. And what happens? I'm the one who gets arrested! Can you fucking believe that?!

The Forth

Pink Lane, NE1 5DW
'Raspberry headfucker'

The Forth is a bit of a strange place in that it alternates between a relaxing, intimate, friendly, down-to-earth, modern bar with a great jukebox, and a cliquey, chokingly smoky, smug wankfest full of irredeemable cunts. No word of a lie. I've witnessed it many a time. Always a Dog favourite for at least one pint on a night out – apart from when it burned down a few years ago - The Forth has a good choice of exotic beers, plus economy lager for the student in your life. It's one of life's great hoots when you drag your work 'mates' in to see that pubs other than Pacific and Bar 42 do exist, let them develop a taste for some Belgian raspberry headfucker and then watched them shit blood when they've seen the price of their round. The latest post-blaze decor consists of massive chandeliers, some alarming wallpaper on (fashionably) one wall only, and work from local artists on the upper level: did they ever flog that painting of the Gateshead multi-storey car park? I certainly hope so, since it's bad enough having to pass it every day, without seeing it on the walls of the bar, too. There are big windows to illuminate that lunchtime session and to give you an unparalleled view of the dossers and crackheads in Pink Lane, and while the outside paint job seems to be stuck at the undercoat stage, I'm not entirely sure if that's permanent or not. What I really like about the Forth, though, is the way that, whatever design foolishness they care to throw at it, it always looks like a knackered old boozer. You can't buy qualities like that, you know. But, hell, it wouldn't be a Dog review without a bit of griping about something. And here it is: I despise, fail to understand and try to avoid DJs at all costs, as anyone will tell you. I'm an old fart who's long past his peak, and I'm only a cardigan's throw away from shouting 'Turn that bloody racket off. Call that music? You want some Big Black on, something with a proper tune'. But what I will say is this: there is absolutely no need, ever, for the Forth's Sunday AFTERNOON DJ to ruin my day and my under-crackers by booming out shit-loosening bass under Top 40 standards. What the fuck were they thinking? But all this is just minor carping about a place I really like and end up in more often than not. Go on, give it a whirl. You might even like it. And if you're feeling a little uncertain about your freedom of expression and the individuality of your dress sense, then rest assured: there's always someone in here who looks more of a dick than you ever could.

For: One of the few bars in the town to still have a decent sized, fully functioning real fire.
Against: Said fire is always surrounded by total helmets who'll hog it all night, especially when you're frozen to the marrow.

It was a while back now when they did it, but The Forth was also one of only two bars to acknowledge The Burglar's Dog website, plugging it on their menus and on the boards in the doorway. The other pub was the closed-on-police-advice Cage Bar. I try not to think about that too deeply.

Gengis
Grainger Street, across from Central Station, NE1 5EN
'Stand up for the murderous tyrant'

The woman we bought our house from was a heavy smoker. And she was a lunatic, one who seemed to have dedicated her entire life to spreading Artex over everything and then sitting down with twenty Bensons to admire her handiwork. Her idea of the perfect living room ceiling was one with two-inch thick asbestos-peppered icebergs that laughed in the face of the smooth-over or the abrasive scrape, and were only prepared to talk business with the wallpaper steamer, the chisel and the fucking six-pound lump hammer. Weekend after weekend we spent up those damn ladders getting the poisonous shite off, the steam dripping boiling hot liquid nicotine down the backs of our necks, until we could finally relax with a battered - but healthy - starting point for our B&Q dreams. And that, the stained, cracked, riddled, distempered, tobacco-streaked shell of a room we were left with, is more or less what Gengis is like. Sure, there's a couple of other features, like the wallpaper that's supposed to look like peeling paint - the stuff with the comically fake studs glued to it - plus some oriental pictures and ornaments and other crap bought on eBay when they were desperate. Aye, there's a mix of wood and slate, and some laughably unconvincing flickering flames behind the bar. But what the fuck's that on the wall over there? Is it an exotic logo, or is it mould? I'm going to stand up for the murderous tyrant here because, let's face it, he gets a bit of a bad rep. I'm going to state quite boldly that the sheer ineptitude of the design concept in this bar is an insult to the memory of Genghis Khan, especially since they haven't even spelled his name right. What are they trying to imply? That, if he came back from a few months' hard marauding, the first thing he'd want to do would be come in here and relax with a gloopy cocktail or a business lunch? And there's a DNA statistic that I misheard once that says, like, 45% of the population of the western world are direct descendents of the Mongol Overlord. In that case there must have been a rogue gene on the loose somewhere down the line because, instead of being fiery warriors, the berks responsible for this bar were clearly not just effeminate, but bone bloody idle too. And if Genghis had known that this was his legacy, this tatty, cardboard haven for red-faced and silver-haired executives, he might have kept his pecker in his pants a bit more often.

For: At least they've had the decency to abandon their initial super-priced pretensions from when they first opened all those years ago.

Against: I haven't seen them switch on the - whoo! - flaming torches outside for a while. That might be because I haven't even glanced at the place for a while.

The Burglar's Dog on... studs. Slippy metal studs beside pedestrian crossings. Why? I'd assume it's for the blind, but I fail to see just how putting death traps in the pavements can be a positive step for the visually impaired. It's almost like they're saying, in some bizarre form of foot-Braille, 'Hey! Stevie Wonder!

*When you're flat on your face with your head in the bus lane,
then you'll know you're at a safe place to cross.'*

The Globe

11 Railway Street, NE4 7AD
'The best shag I've ever known'

Sometimes, when forced by friends with no taste, no bus fare and
certainly no mercy, I can be seen supping on Gateshead's Low
Fell. It hurts, but it's not life threatening. A couple of years ago
the Fell's drinkers were witness to the debacle of Smart, where
the scuzzy Gateshead Arms was modernised, refurbished and
transformed into the sort of luxury bar that pub designers think
everyone on the planet wants to chill in; erroneously, I might
add. Heads were scratched and wallets kept firmly in pockets as
Smart's owners tried to force the concept of the blissed-out
lounge down the throats of people who simply could not give a
monkey's, then watched in despair as their takings plummeted
before giving in, shutting up, and changing it all back - name included - to the way it was before. Four months Smart lasted, if
my memory serves me well. And I can see that sort of thing happening here. It's a shame, really, because the brand-new Globe is
much better than Smart ever was, and certainly has a lot more
going for it than some other spruced up bars I could care to mock.
Why the worry? Mainly the site of the building, which does them
no favours whatsoever; it's less location, location, location, and
more oh-fuck, oh-fuck, oh-fuck. Stuck in the middle of nowhere,
with the gay bars on one side, Benfield Motors across the way,
and no more than a handbrake turn from Scotswood Road up
over, the Globe has got its work cut out to drag in the customers,
unless they strike a deal with the Jury's Inn nearby, making it a
compulsory condition of sale to nip in here for a couple. I'm not
going to pretend it's revolutionary; black slate, black leather,
wooden bar and floor. There are modern photos and artworks of
the Quayside on the walls - purple, I'm afraid - with sections
painted to look like polystyrene tiles. The carpeted area has the

best shag I've ever known on a pub floor, the lamps have been made out of old black tights, and the posters for live music feature the Ukulele Allstars, for whom it's simply not possible to be as bad as their name suggests. The bogs are up some stairs, through some doors, up some more stairs, through another set of doors, out through the yard, DOWN again, across the hall and up again. At least that's how I got there. But it's helpful that they've acknowledged the maze by sticking up arrows to take you back to your pint. That's it: no surprises, no wacky gimmicks, no horror show. It's a nice bar and I bear them no malice. When there's a gig on at the Arena round the corner they should hopefully be coining it in, but I fear - and it's proper pants-pappering fear - that if the punters there prefer officially sanctioned Arena beer at twice the price of the Globe's, then it'll be bankruptcy and ruin, with dogfights on the pool table and the Scotchy charvers dancing triumphantly around the smouldering ashes.

For: Got a joke for you, if you're interested. William Shakespeare walks into a bar. 'Oi,' says the barman, 'You're a poet and playwright, generally regarded as the greatest writer of the English language!' You're not laughing? I think I must've fucked the punch line up somewhere.

Against: Maybe I should have made reference somewhere in the review to the Globe Theatre where Shakespeare's works were performed. That might have helped the 'joke'. I'll never make it as a comedian.

For the benefit of non-locals, I'd like to clear up a misunderstanding here. When I use the word charver, you think I mean 'chav', don't you? Chav is a media twit buzzword, a way to poke fun at the working class for wearing last season's clothes, and for dropping their Gs, Hs, and Ts because that's how they've always spoken and not in the patronising way that that prick out of Coldplay does. Chav is a fashionable term, as if when the papers decide it's unfashionable, it'll be Jimmy Choos all round. Chav is Danniella Westbrook getting the milk in, and chav has fuck all to do with charver. Charver is born stupid. Charver is murderous for kicks. Charver is pure evil (pronounced pua, as in puarly ladgeful). And if you don't understand the difference, you're in for a fucking shock, let me tell you that.

Gotham Town

Neville Street, NE1 5DF
'Four 'K' a day plus expenses'

The last time I was in here was on a work night out and there's something about the philosophy behind this pub that reminds me of work. I think it's the concept of 'Look, I know it's a stupid idea, but we've paid some pompous consultants four 'K' a day plus expenses, so we'd better go through with it or we'll lose face.' So, like the city really needed a mediaeval theme bar, here's Gotham Town to add its two groats-worth to Newcastle's nightlife. Despite the wall of windows facing Bewick Street, the pub is pretty dark and gloomy, especially on the various split-levels and pulpit-type areas towards the back, and while someone probably spent ages on all the carvings and eagle's heads and the like, I'm sure they're supposed to be terrifying rather than just terrifyingly bad. Still, this place seems popular enough, though whether that's down to the atmosphere in here or the fact that its proximity to Central Station makes it a good first pub for the straight-off-the-train brigade, I'm not really sure. One thing's for certain, though: it's not down to the quality of the beer, which is little short of piddle. Another thing: It always amazes me, that in the early days of the Twenty-first Century, when Internet technology means that people can communicate at light speed across the globe, that your average DJ's PA system still makes him sound like a haemorrhoid-stricken baboon with his head stuck in a chamber pot. Huh? What the fuck did he say?

For: It filters off the lunatics straight from the train before they get as far as the Forth.
Against: There's a branch of Subway round the back, so this bar - like everything else within a 500 yard radius of that planet-straddling superbrand - stinks of puke.

Now I remember. When I came here on that work night out they had some geezer with a mullet and a waistcoat playing the saxophone, parping his way through dreadful busker versions of '80s hits. I think he was aspiring to be Kenny G. Ambition, that's what I like to see. Arsehole.

The Head of Steam
2 Neville Street, NE1 5EN
'A good sprinkling of numpties'

Buried under a gruesome office block, and proving that you don't need to desecrate an important piece of local architecture to site a successful pub, the Head of Steam is Newcastle's number one bar for indie saddoes, emo kids, student wankers, call them what you will. It's also one of Newcastle's most popular small venues, and a damned fine boozer to boot. The punters on any given night are exactly the same: sullen kids dressed in the standard I'm-an-individual-and-so-are-all-my-mates-who-look-just-like-me gear: heavy-rimmed glasses, too-small T-shirt, and a scarf indoors. The girls all wear men's shoes and the lads seem duty bound to sport women's bags, for some reason. Like, kewl. Me, I gave up reading the NME years ago - on account of trying to match up their praise of The Datsuns with the actual band called The Datsuns, mostly - but if you're looking for an indie rock ghetto, or somewhere to hear people squabbling about whether the latest over-hyped skinny white boys were better when nobody liked them, then this really is the place for you. In terms of layout, the pub is on two floors - upstairs and basement - with only the vile pissers and a windowsill full of jumbled-up club flyers on the ground floor. The upstairs bar - the main bit, if you like - is a laid-back, friendly, theme-free room done out in cream and red and with a load of paintings on the walls; stylistically I'd put them somewhere between Roy Lichtenstein and Julian Opie, but that's only 'cause I'm a git. Here you'll find the full range of the pub's cracking choice of beers, together with a good sprinkling of numpties of all persuasions at any time of day or night. And the downstairs bar -

open only when there's something on - is the venue where, to-gether with what the pub management themselves tactfully refer to as 'entry level' live music, you can see any Newcastle band that will ever make it big. Well, by 'see' I mean 'be there when they play', since it's nigh on impossible to get a decent view of any band on a stage that's no more than a foot high, and if you're stuck round the corner you're doubly fucked. There you are, then: a halfway positive review, which is something the Dog doesn't do every day. I've got a lot of time for the 'Steamer' - as I've been told the kids call it - and if you catch me saying bad things about it, it's only 'cause most of the punters in here take one look at me and wonder whose fucking fatha I am. Cheeky little cunts.

For: 99.9% of the arseholes who pour off the train and along to either the Bigg Market horror pubs or the nearby premium-rate haircut bars wouldn't even consider nipping in for a spacer in here, and the few that try normally walk straight back out again when they see what's inside.
Against: Fair enough, they're accessible to the street as well as the customers so they get a heavy duty pounding, but the toilets are absolutely honking.

Picked up a flyer in the Head of Steam for an indie club night, which gave a long list of band names with the promise that they would actually play the groups they listed. I couldn't tell you which venue it was; when I said, 'picked up', that was immedi-ately before crumpling it into a ball and launching it across the room. But it got me thinking about the competitors of that club night, the ones they find so appalling. Why WOULDN'T you play stuff by the bands on your adverts? Why would you lie? To haul in the punters and then - once you'd got their entrance fee - tell them, Sorry, the CDs are double booked?

Long Bar

39-47 Westgate Road, NE1 5SG
'Christ, I didn't think I was that drunk'

I was in the Cub Scouts when I was a boy. Don't like to talk about it, but it happened. Every FA Cup Final weekend - the cheapest weekend of the rental calendar - we'd trudge dejectedly to Gosforth Park to build huts out of brushwood and then try to set them aflame. The rain drilled holes in our heads, the games were insulting and the cooking was inedible, so the only highlight of the entire weekend would be a trip to the wooden shack they laughably called the 'tuck shop' to stock up on E-numbers and nutrition-free food. And that shack, give or take a few optics and a cash machine, was exactly what the Long Bar looks like to me. Genius. The Long Bar is named after the long-gone real pub around the corner from here called, uh, The Long Bar, that was used as a set in *Get Carter*, giving them license to clag up loads of stills from the film, blurred almost beyond recognition by some idiot with a hooky copy of Photoshop. It also looks fuck all like the long-gone real pub around the corner. If my tuck shop comparison left you baffled, then try conjuring up the image of a '70s Swiss fondue restaurant, maybe on a telly advert with Chris Tarrant ripping the piss out of it. Think bare wood, stone pillars, cacky browns and subdued lighting, with two whole walls of 'Christ, I didn't think I was that drunk' wonky mirrors, and you'd be bang on. Quite like the choirboy pew seating next to the downstairs bar, though. Reminds me of when the Bishop of [anecdote deleted following legal advice]. The bar upstairs seemed to be the more popular when we were in, though it's probably not a good sign if all the punters are ignoring your flashy decor and gazing ruefully out of the window at the Union Rooms, wishing they'd gone there for a better - and cheaper - pint instead. I was bunged up with flu and an ear infection, so I can hardly be relied upon in the Jilly Goolden stakes, but to me the beer tasted of... well... nothing whatsoever. Our lass says it was pretty average, though. Average food menu, average atmosphere, average prices, average everything, really. Overall, then, not impressed. And to think they closed a betting shop to make way for this? Disgraceful.

For: A reasonable standard of topiary outside.
Against: That flaming Ingrid woman from Metro Radio does Thursdays '@' the Long Bar. I'm not bothered about her DJ sets - I won't be there to listen, ever - but I am deeply disturbed by the posters of her all over the place, grinning like a hospice child when the Toon come visiting. Put your teeth away, girl. Your life's not that bloody joyful.

The Long Bar is popular with the after-work crowd, with suits a-plenty. How come everybody in the world - except me - looks at least halfway decent in a suit? I pull mine out of the wardrobe, and I'm thinking Reservoir Dogs, I'm thinking George Clooney in Ocean's whatever, and I'm even thinking the fat kid out of The Hives. And what do I see in the mirror? Fucking Paddy MacDee, that's what.

The Lounge
8 Neville Street, NE1 5EN
'Love and hate across the knuckles'

Once upon a time we thought this place was half-decent. Call it youthful exuberance, the shock of something so unfamiliar to our codger-bar loving palates, or just plain stupidity. Returning five years later, we find that, aside from the inevitable slide into tattiness that goes with any pub that doesn't have a spring clean every eighteen months, The Lounge has a problem and it's that fashion is leaving it behind. Without actually changing one little bit, the fixtures and fittings have crossed the line from arty to cheesy, never to return, and the purple paint that was the absolute must-have when it went up now looks as clichéd and dated as love and hate across the knuckles. And they know it, that's for sure. That's why I'm certain they're trying to soften the blow of losing their hip status while still hoodwinking the remaining few devotees, by using a drinks tariff that would make British Gas blush: by the time you've worked out how much your cheap pint is going to cost based on what time you arrived divided by the number of staff on multiplied by the number of pumps no longer functioning, your beer has gone up another 50p. Look, I don't really want to hammer the place. It's no better and no worse than average and they serve a decent enough pint, but I can think of at least another five bars within a hundred yards of here that I'd sooner go to. Maybe it's just that, after spending so long writing bollocks about pubs and constantly having to look for new ways to be abusive about life's trivia, I now feel every cubic inch of the office block above weighing down on my soul. Maybe it's that I've really only been here lately in the daylight, and so I'm missing out on the bar's primetime, the after-10 hours when it turns into a nightclub (where the first 500 ladies get in free every weekend; get yourself a frock, lads, you'll save a fortune). Perhaps if I gave that a try instead of sticking so rigidly to the hipster bars or, more likely, lying tucked up in bed with a hamster feeding bottle full of absinthe clipped to the headboard, I'd appreciate the finer points. Can't see it happening myself, though; can you?

For: The summertime terrace - or fenced off bit of the pavement, to be exact - outside.
Against: British weather, the traffic fumes, and the city's alcoholics and other assorted riff-raff, all of which will ruin your alfresco lunchtime pint on that very terrace.

Oh, how I laugh when I think of all those crazy students sitting at the tables along the massive window wall, plotting which amusing attachment they're going to add to the three public art sculptures that form the piece Man With Potential Selves (or, as you probably know it, Man with Traffic Cone On Head) that stand outside The Lounge. I could chuckle and chuckle, and chuckle once more, until every last breath is squeezed from their limp bodies and I can get on with digging another shallow grave in St John's churchyard round the corner. Knobheads.

Newcastle Hero

Central Station, NE1 5DL

'A genuine tuppenny whore'

Just as people don't often feel the need to go to their own city's tourist office, they very rarely see the point in drinking in their local train station bar. I'd never been in here before the review visit, and I see absolutely no reason to go again, unless failure to wave off a distant relative threatens my inheritance. Approaching the door of this place I expected nothing, and nothing is exactly what I got. Lots of it. The Newcastle Hero is a big, unremarkable room with no real distinguishing features worth ridiculing. There's just the bare necessities of any station bar; somewhere to sit, something to pump shrapnel into, and something on the walls to look at if you can be arsed. The threadbare collection of portraits of Newcastle heroes along the wall opposite the bar runs to the likes of Sting (honorary doctorate of everything, ever), Neil Tennant, and our old beige-bar friends, the fucking Lighthouse Family. And if you're skint, I'd advise you take along a screwdriver when you go, because their signed photo of the legendary Brendan Foster has got to be worth a mint on eBay. That comprehensive gallery won't keep you occupied for long though, so you're bound to find yourself gawping at the customers just for something to do. What you'll see is a whole range of people united in their need to be somewhere else; backpackers, laptop slaves, pensioners picking the peanuts out of their upper dentures, plus - when we were in - a genuine tuppenny whore awaiting the call for her next lonely punter. How am I so sure about this? I'll tell you: any half-attractive woman looking expectantly in my direction and retaining her gaze even after making eye contact with this greying, beer-gutted, badly dressed, carrier bag-toting sack of shit loitering by the quiz machine, has got to be on the game. Simple when you can read the signs, even if those signs mean my youth has gone and I now look like a dirty kerbcrawler. But that's it; that's all there is to the Hero. I suppose it serves its purpose well enough, and it's at least a civilised alternative to the brain-dead hollering in O'Neill's, but there's really only a scabby pigeon's difference between a pint in here and sitting on the platform with a can of Stella.

For: Massive chandeliers...
Against: ...hanging from a polystyrene ceiling.

For all that The Lighthouse Family are up on the wall as Newcastle Heroes, it has to be made clear that they are adopted Geordies: the singer - the one that every fucker does on Stars In Their Eyes because you don't have to put any effort in - and the other bloke that not even his mother would recognise were both born in London. And you can take that as evidence of the warmhearted nature of the people of Newcastle, since every other city would have had one listen to their anaemic, GI-diet soul pap and run the cunts out of town.

North

The Old Ticket Office, Neville Street, NE1
'Balls'

The tiny North bar in the Central Station is possibly one of the least inspiring boozers I've ever encountered. I don't mean that in a bad way, like; it's just that once you've clocked the 'theme', the posters and the stuff hanging from the ceiling there's not a whole lot left to deride. And that doesn't keep the wolf from this moaning sod's door, I'll tell you that. North lists its address as 'The Old Ticket Office' and having the bar counter in the middle set in what looks like - or might even be - a ticket booth can conjure up a feeling of nostalgia for the more personal days of rail travel before the keyboard-pummelling frustration of internet booking. It also makes it an utter bastard to get served when the damned barman can't see you past the corners of the booth. Mind you, it's probably halfway your own fault, since while he's shouting 'Next' you're too distracted by the porn film posters on every wall publicising American classics like *Debbie Does Dallas*, *The Devil in Miss Jones*, plus such home-grown favourites as *Now Then*

Mrs Armthorpe, Tha's Got Lovely Tits. North's real claim to fame is that it holds the world record for having the most mirror balls in a bar. There must be, what, literally dozens of them, all different sizes and collecting different amounts of dust and dead moths. And, in a stroke of design genius, the mirrored theme is, uh, mirrored by the DJ enclosure in the corner, the one lined with peeling stick-on tiles reflecting the cardboard boxes and junk they're too chilled to chuck in the wheelie bin. I think that's your lot for North. No wait, there's a beer garden out the front, off to the side of the steps; I wouldn't say it was small, but if you're in it, it's full. Back in the bar and struggling for inspiration, I'm reduced to griping about the music, mainly because North's legendary 25-CD randomizer seemed to be stuck on default Red Hot Chili Peppers setting when we were in. Forty minutes straight of funk-rock stodge with that tit Kiedis going, 'Hut-AH hip-AH itty-itty-oop-AH' like he does in every fucking song they've ever released. Thanks for that, Mr North.

For: The music for the rest of the time may be the usual DJ-centric crap, but at least they've got a written policy of keeping it at a level where you can hear what people are saying to you.
Against: I always head up the stairs, peer through the wrecked doorway and into the abandoned unit and wonder what the hell happened to North. That's usually shortly before realising that I'm in the wrong place and the bar itself is another twenty feet along the road.

You can do a degree in porn films now, you know. Well, maybe not a full degree, but certainly a module or two as part of a media studies diploma. Media studies: possibly the most evil course of all time. It's not just that it's such an unbelievable skive, getting a certificate for watching telly for three years, but more that these gits are guaranteed a cushy number at the end of it, with the industry creating jobs for suitably 'qualified' graduates whether they're needed or not. Another 20,000 2:2s with mitigating circumstances? Fine, we'll just set up a few hundred extra channels; there's bound to be an audience for BBC67. Where the hell is the talent these days? I'm sure that in the golden age of television, students had to produce no-budget projects just to get a tick from teacher. Now those projects ARE the fucking programmes. Here's an idea for primetime telly: take everyone pocketing their wages from the licence fee for doing naff all, tell them they've got an hour to auction off their AV equipment for at least half of what was paid for it, or they'll get an icepick between each vertebra for every quid they're short. I'd watch that. Will there be an omnibus edition?

O'Neill's

38 Neville Street, NE1 5DF
'I am a Jarrow Marcher'

There was an advert when I was kid for, I dunno, McEwan's Best Scotch or something, which implied that, no matter where you may have roamed, their gassy, tasteless piss was the 'One you gotta come back for.' This pub, this terrible Irish theme bar opposite the Central Station is the exact inverse of that, in that it's the last place people go before they get the hell away. This is what I imagine limbo to be like, lost souls awaiting their final destination, only with Van Morrison as every other song over the PA. The first thing you'll notice, kick and curse when you brave the fug and venture into O'Neill's is the huge pile of bags all over the floor. And the second thing to strike you will be the complete lack of anyone from Newcastle, since O'Neill's is almost exclusively home to ex-pats, stag weekenders, sectarian sympathisers and other assorted idiots tearful for the aul country, as if their piddle-poor Irish chain bars are so much better than ours. Night after night you'll see dickheads in their Celtic tops, waving their pints, hollering their rebel songs and promising each other 'tiocfaidh ar la'. It's not the rebel songs I mind - anything that drowns out the frigging Cranberries is fine by me - but more the cast iron guarantee that these fuckers would shit treacle and go running to Ma at the first sight of a black balaclava. Oh aye, they're happy to act the bad boy here, far from home and safe from harm, but they're clearly no more part of a post-ceasefire

Republican splinter group than I am a Jarrow Marcher. Fucking leave the past behind, you imbecile. Quit glorifying some cause you read about on a gable end. We're not terrified of your dubious connections or your kneecapping glances, you tit. We just find you tragic. Now sit there quietly while you wait for your train. Have a little nostalgic weep to yourself at the hurling sticks, the tricolours and all the bollocks about 'craic' daubed on the walls. And shut the fuck up and behave yourself, like you'll have to when you get home. There's a good little boy.

For: At least O'Neill's have woken up to the notion that if someone broke a fiddle in a pub in Ireland they'd put it in the bloody bin and not in a glass case behind the bar.
Against: The place has far and away the most evil Gents toilets in the civilised world. The open-air troughs in the old Gallowgate End at St James' Park were better than the ones in here.

I have absolutely no gripe with the Irish, honestly. One of my best mates comes from Strabane and he's sound, even if I can only understand one word in five he says. I tend to view him more as a representative of his nation than the fuckpigs we encountered in O'Neill's. My problem is with anyone - from anywhere - who's away from home and who puts themselves forward as their country's voice simply because they can't handle their ale and like shouting shit. I'm aware that right now in an English theme pub somewhere there will be an equally vile bunch of retards yelling 'No surrender to the IRA' before scuttling back to their meek hometown chain bars. And I fully understand that you can't judge a country on its travellers. National stereotypes - wherever you're from - are what come about when our scum meet their scum, scampi-faced and rat-arsed beside a pool in Benidorm. National stereotypes have got fuck all to do with 99% of the population, and anyone who believes any of that cack should be beaten soundly. Just thought I'd clear that up.

Perdu

20 Collingwood Street, NE1 1JF
'Wrong, wrong, wrong'

If there's one thing more ghastly than a 'fun' pub, it's a pub that's so far up its own arse that any kind of enjoyment can only be permitted if it fits in with the colour scheme. Perdu is such a bar. It's difficult to know where to start in pulling the piss out of this ridiculously toffee-nosed establishment, but I think I'll just jump right in regardless. From the barmaids prowling about dressed in stupid lace collars like Victorian dandies, to the cocktail prices that make the likes of Popolo look like a soup kitchen; from the pretentious French name (it means lost, as in dignity and your entire night out budget, more than likely) to the *soi-disant* (ha!) opulent chandeliers on a par with your office Christmas deccies; from the psychiatrists' couches to the dead trees in pots, it's all a load of contemptible bollocks and woe betide anyone who cracks a fucking smile. I pinched one of their stupid booklets that were strewn on the tables, just to prove to myself that I hadn't been dreaming when I got out of bed the following day. Get a load of this risible guff: 'His neck lowered in a phrase, his heart sways to her rhythm, as she lifts an amber glass and falls into a smiling cloud'. Hoo hoo hoo! David Blunkett with a box of fridge poetry could hardly come up with worse, and at least he'd have the sense to not get it printed and stuck in front of the public. Ah man, you've got to see the place, just to see how fucking utterly wrong, wrong, wrong it all is. Take a gander at the minimalist lighting in the bead-curtained booths. Notice how there are no pictures on the wall, just frames around 'interesting' bits of the wallpaper. You'll have ample opportunity to see all of it, since it was - and will remain, if there's any justice - so bereft of customers. And the music's a pile of shite, an' all; a seamless - i.e. the same beat all frigging night - mix of DJ grooves and smooth jazz, with some berk tootling and skronking away on his sax to the general bewilderment of all present. Speaking as a local, I'd say this bar is a perfect example of how to feel disenfranchised in your own town, and any visitor hot off the train is going to think we're all a bunch of desperate, aspirational morons in utter denial of our city's own character, and that THIS is what we want. Plus, I'm hearing that scowling celebrity chef Gary Rhodes is involved in Perdu somewhere down the line: if he did anything beyond e-mail them a lucky dip menu and charge them a king's ransom then he, too, can fuck right off. I'm still shaking my head in disbelief. Absolutely horrendous.

For: Surely there can be no bigger insult to head my way this year than being charged Scandinavian prices for a pint of fucking Foster's.

Against: The soap in the lavs started off smelling of fresh apple with subtle coriander notes, but by the time I'd got back to my seat my hands were honking like a stale flannel. And it took three more scrubs with the Fairy Liquid to get rid of the stench.

You can never have enough rants against pub DJs, I feel. In the same way that Britain is rubbish at sport because of the idiot notion that winning is irrelevant and it's the taking part that matters so everyone must get a prize, the year two-thousand-and-whenever-you're-reading-this has been the worst for British music simply because any two-bit arsehole with some decks and a record bag is allowed to call themselves a musician. And because they're abundantly available, they're cheap, so the punters get stuck with them whether they like it or not. It's a shocking state of affairs, it really is. If you're shit, you're barred: that's the way it should be.

Rafferty's

29-31 Pink Lane, NE1 5DW
'Burn it'

Now sandwiched together under one name for convenience but still effectively two separate bars, in either guise this place has always had a reputation for being a bit rough. The right hand side of this building - the old Rafferty's - is a haven for old codgers in overalls, while the left hand - the old Quin's - caters for the younger customer. Clutching our pints we chose left, not out of any preference for decor or jukebox selection or any of that non-sense, but simply to get away from the snogging couple in the right, slavering and licking and gnawing on each others jawbones at five o'clock on a Friday afternoon. And because it was so early, we made a conscious attempt to do the review properly, instead of digressing into the usual tangential ranting. These are our find-ings or, more specifically, How to do a bar the Rafferty's way. We've all been in bad Italian restaurants, haven't we, chowing down on tomato-based mush with no real taste but which leaves you with garlic breath for a week and a half. Picture your local pizzeria, with its pretend taverna roof under the real woodchip ceiling, with fake beams and pillars, and with Artex swirls six inches thick. Imagine the lies they tell you to make you feel like you're in rural Tuscany and not above a hardware shop on some dilapidated backwater High Street. Is the image fixed in your mind? Yes? Right, now set it on fire. Burn it, char it, blacken it. And leave it for a couple of years. Trust us on this. Now throw up some plastic - I'm guessing - honeysuckle round the roof, clag some old adverts and Far Side cartoons on the walls, and get busy with the dullest paint colours you can find; trying to recall it this morning our lass says terracotta, while I say goose shit green. Add a few rails, a jukebox and a quiz machine, and you're almost ready. OK, fling open your doors to any old nutters, lepers, pass-ers-by and headcases, serve them cheap beer and let them get on with it. And you'll have - hopefully, if it's all gone well - a de-cent, no-fannying-about little boozer. Aye, you say dregs of hu-manity and slippery customers, but I prefer to think that it's just full of real people, or at least anyone who hasn't had an insulting niche bar tailored specifically for them. You thought this was going to be a panning, didn't you? Ridiculous notion.

For: Good for a post-work token visit, full of beans and looking on the bright side.
Against: I wouldn't fucking DARE go in later than half seven. Come on, man. It's a fucking loonies' bar.

Did someone mention sandwiching? The first two pubs on our punishing review schedule today were The Long Bar and here, and between them as you walk up Westgate Road is a well known sandwich outlet, whose Unique Selling Point at the time of writing this crap is that their products are 'hand cut'. Eh? Fair enough, I could understand that sort of trumpeting from a diamond merchant or a one-man company making acoustic guitars using only traditional tools, but fucking hand cut butties? How can that be a luxury service?

Revolution

Collingwood Street, NE1 1JF
'Sticky crap for the kids'

Housed in an old bank and replacing the laughably short-lived wank-fest eatery that was Café Chinois - which you won't remember but we must keep on mentioning as a lesson to anyone with high-falutin' ideas for the catering trade - Revolution has been around longer than any chain bar has the right to be, probably because it's yet to even approach being truly shit. Typically - as part of the cod-Russian-themed chain - this place advertises itself as a vodka bar, and while their initial 90-distinct-types menu of traditional imported vodka has now been reduced to a glossy list of pop-flavoured sticky crap for the kids, there's still enough for alcohol snobs like me to be happily shafted for a shot of something unpronounceable. But, strangely for a bar, it's not the drink that's the main reason to come here, nor is it whatever bollocks the Revolution chain are claiming as their brand values this month. What we like most about it is the building itself. Serious money was obviously spent here on restoring the bank's old décor, with magnificent carved pillars, high, ornate ceilings and enough cold marble to rival Lenin's mausoleum (no, of course I haven't been, you daft bastard). And they've definitely been keeping on top of the spring cleaning, so it looks just as fancy now as it did when it first opened five years ago, and that's not something you can say too often. The only differences I've really noticed over time are the plush new booth seats on the lower level, and the angled mirrors above the bar counter, the ones that let you see the pained, unserved expression on the face of whichever poor sod's been sent to get the round in. With the bar counter running virtually the entire length of the window wall, they never, ever seem to have enough of their snooty staff on to man it, and you find yourself thinking that a bit less of the cocktail-aerobics and posing, and a bit more speed on the service wouldn't come amiss. Plus, with that huge display of bottles in the window looking like an upmarket target for lob-the-beanbags at the fair, I wouldn't like to be around the next time Newcastle United lose a Cup Final. I imagine their lease will be up long before that happens again, though. Still - looking for positives - as well as the attention given to the decor here, Revolution's other plus point is its location; the sunlight blazing down Collingwood Street and through the huge windows makes it an absolute spunker of a bar for a spontaneous payday afternoon session, knocking off early and pissing your flexitime up the wall. Obviously, from my cantankerous point of view, the place becomes slightly less attractive when the pink-ties and pin-stripes arrive once the sun's over the yard arm, and is a definite no-go zone when the fake tans start snaking round the block waiting for their eclectic beats. You might like all that stuff: I don't, but then you knew that already. On top of that, I'm deeply and sensibly suspicious of any bar that will grant admission to people who are prepared to queue up to get in. And I suppose that sort of sums up my attitude to the place; it's a fantastic-looking bar with decent beer at a manageable price, and it only has one major down side, namely the people - staff and customers - in it. Shame.

For: Afternoon, sunshine, nice pint, good company, half empty, no flaming DJ.
Against: All other times. And the over-attentive daytime table service gets on your bloody wick after a while.

It was with a sense of great joy and a hmmm of strange coincidence that our review visit came exactly one day before the start of demolition of that bloody monstrous Westgate House next door, the hideous office block that captured the feel of the pre-Glasnost Soviet Union better than any carefully researched Russian theme bar ever could. Obviously, I know 1980s Vladivostok like the back of my hand.

The Sports Café

19-25 Grainger Street, NE1 5JG
'I'm mad, me'

The Sports Café is also in an old bank, the former TSB at the Station end of Grainger Street, the one that some bright spark knocked the wrong wall out of, almost sending the whole building sprawling all over the road. After spending years and a whole boatload of cash on doing it up, the building's new occupiers have produced, well, something that's a dead ringer for Sports Soccer on Eldon Square's Blackett Bridge. Even if you're not from Newcastle, there'll be one of those shops on your High Street, hawking cut-price training gear to lard arses who've never done an hour's exercise in their lives, except maybe the walk from the bus stop to the chip shop and up the road to the bar. This is the store that gives us proud Britons our national dress. The public wants what the public gets. And, if you take away the mountains of unsellable Donnay sweatshirts from those retail units and replace them with a few beer pumps and that, then you'll know, more or less, what the Sports Café looks like on the inside. Yeah, there's a few pool tables and some rubbish autographed gear in frames, but there's not a lot more. I had, I'll grant you, the most shocking hangover when I came to do the review, but it just seemed to me like staircase after staircase, leading to more and more laminate flooring, round and round and up and down; we got lost on the way out, for crying out loud. Look, I'll be honest with you: we're sick of just slagging off bars willy-nilly, so we're going to try to look for some good points here. Even though the Sports Café is part of a chain - and we fucking hate those on principle - I didn't mind the place when it was full before the match, with sports fans watching, like, sport. There: a positive comment.

But it's the adverts they're handing out about what they do for the rest of the time that make my blood freeze. Namely: The Sports Café Office Party, on Fridays where you 'drink, dance and flirt' and 'where office rules are made to be broken'. This, I assume, means the same gaggles of 'I'm mad, me' arsewits and blubbery brood-mares in hastily-applied slap squabbling and cackling about sweet fuck all over a sickly cocktail or a special offer bottle. Look at the plight of them, if you can bear it. One's crying; one's been sick down his shirt; he's trying to get in her pants; she's about to belt someone. All human life is here, stapling open the eyes of evolution and photocopying its face. And as ever, they're the only people in the entire bar who have yet to realise they have nothing whatsoever in common, besides utter despair. Saturday they'll be livid and thumbing out the poison texts, Sunday in a sulk, Monday looking daggers, Tuesday's a bit of a thaw, and come Friday they'll all be back here again, the same repression causing the same social disasters among the same otherwise-unemployables over and over again. It's a tragedy, it really is. And these jokers want to make a theme night out of it? It beggars belief, I tell you.

For: They've swiped that DJ from Idols and he's brought 'the fanny' - his words, not ours - with him.
Against: When is someone going to cotton on that poledancing podiums should be more than a foot off the ground? If I'm being deafened in a bar that advertises titties, then titties are what I want to see, not the back of some lanky twat's head.

That hangover I mentioned earlier? After an office night out, it was. Hence the bitterness about office workers, about institutionalised madness, and about my wasted life amongst fools. You think I just rant like I do to whack the beehive, do you? You think this is fiction? Write about what you know, they say. I've lived every fucking second of this nightmare and I'm whining about it as a warning, to you, because nobody else will.

The Star

79 Westgate Road, NE1 1SG
'A pig in shit, a sand boy, or even the proverbial Larry'

There's no point beating around the bush: The Star is as rough as fuck. On a match day, you can't move for screaming, scowling, glass-throwing headcases, pushing and shoving and daring you to say something. And that's just the bloody staff. The punters are the grimmest crowd you could ever imagine this side of the Grainger Market radgie bars, and would scare the living shite out of any stray tourist who got lost on his way from the Centre For Life to Eldon Square. And this, for reasons I'm far too innocent to comprehend, is a pub nicknamed the 'Shooting' Star. Still, at least all that gives me something worth criticising, rather than the complete mental vacuum caused by this place for the rest of the week. The Star between games is an average, run of the mill, lowest-common-denominator, desperately dull, drab, gloomy little pub with absolutely no atmosphere at all, which means that I'm probably going to have to resort to character assassination just to pad this out a bit. Maybe it was because I was three days away from going on holiday when we visited, and was in the sort of mood where, if I'd seen a pig in shit, a sand boy, or even the proverbial Larry, I'd have told them all to cheer up, but I did get the impression that if the Samaritans did personal visits, they could do worse than start off in here. The punters in the front end seemed to be one step away from belting each other, while the back of the pub was full of people who looked like they wished they were dead. Fuck it, man, I wished they were dead myself. So, to sum up: The Star - you need it like you need a hole in the head.

For: If you're serious about topping yourself, rather than being in the middle of a drama queen sulk, then get yourself in here.
Against: Everything between entering and leaving.

Even being situated right across the road from the Academy won't do this place any favours, since your average gig-goer there is either posing in the hipster bars round the corner, or huffing and puffing at daddy for not being able to find a parking space quickly enough to allow them a sly underage swig of vodka from the hairspray bottle and a tweak of the eyeliner before the venue doors open.

The Telegraph

Orchard Street, NE1 3NZ
'Five quid a pint'

Time for me to revisit the Telegraph now that the refit they had a while back looks just as shabby as the lovable dive it replaced. L-shaped, with stripped wood, retro-kitsch lighting, red and cream walls, and cosy booths, the Telegraph is clearly one of the best bars in Newcastle. There's a range of original pictures on the walls brightening the place up with a contemporary touch, and while I was absolutely smashed the last time I was in so I didn't really notice, I'm fairly sure they've still got that one of a huge Elastoplast. Oh aye, the beer's always decent, the atmosphere's usually good, and as for the punters, it depends what time of day you go, really. It's postmen early afternoon; four bells onwards it's disgruntled office workers from whichever call centre in the area is counting down to overseas outsourcing and redundancy this week; and after that it's hipsters, heavy of spectacle frame and grating of voice. But at least you have to suffer neither charver vermin nor moneyed fools who're unable to entertain the notion of a good time unless they've paid five quid a pint. Upstairs is the pub's major selling point, the fantastic rooftop beer garden where I've spent many hours watching the trains whilst pretending to listen to our lass wittering on about nowt. Well, I say many hours: all those hours were on the same night, on one of the rare occasions in this town when it actually stopped pissing down. And the Telegraph's upstairs room, if rain stops play, features bands (yay!) and DJs (take a wild guess!) throughout the week: check local press for details, and don't be asking me, 'cause I'm far too old and apathetic for that sort of thing. So, aye, The Tele needs a wipe-down every once in a while and, aye, there's always some penis-head getting on your nerves, but it's certainly one of the top five in the city. Watch them ruin it again.

For: What they used to call a well-stocked jukebox, possibly the only one in the town that actually plays what I tell it to.
Against: Having to walk through that piss-stinking tunnel under the railway tracks to get there.

DJ rant #762. How come, when you see a promo poster these days for an evening's entertainment in a bar like this, the DJ - the bloke who plays records, lest we forget - now occupies top billing with his 'set', while the bands have to make do with a lowly spot further down the page in smaller font? When the fuck did that start happening?

Tilleys
105 Westgate Road, NE1 4AW
'Your average pitch black wankbar'

Now part of the sinister Head of Steam global conglomerate, Tilley's has been smartened up a bit from the stinking student ashtray it was before, and it's a damned sight better for it, too. Aye, the colours are pretty bloody awful - purple ceiling, mustard walls - but it still manages to be cool without being pretentious and buzzing without pummelling your bloody eardrums. And any pub that has big windows so you at least know what time of day it is when you're there is good for me: try telling that to your average pitch black wankbar. And while it's probably expected in a pub review to talk about the stuff that goes on inside, the beer and chat (In a bar? Controversial, I know.) often takes a back seat to the life outside. Those windows are just the ticket for spying on the endless parade of scum that seems to wander aimlessly up and down Westgate Road at all hours: there's nowt like seeing some pissed-up spotty oiks in Helly Hansen gear practically humping each other in a shop doorway at two in the afternoon to make you feel so much better about your own upbringing. And watching the police cracking down on the town's alkies over the road is always good for a grin. See the drunks wazzing away their dole money in the 'plaza' by the city walls, the one with the big fuck-off silver spike stuck in it. Laugh like a fart from a cyclist in the Tour de France home stretch as Plod pounces and pours away another two litres of economy lager before moving the miscreants along. And when your eyes return to the interior, instead of gazing dejectedly at the floor like some floppy-fringed emo twat, why don't you glance up to the wall next to the window, where you'll see the big cartoon picture of Tara Palmer-Tomkinson looking foxy, demure and far more human than the appalling 'famous for what, exactly?' giggling nincompoop on the telly. Absolutely tremendous, that. So aye, I've seen a thousand refits, and they've all been far, far worse than this. From high street-standard dull-fest to stylish toss-free bar is no easy step to make, but I think they've done it. I suppose I'd better mention the customers, finally: they're more or less the same punters as the Head of Steam, The Forth and The Telegraph - it's all a bit bleeding incestuous if you ask me - but I'd still rather relax and sup with people who are just a bit dopey looking and/or snooty than sit shaking like a shitting dog among identikit Geordie Boys and Bacardi Bruisers looking to kick my fucking head in. For nowt.

For: Liefman's Kriek beer on draught. Oh, that sweet cherry poison.
Against: The new sign above the door belongs outside a prissy hairdressers and not a boozer.

What? Aye, man, aye. I KNOW the Head of Steam is a small company trying to take a stand against the unimaginative corporate bar chain. I was trying to be ironic when I called them a sinister conglomerate. Jesus, take a joke, will you?

Tokyo

17 Westgate Road, NE1 1SE
'Ever-spreading backsides'

Tokyo: formerly Po Na Na, Jakks, Berlin's, and always, always a bar for strokers. Let's see if this incarnation is any less annoying. Well, for a kick-off, having no names on the beer pumps may place them at the very forefront of bar design, but it can be a little irritating for the poor punter wondering what the hell he's going to get served. And it's alright forcing the bar staff to tell you what's on offer when it's quiet, but as soon as the inevitable beanie-hatted-goatee-bearded idiot turns up with his tunes it'll be a fucking nightmare. The bar started off being merely gloomy when we were in and then descended into pitch-blackness when some bright spark decided it was time to get a little moody, but I did at least have a chance to clock the decor before the eyestrain popped my lenses out. Curtains hanging from strange places, intimate booths along one wall, floor-to-ceiling mirrors along the other; all very tastefully done I agree, but I still couldn't help but feel like I was drinking in the Blackie Boy, and I'm sure that's the last thing the designers wanted. The call of nature forced me to check out the bogs: the usual expensive bar stuff, all polished wood and gleaming chrome, tragically offset by the beer belly-defying unpleasantness of having to piss into a hole in a cupboard, not to mention the indignity of hockling on your cock instead of in a trough. And it was only when I went for a slash - up the staircase that looks like my fucking bathroom did when I trusted the plasterers not to make a mess - that I came across this bar's real selling point: the beer garden. Enclosed by the neighbouring buildings on three sides, protected by a muckle sliding door on the other, and with fairy lights twinkling among the weeds, you can finally see the attraction of the place and maybe forgive them for their exorbitant prices. Slouching on the outdoor settees and ripping the piss out of the latest fashions as a cool breeze ruffles your hair is almost enough to make you forget that your bar bill has just sneaked in under a fiver for a pint and a half. To be honest, pretentious toss though it was, I didn't mind the bar itself. It was the punters who got on my tits - sour-faced office girls bemoaning their ever-spreading backsides over a pricey cocktail, and Celtic-tattooed chumps making the most of their footballer's mullets before the stranglehold of male-pattern baldness. Plus, if I'd just spent a fortune buying drink in a place like this, I'd at least try to make it look like I was enjoying myself. Miserable bastards.

For: I'm a sucker for beer gardens, so that's a definite 'For'.
Against: Oh, do cheer up, love, will you?

If you've ever wondered why it costs £50 for a solicitor to take a piece of paper from this pile, write their name on it, and then put it on that pile, then Tokyo's smug, corporate-laptop-bagged, expensively spectacled customers will provide your answer. Greedy, pen-pushing, arrogant, bullied-at-school, overbearing, PA-molesting, pin-striped needledicks, the lot of them.

Union Rooms
48 Westgate Road, NE1 1TT
'As bad as Fred West'

Thanks to the marvellous building in which it is housed, the Union Rooms is the least horrible of Newcastle's Wetherspoon pubs, even if that's tantamount to saying that Dennis Nilsen wasn't quite as bad as Fred West or Peter Sutcliffe on account of his skill with the paint roller. Once a jewel in the Wetherspoon crown, this bar has quietly frayed around the edges over the years and now looks like a stately home gone to seed, or the sort of place Griff Rhys Jones would goggle his eyes about on that Jolly Middle-England begging show of his. I can see him now, leaping from room to room, bounding up the stairs, fixing his gaze upon the stained glass windows at the top of the staircase, and then falling flat on his extra-chinny face over the tatty carpet that lines the steps. That'll teach him. A haunt for students and paupers, tightwads and skivers, the Union Rooms serves up a reassuringly drab pint of cut-price fizz to go with your something and chips, and provides ideal respite for punters who aren't necessarily out to enjoy themselves, a mindset I fully understand. On any afternoon you care to name, you can pull up a battered stool, have a window to yourself - there's enough to go round - and stare at your own personal rain. And if you're really lucky, you can treat yourself to the best graveyard view in the whole town. That, believe me, is its prime feature. I don't hate this place, though: it's not that bad, really. I just tend to view it as an acquaintance I don't see too often, one whose name crops up in conversation, but never provokes enough interest to have me reaching for the phone or digging out his e-mail address. He's fine as a memory or an entry on the Christmas card list, but by Christ is he boring if you actually meet him in the street.

For: Astonishingly, the first time I became aware of the pub's range of Polish lagers - Żywiec, Okocim and Tyskie - was the very day after I returned from a brief jaunt to Krakow.
Against: Oh Lord, not fucking Żywiec...

The Burglar's Dog guide to Krakow: Contrary to popular opinion, Poland is not permanently six inches deep in snow, nor is it in black and white. It is a country determined to throw off the shackles of its communist past and show its true colours alongside the greats of Europe. Here's our suggested itinerary for its historical showpiece, Krakow. Day 1. Morning: Wake with hangover. Spend five hours in 37-degree heat at Auschwitz-Birkenau. Fail to take bottled water. Or food. Afternoon: Travel on sweaty minibus to salt mines of Wieliczka. Queue in blazing sun for an hour. Let salty air of mines remove all healthy toxins from body. Evening: match usual Foster's consumption pint-for-pint with strong Polish beers, add celebratory cocktails and a splash of bison grass vodka. Collapse. Day 2: Stay in hotel toilet. Day 3: As day 2. Mind, those Poles don't half make you feel welcome. Not only do they know all the English phrases that could ever be needed in the service industry, but they were kind enough to offer to take me to hospital, too. Cultural ambassador? Me?

Maybe if I got my fucking dribbling, weeping face off the pub doorstep, aye. What a mess.

Yates's
30 Grainger Street, NE1 5JG
'The finest bar Newcastle has ever seen'

If there was any justice in this world, then this would be the finest bar Newcastle has ever seen. Housed in a truly remarkable French Renaissance building built in 1886 by John Johnstone for the Newcastle and Gateshead Gas Corporation, one of the most impressive sites in an already astounding area of architectural excellence, this bar deserves to be nothing less than a sumptuous Grand Café to make it the envy of cultural cities the world over. Instead it's a Yates's chain bar. And it's bloody awful. From the problem-estate youth club colour scheme, to the sticky carpet remnants; from the stodgy nachos and burgers soaking up the average beer, to the dog-rough punters, you know exactly what you're going to get before you even walk through the door. We can safely say that this branch of Yates's is identical to the one in your town, except that this one has probably got a few more floors of mediocrity. You can't even make the most of the large screen TV, since Sky's afternoon matches are bleached out by the pub's only good point, the sun blazing through the windows for most of the day. An over-abundance of promo material advertises tacky theme nights throughout the year and highlights their seeming inability to use the word 'party' without sticking two exclamation marks beside it. And above the pool tables on the top floor, there's a patronising poster of beautiful people standing, cue in hand and grin on immaculately painted face, helpfully showing the general gist of the game. Listen: I don't need to be told that a pool table is where you play pool, and I certainly don't need some fuckers telling me what sort of time to have. Simple rule of thumb: if they need to show you people (pretending they're) enjoying themselves, then it's a guarantee that you most definitely won't. This place is an absolute barrel of dross. How the hell has even one of these bars survived, let alone a nation-wide chain of the bastards? I promise you now: when my lottery numbers finally come up, I fully intend to give this building the pub it deserves. And you're all barred, the fucking lot of you.

For: Get a seat in the windows on a sunny day when you've got a thumping hangover and no real thirst for the drink, and it's just about bearable.

Against: They boast of being an 'unrivalled meeting place'. Fuck alone knows what that spurious claim is based on, but I'd sooner meet up at the bus stop outside, in the pissing rain if necessary, than ever set foot in here again.

Theme nights: the work of the devil. And no theme night could ever be worse than the humiliating spectacle of St Patrick's Day, whereupon the feckless, pissed-up inhabitants of this country attempt to compensate for their own lack of national pride by hijacking someone else's. I'm sorry, but you can't write off 364 days a year of jingoistic abuse simply by wearing a stupid Guinness hat for the remaining 24 hours. St Paddy's Day should be exclusively for the Irish, and the rest of you sad twats can fuck the fuck off.

4

BURGLAR'S DOG DESIGN SOLUTIONS PLC

Everyone has, at some point in their life, fantasised about opening their own bar. Whether it's to escape from the drudgery of the nine-to-five, to relive the easy café-bar life they experienced on their last European holiday, or to altruistically provide a place for live music that's a little different from the usual dive, we've all had the dream.

But where would you start? What would be the things you'd need to consider before you even approached the bank for your business loan? Surely there are things you need to do other than polish the wine glasses and rake in the readies. We imagine you really, really want to open a new bar but just lack the wherewithal to get your project off the ground.

And that's where Burglar's Dog Design Solutions Plc can help. We aim to provide a service tailored to your every desire to help you through the planning and design of your dream, so that you can enter the modern bar market with confidence and optimism. And we can give you the tips you need to keep up with the professionals on the scene, those skilled designers who really have their finger on the city drinker's pulse.

All new bars that have opened in the past year in Newcastle upon Tyne have been meticulously studied and all aspects of the modern pub have been carefully considered, giving us the expertise to place you in pole position.

We will also provide a name for your establishment, individually crafted to suit your answers to the questions below. Simply circle the options that most closely resemble your plans, and let us take the strain.

Please take the time to consider your answers to the questions in these ten sections for your obligation-free consultation.

SECTION ONE: LOCATION

The location and setting of a new bar are often crucial to its success: get these things right and the customers and their money will just flood in. To create the proper ambience for your business, you'll ideally be looking for a building with a sense of historical propriety, a tradition that cannot be bought, and character far beyond mere bricks and mortar. The site you choose could already be a bar with real local charm; or it could be a location with strong links to the area's past.

Let's assume you've already found a place that meets these essential criteria. In planning the building's heavenly makeover, how many of the original features do you plan to keep?

- None of them
- The troughs in the gents
- A tiny bit of the facade so that you can claim to be showing respect, much in the same manner as you'd respect a grave by shitting on the headstone and pissing on the flowers

SECTION TWO: COLOUR SCHEME

The colour scheme of your bar will be of paramount importance. Contemporary, complementary and sometimes controversial, the colours of a modern bar can determine the mood of your customers, and care must be taken to select the apposite hues to excel in a saturated market. Why just paint when you can impress?

Please pick two exciting colours from the extensive Contemporary Bar range, shown here in its entirety. Remember to select one from each palette for contrast.

Palette 1

- Hi-Fibre Diet
- Autumn Decay
- Midnight Slurry
- Impacted Fudge
- Easter Vomit

Palette 2

- Hammered Thumb
- Tourniquet Twist
- Tainted Throb
- Soft Melanoma*
- Classic Bruise

* not available in Vinyl Silk

SECTION THREE: LIGHTING

Young love: there's nothing more gladdening to the heart. And if a meeting of kindred souls occurs in your bar, then that's a feather in your cap, not to mention a cut of the takings from the blob machine in the crappers.

Which of these lighting systems will you install to bathe your customers in a warm, zit-covering glow and increase their chances of copping off?

- A 40 watt bulb
- A state-of-the-art rig with a total output on par with a small child's first torch
- One thirteen lux neon lamp at which even the most desperate moth would scoff

SECTION THREE: FACILITIES
One-upmanship in modern bar design should stretch as far as the lavatories, don't forget. Expensive beer deserves to be micturated onto expensive stainless steel, after all.

You envisage the very acme of stylishness to accompany your customers' bodily functions, but what will your construction team actually provide?
- An MDF-lite chest-high box that requires a seven foot distance and a finger on the prostate to reach with the golden stream
- Gleaming platinum-plated taps and hand-dryers, none of which will ever work
- A crotch-soaking contemporary artwork. Painted brown

SECTION FOUR: DRINK
Modern transportation and global industry mergers have put within the bar owner's grasp a whole host of exotic beers from the four corners of the globe.

Which of the following will you serve in your establishment?
- Foster's

And how much will you charge per pint?
- £3.50
- £5.00. It says 'Foster's' on the glass, though, with a pretty map of Australia
- One arm. One leg. Payable in instalments. Through the nose

Thinking of the customer and his desire for value-for-money, what incentive will you be offering at point-of-sale?
- Change on a tray
- Corporate doily
- Superfluous napkin that sticks to the bottom of the glass and makes the punter feel like a right tit

SECTION FIVE: FOOD
Peanuts, sandwiches, lasagne and chips: all yesterday's news to the contemporary bar owner.

What will you be offering to your customers from your lavish Michelin-style menu?
- Alligator truffles
- Braised pomegranate mash with chilli and grass
- Flash-fried placenta and crushed potatoes

SECTION SIX: SECURITY
Your business needs customers to thrive, and customers expect a pleasant greeting from your front-door representatives.

What type of security will you employ to stop anyone getting in, ever?
- Old-skool sorry-no-denims
- Initially friendly butch lesbian ballcrusher
- Psychopathic crack addict with a hair trigger temper and a blade up his sleeve

SECTION SEVEN: STAFFING
Recruiting the very best staff is essential: it stands to reason that the finest employees in the land would reject the chance of a cushy office job and would prefer instead to work for you like a single-parent-family carthorse, with minimal employment rights and appalling conditions, all for £2.25 an hour.

The following sentence is a typical extract from Thursday's Chronicle jobs pages:

'We are actively seeking giddily enthusiastic individuals who can display (blank) to customer service.'

Which of these words would best fill in the blank in your job advertisement?

- Dedication
- Obsession
- Psychosis

And which characteristics will your successful applicants actually show?

- Indifference
- Surliness
- Outright hostility

SECTION EIGHT: YOUR TARGET MARKET

Knowing the carefully researched demographic tastes of your desired customers gives you the edge in providing the perfect service to them.

Which of these social subdivisions will comprise your target market?

- Pre-club young adults with high disposable income
- Acorn type C, subset 7.19, group 7
- Complete helmets

SECTION NINE: EXCLUSIVITY & THE VIP

Your most select customers like to feel they're enjoying special privileges away from the rank and file, even though they're drinking in the same bar and breathing the same filth from the same air conditioning.

What will you provide to cater for their elitist whims?

- A roped-off VIP area
- A DNA-testing entry pad
- Cold War spy exchange, like in fucking Germany circa 1963

SECTION TEN: MUSIC

All bars need to find the right mix of sounds to cater for all tastes and for people from all walks of life. But over and above this, you're going to need that special something to draw in the crème-de-la-crème of partygoers.

Which 'sounds' will you focus on to make you stand out from the crowd?

- Wallpaper soul and R&B
- Indistinguishable blissed-out beats
- Panpipe Bossa Nova

Your DJ is one of the most important people in your bar. After all, who else in the place has the innate skill required to play other people's records one after the other, and the self-assurance to believe this talent makes them a superstar musician?

What kind of disc jockey are you looking for?

- Some skinny mammy's boy with an autistic knowledge of Marvin Gaye b-sides
- A jumped up chancer who'd staple his own mother to a four-to-the-floor beat if he thought it'd get him top ranking on a roadside billboard
- A hollering cretin who waits until the floor is knee-deep in punters' shite before realising that volume can go down as well as up

TERMS & CONDITIONS

Please read the following terms and conditions before submitting your application:

In entering into a contract with Burglar's Dog Design Solutions you are confirming that you are hopelessly optimistic, have absolutely zero understanding of the law of diminishing returns, and are prepared to file for bankruptcy before the end of the year. You also confirm that you blame the following for your imminent failure in business:

- The government
- The breweries
- Al Qaeda
- Two-bit pub review websites
- Anyone and everyone except yourself

LET US NAME YOUR BAR

If you accept our terms as outlined above, then please follow these simple instructions:

Stage 1: Take potluck with one of these perfectly feasible names, listed A-Z, capital letters verboten.

aspire; barramundi; capybara; bar dado; enculer; flange; gnu; hubris; impetigo; jodhpur; komodo-modo; the.laundry; mauve; narcissus; obloquy; pudenda; quinquereme; résumé; sputum; threeesome; underlay; varicosa; whelk; x-crescent; yarmulke; zabaglione.

Stage 2: There is no stage 2.

That's it. That's the sum total of our service. What the hell were you expecting, like? A personal visit? A dossier? A PowerPoint presentation? Don't be ridiculous.

Just get on with choosing a name from our list and quit wasting our time. We don't care how you do it. Prick the page with a pin, skewer it with a dart, launch a fucking nuclear warhead at it from the other side of the globe if you wish; it's all the same to us.

Just be aware that you can't call yours Taramasalata, since we've copyrighted the name ourselves ready for our bar's launch. We've spent a small fortune on the @ signs, too: one for each 'a'. It'll be class, you just wait. It's in an old post office, see; it's, uh, dark, chilled, luxurious, and exclusive, and it has nationally renowned DJs. And if you look happy, you're out. Don't tell me you had a bar like that planned too? Great minds, eh?

Feel free to try again tomorrow if you think our choice of name is unsuitable for your bar. There will be no additional charge for this extra consultation.

Good luck with your new venture.

You tit.

5

City Centre

'Described as the "city of palaces" when completed in 1842, Grainger Town is the historic heart of Newcastle. Recent restoration projects mean that the elegant stylish Victorian and Georgian architecture can now be enjoyed to the full. The area takes in the magnificent classical Georgian buildings of Grey Street – including the famous Theatre Royal – Grey's Monument and the Edwardian Central Arcade, and leads to the city's main shopping thoroughfare of Northumberland Street, as well as the bustling Eldon Square centre. And Greggs.' – Norman Undercroft, Historian.

Adelphi
20 Shakespeare Street, NE1 6AQ
'Crocked and hopeless'

Newcastle's premier hooligan bar and helpfully just a bottle's throw from the cop shop, the Adelphi is the sort of place you admire from afar for its integrity, and then stay the hell away from for fear of a kicking. Me, I've never had any bother in here, but that's because I always wear my Toon top when I go, and 'cause I try to swagger like I'm some sort of fucking hard case rather than the spineless little wanker I know myself to be. How man, I'm squit-shit scared of the puppet Gremlins out of the '80s films, never mind the human ones with the knock-off Burberry who get in here. There's not really much point in trying to have an in-depth discussion of the Adelphi's decor: there's the bar counter in the middle, a bog door through an arch somewhere at the back, a floor and a ceiling, and that's your lot. Every single other square millimetre of space has been covered by Newcastle United stuff. Photos, posters, mirrors, scarves, flayed tattooed skin; it's all there. From the dawn of time when we were a club that won things, to the charity fund for the crocked and hopeless we've been recently, there's a framed snap to celebrate it or make you cuss like a fucker. It truly is a remarkable display, comprehensive enough to feature the Judases and turncoats of Newcastle United history as well as the likes of Shearer and Milburn. Whether they'll ever stick up a picture of bloody Bramble is another matter entirely, though. Look, we don't often get in here, so it'd be stupid to prattle on at length about the place, so we'll just tell you that, depending on your point of view and the colour of your shirt, it's either rough as fuck or a no-nonsense bar with cracking atmosphere. And because it's obviously not match day every day, what we'll say about the Adelphi for the rest of the time is this: if you want to spend time amongst chain-smoking codgers, harassed businessmen and slumming-it luvvies from the Theatre Royal, then this'll be right up your street. We're a good few years too young to enjoy it now, but time stops for no man.

For: The opening hours, which, for as long as I can remember, have been whenever they fucking well feel like it.
Against: If you're ever charged with taking a photo of the Adelphi there's always some bugger parked outside, making it nigh-on impossible to get a decent clear shot of the place. Instead, you'll be reduced to standing with a massive zoom lens across the other side of Pilgrim Street, and made to feel like a junior Chronicle smudger covering an unsolvable hit-and-run case where the accused's family are hard as fucking nails.

Club v country: I can never get as fired up for England as I do when it's Newcastle United. Who does? Who would actually choose the national side over their own team, apart from club-hopping Cockneys or racist morons? Actually, I know fine well who does. It's the berks who believe that the more shitty merchandise you display, the more of an expert you are on the game. I dread the European Championships and the World Cup: every two years you get the same imbeciles who'd spit at you for the rest of time boring you to death with their borrowed platitudes and unrealistic expectations. And all this drivel about reclaiming the flag of St George? It was better when it was only the BNP who waved it: at least they have half an idea why I fucking hate them.

The Bacchus

34 High Bridge, NE1 6BX
'Mayhem and murder'

People keep telling me I'm too negative; in fact everyone I know has been saying that lately. So, just for a change, I'm going to try my hardest to give a positive review, despite the fact that the Bacchus is where I first met our lass, back in the days before decimalisation. If you haven't been in here for a while - and, believe me, I still see once-a-year punters spinning round and looking confused - then you'll notice a few changes from the old place. Firstly, and most importantly of all, it's a completely different pub. The old Bacchus was razed to the ground and the new one is essentially where that flaming rancid Goth shop Phaze used to be. Got that? Good. Now that we've established the basics, maybe you can stop waving your fucking arms about and smacking me in the teeth. Secondly, there's only one room now - if you don't count the little snug area off to the left where the grannies gather to plot mayhem and murder - with a huge bar slap-bang in the middle, a bar permanently encrusted with the fattest of fucks in the sloppiest of suits. If there is one thing that's remained from days gone by, then it's the emphasis on conversation and relaxation, with comfortable armchairs by the windows at the front, although I don't know why I bothered to mention them, since you'll never get to slump there. Take any lunchtime, any post-work swifty, or any evening session and see if I'm lying: there'll always be some gopper from a cosmetic counter sitting in one chair, with her shopping stuffed into another three. Her mouth will be Botoxed into a permanent pucker of rage and her habitual theft of her merchandise will leave her stinking like a whore's drawers. And you will never be brave enough to ask her to shift, no matter how many pints you've necked. Speaking of whores, my 'thirdly' is this: if the old Bacchus decor was what drew you in, making you feel like you were next in line in the brothel you'd never have the balls to visit, then I'm afraid all that's changed, too. Instead there's a vague cruise-liner theme - a bit like the Poseidon Adventure but, like, the right way up - with nautical photos all over the place and tons of fancy wood-work. Other notable decor items are the Burberry tartan carpet on the raised bit at the back and the massive wine glasses on the way to the bogs upstairs, though I must be going frigging blind 'cause I it took me three visits and someone saying, 'Up THERE, you moron' before I saw them. I could prattle on all day, to be honest, about this, that, and the other, but the overall impres-sion is of a pub that purely wants to be just that: not a leisure venue, a 'luxebar', or a 24-hour party palace, complete with thumping four-to-the-floor when you're trying to eat your dinner. It's just a boozer, and a pretty smart-looking one at that, but it sure makes a change to have a quiet pint in here after putting up with the identikit bars that reared their coiffed heads in the time the Bacchus was in ruins. There. Is that positive enough for you?

For: If you're drunk enough, and you squint through the right bit of window, then the sign on Pani's Café over the road clearly says 'Penis Café'.

Against: During the Bacchus' eighteen month demolition-and-resurrection there was an internet newsgroup set up to cater for the people who were missing the place. The sad bastards. Who'd be tragic enough to go on the internet writing about pubs, like?

That Burberry carpet prompts me to give my bigoted two-penn'orth on this matter: I saw an entire family - average age seventeen - of charver filth in the town on the weekend of the review visit, clad top-to-toe in stolen designer sportswear, and pushing a pram up the Bigg Market. I failed to catch the name of the child for all the 'Heeyah man's and 'Y'daft cunt's, but following the pattern of the-posher-the-name-the-scummier-the-child, let's assume it was called Pronuptia Jade. And what was this future shoplifter travelling in? A fucking Burberry-effect pram, that's what. Why, it must've been the envy of the whole of the courthouse steps. Vermin.

Bar 42

16-18 Hood Street, NE1 6JQ
'Great meeting place'

I'm an early starter when it comes to the lash. And because I'm a lily-livered jessie, that also makes me an early finisher, tottering home having clearly had enough just as the rest of the town is getting warmed up. And that's how, from my bus-stop vantage point across the street, I've witnessed the bewildering spectacle of Bar 42. Countless are the times I've stood there in my big coat, cowering from the wind and snow battering down Pilgrim Street, and watched the procession of scowling, semi-naked trollops heading for this place. Time after time I've seen the endless queues of deep-frozen imbeciles in thermal chiffon, and been completely unable to fathom why such an awful bar is so bloody popular. It can't even lay claim to being a 'great meeting place', since once you enter you'll never, ever leave. And this is something I know to be true; Christ knows I endured it enough times before I put a blanket ban on work nights out. This is how it happens: 'Eeh, I'll meet you in 42 at 4.30. Hee hee, trebles! But Donna won't be there until 6, and Simon can't make it until half past. Me sister's not out 'til 8 and she's meeting her mates there at 8.30. And Linzi doesn't get off 'til...' So they stand in flaming 42 all night, waiting for fool after fool to arrive, none of them with the wit or intelligence to suggest that, just once in their lives, they might try somewhere else. Because that would be heresy: they go there because that's where they've always gone. Simple as. Night after night and year after year they waste their evenings in here, pretending to be happy. The music's crap, the atmosphere's terrible, the beer's over-priced piddle and the first thing any sensible person dragged in against their will would do is make a frantic search for the fire exits. Even the decor is depressing in that tatty, holes-in-the-carpet, grim late '80s way. But it doesn't matter what the management plan to do to it or how many refits they attempt, this place will always be the same: a dark, claustrophobic, low-ceilinged, punters-jammed-in sweatfest. And whether it's early doors or lasties, a lunchtime pint or an evening blow-out, if you drink in here you're an idiot. And you always will be.

For: The cats' litter tray at the bottom of the stairs.
Against: When I am king, closing down Bar 42 will be the second thing I do. The first of my regal decrees will be that there is a standardisation of the girl's name Lindsay. I mean it. And all the Lindseys, Linseys, Lyndsays, Lyndseys, Lynseys and especially the Linzis – with circles over each 'i' – who pack out this bar every night will have ONE WEEK to change their passports, their driving licences, their bank details and their e-mail accounts – 'let us no if u want the meal thanx linz xxx' – or they will be incarcerated. With no telly. And no legs.

'Why do you never come to office nights out any more?' they ask. Repeatedly. So I tell them, with as much patience as I can muster. 'It's because whenever I ask you a question at work about work, all you want to do is act the goat about how great Friday night will be. Yet when you actually hit the bar - to let your hair down, remember - all you can think to talk about is your damned spreadsheets and flexitime squabbles.' Got me, fuckhead?

Bar 55°

55 Degrees North, Pilgrim St, NE1 6BJ
'Describe the ambience without using the word 'wankers'...'

I like small pubs. A counter, a few tables and a reasonably clean bog, and I'm as happy as the day is long. Warmth and intimacy are the things I look for in a boozer. And that's why I doubt I could ever fall in love with Bar 55°. The place is HUGE, bordering on cavernous - think of the beer-and-nachos area of the Newcastle Arena and you'll be on the right tracks - and is hardly the ideal setting for a cosy pint. You approach the bar through some of the most optimistically clean subways in the northern hemisphere, and pass a smart little fountain next to that stupid pink wedge thing that's meant to take the prospective homebuyer's attention away from the fact that they'll be living in the middle of traffic carnage if they buy a flat upstairs. The doors in the glass-fronted exterior weigh half a hundredweight each, and by the time you've wrestled with the bastards, you're in the mood for something special. Tough titty, folks. The bar is certainly one of the largest in town, and it's easy to admire the architectural design of the Royal Arcade - as I used to do many years ago before going upstairs to sign on with the rest of the dole wallers - that forms part of the pub, but I can't help feeling short changed, and not just because of the beer prices. The big palm trees and the grand piano challenge you to describe the ambience without using the word 'wankers', and the low cylindrical dropdown lighting is so subtle and unobtrusive that you clonk your frigging head on it no matter how much you try to avoid it. Widescreen TVs in pubs: a good thing. Widescreen TVs in pubs showing some sort of fashion channel: rather less good. The question I ask is, why? Are catwalk models the type of punters this bar wants to attract? Is that what they're trying to convince you you'll see the next time you're in? Horse shit. And wheezing saxophone jazz over the speakers? Give me a fucking break, will you? Mind you, come the summer I'll be sitting outside on the terrace overlooking the Tyne Bridge, especially if it stops raining, so ask me what I think of the bar in the middle of June and I might give you a different opinion.

For: The padded headrests above the urinals in the gents. Now you can have your Pythagoras piss - drunkenly forming the hypotenuse in his theorem - in absolute comfort when you're running your length.

Against: My bus passes 55 Degrees North every morning. Half asleep the other day, my brain misinterpreted the sign above the pub's door as saying 'Barse', the layman's term for the perineum: i.e. the bit between the balls and the arse. Quite appropriate, I thought.

Further research - well, more like fortuitous internet stumbling - has brought to light the fact that architectural splendour of the Royal Arcade inside this bar is, in fact, fake fibreglass bollocks. The original bit the dust when much-reviled politician T Dan Smith and his mates went on a five-year bender with the wrecking ball and destroyed most of the town's heritage. Fun Fact: 87% of blame for anything in Newcastle can be attributed to T Dan Smith. Concrete monoliths, dilapidated tower blocks, the debacle of the Souness era: all Smith's fault.

Barluga

35 Grey Street, NE1 6EE
'Boxing Day sales'

Formerly The Metropolitan and still the lunch venue of choice for Grey Street's expense account business bores, the recently (well, since the last time we gave enough of a shit to go there) refurbished Barluga is still smarming away, turning its nose up at anyone with an ounce of sense. Incredibly, after all we've tried to teach them, this town is still burdened with the kind of fools who think sophistication is something to aspire to rather than justification for a public flogging, and all of them drink here. Please, for the love of the Lord, could you get this straight, all you giggling shop girls and balding bank clerks: sophistication can NOT be bought online. And drinking here does not make you a catwalk model or a style guru: it makes you skint. I don't go to Barluga very often, as I've said, but how come every time I go the bar staff always seem to have something more important to do than actually deign to serve me with my overpriced pint? Do I really look like I'm going to appreciate a nice straight line of serviettes when I'm choking for a beer? No. I just look like a very angry man, because that's what this place turns me into. I think the decor's changed a bit since the last time I looked; I'd guess that they've seen one too many Boxing Day sales adverts and they've decided that a hideous '70s revivalist colour scheme is the way to go. I don't remember the pretend snakeskin seats in the booths, but I definitely do recall the fucking beanbags upstairs: how the hell have they survived this long? And they're STILL - and we can only assume that they believe the constant mockery they receive is based on jealousy - trying to flog caviar at £45 a scoop, clearly in the hope that reviewers far more reputable and influential than The Burglar's Dog will mark it down under 'gastropubs'. Will you pack it in, man? Look, if we have to be fair about the place - I suppose it's in our contract, after all - we'd say alright, once in a while, for a single pint on a spontaneous afternoon session, it's tolerable. But if I'd come in here on a big night out expecting it to live up to its insupportable claims of greatness, and seen THIS, I'd have to sup up, leave, head for the bus stop and go straight home. That's how depressing it is. And if you've ever been there and left without feeling slightly grubby, then you have no business reading this. Get yourself over to GQ, you fucking idiot. Barluga: truly a bar that only a complete scrotum could love.

For: In five years time this place will be long gone and you'll be able look back, with the sort of smirk normally reserved for the Sinclair C5 or Andreas Andersson, upon the stupidity that prompted someone to sell caviar in a fucking boozer. Alright, we might be being a bit optimistic on the timescale, but I'll dance on this place's grave if it's the last thing I do.

Against: I think they've even done away with the faux-naïf (translation: shite) paintings of naked ladies on the stairs. What a fucking gyp.

Chilled. If I see the word 'chilled' to describe a bar once more, I'm liable to stab some fucker in the neck. I can't think of a single thing that makes me feel less chilled than a manufactured 'chilled' atmosphere. Tell me, please, what the hell is chilled about beats too loud to talk, lights too low to see the spots on your dominoes, and a temperature so high you end up smelling like a cheese 'n' pickle sandwich before you've even got your (minimal) change back? Come on, TELL ME.

The Black Garter

31 Clayton Street, NE1 5PN
'Sphincter-faced harpy'

Is your life being blighted by some stupid tit who insists on telling you that he's 'street', just because he's wearing some saggy-arsed basketball gear? Then the best thing to do is tell him to keep his embarrassing, Yank-wanking naivety to himself, and fetch him in here. Off the stretch of gum-clagged tarmac between the markets is where the real British 'street' is found, festering away behind the doors of the Black Garter, and it's enough to make the pillock in his FUBU fancy dress and his oversized trainers shit blood and diamonds for the rest of the year. The Black Garter is, clearly, a fucking horror show. It's a dump. And it's full of scum; lazy, bitter, wilfully stupid, career dole-ite scum, state-provided with anything they could ever need and working on a plan to steal everything else. From you. The punters in here are what the newspapers tactfully call 'neighbours from hell', and what you or I refer to as 'those fucking filthy animals next door', the families that you see punching each other's lights out in the garden every weekend trying to settle some perceived slight, or stabbing the bride at weddings for thinking she's summat special. And they want birching, the whole lot of them.

Yeah, yeah, I know what you're thinking; you're thinking, 'What a fucking pompous twat'. Listen, college boy; I was live-and-let-live once. Everyone's a bloody liberal when they're young and stupid, right up until they start seeing everything they've grafted for, and everything they believe in, being shat on from a great height by these fuckers. I crossed that line long ago, never to return. And it won't be long until you're over here with me, I can assure you of that. There's simply no getting away from the fact that The Black Garter, and all the other bars on this street, are cess pits and no-go zones for anyone with a functioning brain or a shred of decency. We turned up to do our review duties and found the way barred by some appalling, shrieking, sphincter-faced harpy in her hooped sweatshirt and greasy trackie bottoms, homemade tattoos and sovereign rings of dubious origin, squab-bling over fuck-knows-which trivial matter with her grunting pack of friends, family, or co-defendants. I didn't even dare ask them to move in case they had me down as some sort of snooper just for wearing matching shoes. This is at 11.45 on a Saturday morn-ing, by the way. And since I couldn't get in, there'll be no plush rewrite or decor-referencing minor update, but none of that mat-ters. I know what it was like when I went ten years ago and had my jacket lifted by some fucking toerag and my face threatened with rearrangement for wanting it back; I know what it was like five years ago when we braved a review visit amongst the shop-lifters and pretend war veterans; and I know what it'll be like after Armageddon hits, when there's only the rats and the scum-bags in here still alive, bickering about fag-ends and sticking pint pots in each other's faces over whose turn it is on the bandit. It will be a fucking crime against decent society. And they will kill you if you try to point that out.

For: The Grainger Market ghetto of here, the Clock, the Fish Bar and the Blackett Arms, makes it so much easier for Plod to keep an eye on the vermin.
Against: The karaoke-running drag artist Ophelia Balls is now plugged on posters as Ophelia B. It seems that it's perfectly ac-ceptable for subhumans to get smashed on dirt-cheap beer before

131

running amok through the town, but displaying a weak sexual pun is clearly more than the general public can stand.

I've had something I want to get off my chest with this review, clearly. See, the thing is, I actually did live next door to the neighbour from hell, for four interminable years while the piss-addled old bitch and her muscle-bound lesbian lover drank themselves nearer - but not actually all the way, tragically - to the grave. Day after day, from eight in the morning, she'd sit there on the front step with her cans, telling the toddlers in the street how she was getting a 'sun tanned pussy' before passing out and being helped onto the settee by people far more tolerant than me. The only amusement we got out of her entire residence was when she fell on the cooker and set her head alight. And those were the quiet times; oh, how I loved it when her extended family used to turn up at night and spend eight angry hours getting hammered and howlingly trying to apportion the blame for their mother's alcoholism before rucking gaily until the police arrived. That was five long years ago, and even today I wake up with the sweats when I hear a car pulling up outside after midnight. I still can't see a headscarf without wanting to put an axe through it. And I have, literally, wept on hearing Boyzone's 'No Matter What', the anthem for all persecuted, evil, drunken shites the world over to play at three in the morning, over and over again until the batteries die. (I was in the dentist's chair getting my teeth drilled at the time, but I'm trying to play the sympathy card here.) And you wonder why I'm such a cantankerous sod?

The Blackett Arms

11 Nelson Street, NE1 5AN
'Cleaning his ears with a beermat'

Following a recent refit, the Blackett Arms has combined a playful sense of chic with a traditional twist. Serving cocktails and cappuccino, and complimentary paninis with oils and balsamic, it's now become a serious rival for Café Royal across the road, and has got the fashionista crowd purring that it's this season's hottest venue. You weren't fooled by that cack for even a second, were you? Can't say I blame you. Take away every word except 'serious' from the first two sentences, and you might have a more accurate description. In fact, if you just used the word 'sentences' and added 'to run concurrently', you'd have most of the punters summed up, too. Even though I've found this to be the least immediately ominous of the Grainger Market bars, walking in here I still feel like I've gatecrashed a gangland wake. Picture me staggering in bollock naked, booling our lass in the wheelbarrow position, with a flashing red nose, a jester's hat and blowing on a party hooter, and then imagine the reaction of the kith and kin of Knuckles 'Knuckles' McKnuckles. That's how welcome I feel in here. The entire pub's clientele is gathered round one table in the room to the left and, foolishly, I catch the eyes of the couple facing me; he's got his feet on the table and he's cleaning his ears with a beermat, and she's stuffed into her top like minced pig's knackers into sausage skin. And they're looking at us as if to say, 'Who are you and what the fuck are you doing in here?' Shit, man: Will this pint ever end? Even the bloke on the bandit doesn't like us; he's dropping his guts like a cornered skunk, probably to keep us far away in case we snaffle his surefire jackpot technique. Cowering nervously beside the doorway, I'm clinging on to the shelf to stop my knees from shaking and buckling under me. I'm laughing at the toothless gimp running the karaoke even though he's churning out stuff that would make Bernard Manning wince with shame and still fucking up the punch lines. Did you just pour yours into mine, you get? Oh, Christ; now they're all crooning 'Happy Birthday' and, in fear of a glassing, we're singing along, even though we haven't a clue whose big day it is. All the same, we're wishing dear Mumbles all the best for her mumbleth, swearing on our mothers' lives that she doesn't look a day over mumblesty. Seizing an opportunity, we sneak into the front room to sit down before we fall down, as some old crone butchers 'Tainted Love' on the stage next door and, glancing around us at the eviscerated seating, we're wondering what the fuck we ARE doing in here. This truly is a rough dive. But hey, this beer's not that bad, and at least we're safe from wankers whose latest haircut cost more than all the clothing in here put together. Another pint? Aye, go on then. Your round.

For: I like the way that the function room / venue upstairs- The Red Rooms - has a separate staircase to shield you from all the unpleasantness of the main bar.
Against: Just because I got out safely with my smart arse intact, doesn't mean you should try it.

At the time of writing, the Grainger Market is due for a massive refurbishment by the council, hopefully to make it - and its pubs - slightly less terrifying. They're planning cultural events and temporary art installations. They are, I shit you not. Maybe one day there really will be that playful sense of chic I mentioned earlier. Or, more likely, maybe it'll all KICK OFF, with pitched battles between the paintings. Who'd win: Perry with the palette knife, or Mackas with the machete? There's a Ladbrokes next door to the Blackett Arms if you fancy a flutter.

Boom!
14-16 Newgate Street, NE1 5RG
''Boom!'? More like...'

SHITE!

For: That's the easiest - and most truthful - review the Dog has ever done.

Against: Fucking '90s Bar, my arse. It still IS the '90s as far as I'm concerned. How the hell can there be a nostalgia bar for something that's only just passed? What the hell are they planning next? A fortnight-past-Tuesday bar? Jesus.

Look, apologies for the brevity of the review, like, but there's really no word other than 'SHITE!' that will suffice. Imagine if Blue Peter tried to build a '90s theme bar for your Action Man, using some old wrapping paper and a few pictures cut out of Smash Hits. That's exactly what we're talking about here. It's a joke. And the beer's dreadful, too.

Bourgognes
64 Newgate Street, NE1 5RQ
'Ash, sauce, puke and nappies'

Bourgognes is owned by the Original Pub Company chain, a firm notorious throughout the land for steamrollering decent little bars and replacing them with pre-packaged pastiches of themselves. I'm sure we've already mentioned - more like ranted - many, many times about the chain bar manifesto, to no avail. But this time, though, it looks like the wreckers have actually done something right. Don't get me wrong; I'm hardly likely to try to persuade you that it's fantastic, since we waited a good five years after the refit before we even thought about going back in to review it. But in giving it a lick of paint - vile orange and green - and bunging in enough mirrors to exaggerate its size and take your mind off its poky under-mall location, they've allowed Bourgognes to make the miraculous step up from absolutely abysmal to merely poor. And in losing the 'character' or, to be more exact, the layers of ash, sauce, puke and nappies, they've certainly made it into somewhere you might not actually commit indiscriminate murder to avoid. Maybe they're cashing in on The Gate-loving halfwits over the road, who like a bit of fake plush with their mediocre beer, I dunno. I'd be interested to hear a more exotic explanation. The punters remain as rough as ever, which is hardly surprising for a bar that's right under the city's branch of Argos; those customers not displaying outright hostility towards you are just subtly shoving their massive, box-stuffed carrier bags under your feet as an ice-breaker before punching you in the throat. And that's probably why - instead of the usual laminate - they've installed extra heavy-duty plastic flooring, making it so much easier to mop up the spilt drink and bodily fluids. But really, and I can't stress this enough, the Original Pub Company should be shaken warmly by the hand for their efforts, even if that's something you will never see me put down in print again.

For: Jesus man, you should have seen it before.
Against: My mate Ray is a fool. He got served on the review visit and then, because he could no longer see 'his' barmaid, he assumed she'd left rather than hand over the pints, so he ordered again. And it was two-for-one. Five bells on a Saturday afternoon, the place is packed to the rafters, and we're standing there like a row of Bruce Forsyths trying to slurp the pints up our chins without knocking into anyone and dropping the lot. I think Bourgognes made this happen on purpose, just to take advantage of our post-match stupor. In fact I'm convinced of it.

Have you ever stopped in the middle of the road outside Bourgognes to pick up your boot of a missus from Argos, simply because she was too fucking bone idle to walk the extra sixty feet to the car park? Or have you pulled the car up anywhere and thought, 'I will stop here, for this is where I want to be', oblivious to the carnage and resentment piling up behind you? You have? Then this is what we'd like to see happen to you: first time you do it the wardens shoot across and fine you; second time they shoot your tyres; and third time they shoot your fucking face. You've had it coming long enough.

Butlers

18 Nun Street, NE1 5AQ
'A cruel, cruel master'

If they're still calling this place Butlers Bistro, then it's about as far from the smug, arty-farty idea of traditional bistroland as you could possibly imagine. This is a bar where people drink when they're barred from the Clock or the Fish Bar. This is a bar where my so-called hard mates refuse to go. And, in spite of my concerns about the rest of the dumps surrounding the Grainger Market, this is the only bar where I've felt directly threatened rather than just worried by reputations. For years I didn't even realise that this was a pub; I just thought it was a greasy spoon café catering to the wall-to-wall pensioners who shuffle in through the day. We reviewed it half-heartedly a while back - just after one of the doormen got done for peddling smack, as I recall - and then spent every moment since steering well clear. They've had a bit of a refit recently but, tiptoeing in for a refresher, we find that it's still, even at five bells on a Friday, on payday, when the sun's out, rough as fucking fuck. At first glance this place is done up to look a bit like a hardware shop at Beamish, but instead of desperate parents dragging round kids who couldn't care less, Butlers is full of angry blokes in steel toecaps, and evil witches plotting hen night degradations. Strewn here and there are strings of Christmas lights, but we'd advise that you don't look at them when you're moving about: Butlers is so damned narrow that any distraction could be harmful, since if there's a four-foot arse wedged into a two-foot gap then you can't help but spill the owner's pint. The barmaid keeps mooching about, dutiful yet terrified, like the faithful hound of a cruel, cruel master. And whenever someone leaves, she's in like a shot, wedging the chairs back against the wall, as if the slightest discrepancy in their interlocking pattern would make it easier to yank them out and break them over heads when it all kicks off. Glancing away from the telly above the optics - the smallest big screen you could ever imagine - I see Father Jack Hackett worrying the bar, and, next to him is the only reason this place is still standing: the clock. Set right in the middle of the bar top and visible from every point in the pub, this gilded, ormolu, Rococo timepiece is surely the work of a benevolent god, and its dazzling array of shapes, reflections and refractions are enough to calm the most furious soul. When tempers are frayed and voices are raised, they simply need to say, 'The clock, Billy. Look. At. The. Clock.' and all is well again. I just fear the day when someone nicks it.

For: Like eating chips from a sumo wrestler's nappy, it's an interesting experience, but not one you'd want to repeat.
Against: No matter how grim it gets inside, it's still better than the hideous breezeblock monstrosity of Wilkinsons across the alleyway.

Father Jack Hackett was, in case you'd forgotten, the drunken old bastard with the cataract in TV's Father Ted. People say it was a tragedy that Dermot Morgan - who played Ted Crilly - died in his prime, and brought a premature end to a fantastic show. They're right, but it was hardly the saddest comedian death in history. That award must surely go to Dustin Gee, showbiz partner of Les Dennis, who passed on just as they were about to make a name for themselves. See, if Dustin hadn't snuffed it, then Dennis wouldn't have been able to launch his fledgling career on the back of the 'Aw, the poor lad' sympathy vote, and we'd have been excused twenty years of his shoddy game shows and embarrassing impersonations that all sound exactly like Les fucking Dennis. Mind, that Ardal O'Hanlon isn't far behind. 'Ah, Ted. Why'd ye have te go and die, sure? Did ye see me in My Hero? I looked like a fecking eejit, so.'

Callaghans
New Bridge Street, NE1 8BS
'Laughable incompetence'

We know it's not exactly professional to review a bar on one short visit. We know we should do it properly if we're going to do it at all, and get a balanced view by arriving at different times of the day. We know it's only fair and just to calculate an average and use that as the basis of the review. But if there was ever a time when a swift and wholly unsuccessful trip to a pub summed up everything about it, then it's the time we wasted in Callaghans. Hamstrung and marooned, waiting for a mate with no mobile to arrive from out of town, we endured possibly the most farcical start to a half-day session the world has ever seen. Never before on a quiet afternoon, in our own city, speaking the same language, have we managed to spend the best part of half an hour failing to get served. Never again will we witness such laughable incompetence in the name of the pint. Looking around - we had ample opportunity - we got to clock the bar's Irish theme, with all the usual blarney and begorrah and bollocks. They've even ballsed that up, since this clearly doesn't look like a real bar where people would drink beer and make a mess. It looks just like a museum piece; like some fake-dirty, cod-historic mock up as part of a brewery tour. I've spent many a tired afternoon trudging round brewery museums all over Europe - Guinness, Heineken, Carlsberg, you name them - and even they, in their tourist-boring, voucher-swapping mediocrity, would be embarrassed by such a sham masquerading as a traditional-looking bar. And in those museums, you often see hologram barmen in historical tableaux, clearly designed to save some poor twat the indignity of dressing up in sackcloth and repeating the same cobblers over and over. I tell you now; those holograms would have been far, far better than the uniformed pillocks from the adjoining Premier Travel Inn who'd been shoved in here to cover the afternoon shift. Christ knows what their proper trade was - tatty peeler or bog roll hanger or something - but they were absolutely fucking useless behind the bar. Couldn't work the till, couldn't pour the pints and, finally, couldn't change the barrel. Give them their due, though. There was none of that 'sorry, no change' carry-on. These clowns had ALL the fucking change. The poor sod in front of us had both hands cupped, and it still wasn't enough to hold all the shrapnel from a twenty. That was the final straw for us. We left, unserved and thirsty, to loiter outside and wait for our mate in the street. What's the craic? Sack this pile of wank for a start.

For: It raised a grin, if nothing else.
Against: How bad can a bar be if a flaming stag do wasn't even the worst thing about it?

We ended up sitting outside Fusion across the Blue Carpet wait-ing for our mate. What a terrible idea that was. Incredibly, their barrel needed changing too, which meant it became forty min-utes without a beer. When the pints finally did arrive they were full of crumbs and floaters, and mine gave me heartburn like you wouldn't believe. And I'm not saying I had a bad tummy the day after being served such swill, but if I'd kept what roared out of my poor arse, I could have stuck it in a tub and sold it as decking stain to the Bank Holiday broom-slaves of at least half the town.

The Charles Grey

118 Grey Street, NE1 6JG
'Arguably the best in Newcastle'

Let's be honest here. FMs - which The Charles Grey replaces - was an absolute disgrace. Imagine a poor man's Hard Rock Cafe, half-heartedly decorated with musical memorabilia of dubious prove-nance, serving up cooking lager and alcopops to a customer base of shoppers and tourists too scared to move more than ten feet away from the Monument. When I saw that the place was being refurbished, I harboured relatively high hopes that the bar on the site that is arguably the best in Newcastle would be overhauled to live up to its location. Imagine, then, my crushing disappoint-ment in finding that the twin evils of apathy and corner cutting have produced this, a Matalan version of the Bacchus down the road and round the corner, with a total refit budget of less than a ton. They've slapped some fake brick cladding on the pillars, tied a few twigs to the ceilings, and bunged a few pictures of histori-cal characters - I suspect Earl Grey may be one of them, but I couldn't be arsed to work out which one - on the walls, but that's about it. It looks decent enough from the outside, but once you get through the doors you'll find the same old tatty carpet on the never-ending stairs; I'm not expecting them to give me a fireman's lift up to the second floor, but they could at least have replaced the missing stair edge. The whole place just seems so half-arsed, and even after racking my brains for an hour, the only things I can really remember are the chairs on the upstairs level that you need a stepladder to get onto. Look, this place isn't the biggest crime in history - the beer's decent enough, after all - but fuck, if they're going to occupy a prime slot you think they'd put some effort into it. The Charles Grey is like every other cynical tourist trap the world over, yet it could have been so much better with a bit more thought and a bit less transparent greed. What a wasted opportunity.

For: The sign outside blends into the surrounding architecture so well that the pub just looks like an extension of the jewellers next door.
Against: The view from the windows of Rockport-clad juveniles legging it from the shops Eldon Square with red-faced store detectives in hot pursuit is enough to dampen the spirits of any decent, law-abiding citizen.

True story: Even though it took us longer to get up those stairs than it did to drink the review pint, our departure was accelerated by the bar's gratuitous playing of 'Angels' by that fool Robbie Williams. Our dear old Queen Elizabeth II is cracking on a bit and, foreseeing the day when Her Majesty croaks, and aware that nobody wants God to save that jug-eared, mumbling loon who's next in line, let alone sing about it before the next England match, I just know that there'll be some sort of campaign to make Williams' witless dirge the new national anthem. Whether by government statute or some misguided attempt by the royal family to curry favour with the nation, it'll be live all night Saturday on a TV phone-in show, probably with Patrick fucking Kielty. I tell you, when that happens, I'm on the next plane out of here and I'm surrendering my passport.

Duke of Northumberland

18 Clayton Street, NE1 5PE
'An Oxfam version of Austin Powers'

If there was ever a bar to stop me bleating about the decline of
the traditional pub and just start loving the deluxe lounge bar,
then it's this one. I knew from reputation that this place was a
bit rough, but I wasn't expecting it to be as harrowing as this.
What a fucking dump. The Duke of Northumberland, aka The
Clock, is not the sort of place you want to take your lass for a
quiet pint, unless she's seventeen stone, lists her hobbies as
'pies' and likes headbutting total strangers. Don't come in with
your mates; their cowardice in the face of terror will only disap-
point you. And don't even come here with a fucking gila monster,
unless you're absolutely sure it's packing a shooter. I am going to
spell it out for you: there is no point in coming here at all. It's
been done, and I did it, to stop you from being so stupid. Drinking
in the Clock is like climbing Everest; unless you're the first,
you're wasting your time. You get all the hardship, but you won't
make the news. This bar doesn't have decor in the traditional
sense. It has walls like the dirty protest of a prisoner in solitary
confinement, plus scattered jumble sale pictures of the Duke
himself that are probably only there to conceal weapons or a
half-finished bag of pickled onion Walkers. I'm not saying they
expect bother in here. But you see those mirrors, the ones you
used to find on the stairs of double-decker buses? They've got
them on the back wall so the bar staff can see it all kicking off in
the doorways. In every corner and on every ripped seat sits a piss-
soiled old bastard, either cursing his luck watching the racing, or
staring into space and swearing at his demons. The gent to our
left appears to have been clutching the same pint since 1973. I
try looking down the back end of the room towards the dartboard. Bad idea. There's a bunch of scrawny whippet-boys sitting
on a hair trigger. They're facing into the room and away from
each other, like the only thing they have in common is their desire to see my teeth all over the floor. Fucking hell, man, it's only
lunchtime. Hearing the smash of glass I turn round, expecting a

shattered pint pot to be heading in my direction; it's just a clumsy barmaid, thank Christ. I laugh quietly and nervously, and pray my grundies can take the strain. And in the middle of all this, staggering about, is an Oxfam version of Austin Powers, oblivious to everything, including the dribble on his cravat. I toy with the idea of helping him out and explaining to him my fears for his safety. Then I think about it rationally and I leave him to it; anyone acting that much of a twat in a bar like this has got to be the simple kid brother of the hardest, angriest, least reasonable motherfucker in the whole town. Even catching his eye would mean the loss of one of mine. I'm sure of that. My pint finally drained, I head for the door and practically kick it open in my desire to get out into the street to mingle with the harmless nutters hanging around outside. And only in the fresh air do I realise this bar's one plus point: when the mallrat crowd around on Newgate Street tire of the protective bosom of The Gate, there's a chance that this will be the first bar they try in their search for authenticity, and it's possible they will finally get the hoofing they so richly deserve. Here, mate. I'll hold your coat.

For: Damn good beer. They wouldn't DARE water it down.
Against: Everything else. I'm not going to praise the place just because we got out in one piece.

I think I've worked out how we managed to stay alive. I thought we'd be killed for turning up with ties on, but as three of us were semi-smart with scruffy jackets and the other bloke was wearing a suit, we must have looked like we'd just avoided a two-stretch on a technicality and were going for a pint with our bent solicitor.

The Duke

High Bridge, NE1 1EN
'The same old deadbeats'

The Duke - or Duke of Wellington as it was known back then - was one of the first pubs we reviewed, and it's an absolute joy to report that it's still there, virtually unchanged bar a lick of paint and a helpful truncation of the name. Defiantly resisting the humiliating attempts at bouffantification of other similar bars in the town - see the debacle of The Lane over the road for a perfect example of what not to do to your boozer - the Duke remains a small, friendly pub with excellent beer and a good atmosphere. And, given its proximity to the piss-swimming butcher's shop that is the Bigg Market, you have to admit that's little short of miraculous. The decor looks, well, just like a pub - if you can remember what they were - with plenty of wood that's just on the right side of knackered, and blackboards that advertise not tartrazine-laden sodypops for drunken teens who don't like the taste of alcohol, but pints. Of beer. The only concession I've seen to the 21st century are a couple of new plasma tellies stuck in the corners that, incredibly, show Programmes That People Might Watch with the volume turned so you can hear what's going on. None of that vacuous Fashion TV shite here, or punters gawping at the screen because they've realised that once they've stopped talking about their haircut they've got fuck all left to say. So aye, it's a pub, like they used to be before the wankbars spread like a cancer through the town. Unpretentious is the word that would best sum the place up. And that's the way it should stay. You can say I'm a miserable old fucker for loving it and I won't care. You can ask where the sushi menu is and I'll laugh in your face. And you can stare aghast, wondering where the decks and the PA are, and I still won't give a shite. Screw you, I'd say. I like a bar that digs its heels in against so-called progress. I like being served my drink by human beings and not giggling jailbait. And I'm proud to say I'm one of the same old deadbeats who've been propping up the bar for the last twen... they've done what? They've got shot of the ancient wooden partitions and replaced the benches with comfortable seating? I bet I look a right fucking tit now.

For: Cracking little boozer at any time of day, except for...
Against: ...can you fuck get served on a match night for all the besuited pricks hogging the bar and pontificating over their halves of guest ale. MOVE, you fat oaf.

The same faces have been behind the bar of the Duke for absolutely ages, and I like that. I'd like to express my dismay at how, while European bar owners show a bit of pride in their work, landlords over here tend to be either surly and grasping, or on the verge of a nervous breakdown, all thanks to the vermin who make up their customers. On the continent (in cities at least) you can visit a bar at ten year intervals and you'll still see the same staff, happily chatting to their punters, safe in the knowledge that theirs is a respectable career in the public service. Over here, you're 'lucky' if a bar lasts a year before the next tacky refit and management reshuffle. And our beer's piss, too.

Enigma
Carliol Square, NE1 6UG
'The Ku Klux Klan'

The previous chapter in this book - Burglar's Dog Design Solutions - was a guide to making your new / refurbished pub look identical to the tiniest degree to every other bar in the town. It was - and we felt certain that this was abundantly clear - supposed to be a bloody JOKE. However, a few short months after we cobbled it together, our consultancy bore its first fruits in the shape of Enigma, a bar that followed our guide to every last misused apostrophe. We didn't know whether to laugh, cry or torch the place. Far be it for me to get nostalgic for this pub's former incarnation of Wilders, shit-stinking tip that it was, but the constant uprooting of bewildered scum like myself to make way for the new breed of identikit punters is a little demoralising. Don't they love me any more? Is my dress sense that poor? Is my dancing really so embarrassing? Bearing in mind that I know as much about the Ku Klux Klan as I do about the clubbing scene, I'd imagine they've tried to create what I believe they call a 'warm up' bar for World Headquarters over the road. Fair enough, follow the trends to the big bucks, and I'm sure Enigma'll be a money-spinner, but did they have to make it so depressingly, cynically obvious? Was it really so necessary to go for the lowest common denominator in every single aspect? From the artwork that looks like something Paul Klee might have done shortly after being pepper sprayed by a paranoid lesbian, a picture that commits the cardinal sin of being selected simply because it 'goes' with the furniture, to the reds and the creams of the colour scheme; from the subtle lighting to the flat screen TVs, it's all very tasteful in a style-bible sort of way, and very, very, very dull. Plus, for all the financial outlay and attention lavished on the refit, it still stinks of mould and mildew like my old long-demolished Benwell flat. And whichever way you look at it, Enigma's a fucking shite name for a bar.

For: Wilders really was a dump and something - anything - had to be done.
Against: The poster in the bogs says that Monday night is busker night. My fragile, hungover brain can barely contemplate just how much misery that could inflict on the unsuspecting punter.

Buskers, though. Acoustic guitars. For years I've been nagging our lass to learn some chords on the guitar. But after watching a few of the 'North East's finest female singer-songwriters' yelling their way through dirges about their doomed love lives in a bar last weekend I had to tell her straight: Touch my guitars and I'll break your arm. You know why she's always refused to learn, though? Doesn't want to cut her fingernails. What is it with women and their nails? Have you ever heard a bloke go, 'Phwoar, looka the fingernails on hor!'?

Fitzgeralds

60 Grey Street, NE1 6AF
'Chocolate-box scenes your gran would love'

The author F Scott Fitzgerald is once said to have been chal-
lenged to write a story using as few words as possible. This is
what he wrote: 'For Sale. Baby's shoes. Never worn.' Except, he
didn't. Looking it up on the internet, we find that it was actually
Ernest Hemingway who penned that, which leaves us a) looking
pretty foolish and b) without a single noteworthy theme to base
the review on. I'm not going to slag this place off, though. Nor
am I going to throw some pummelling great tantrum. Fitzgeralds
is in no way unpleasant; it just bores the tits off me. And, much
as it shames me to say so, I'm probably just going to have to do
the review properly and make it factual, so you may want to skip
this one. Traditionally furnished with wooden panelling and
brown leather booths, and an ornate ceiling whose centrepiece is
a large, stained glass light reminiscent of a peacock's plumage,
Fitzgeralds combines racing green with muted shades of brown
and purple for a relaxed atmosphere. Fully carpeted throughout,
and with large doors looking out over the courtyard of the newly
built office block on the adjacent High Bridge, there's a spacious
feel enhanced by the extensive use of mirrors. As well as its potential for relaxed business lunches, Fitzgeralds is also popular
with ladies of a certain age, and... this is making me feel ill. Listen to me: 'Wah-wah-wah, ladies of a certain age.' Look, they're
ancient old biddies, and, from where I'm sitting holding my nose,
Fitzgeralds is just a couple of crossed 't's away from a lucrative
sponsorship deal with leading fadge-mop product Tena Lady. And
it's dull: as dull as ditchwater, on a wet weekend, in Torquay out
of season, with John Motson, watching Bolton play a friendly. And
it looks like a fucking brothel. What the hell is all that stained
glass supposed to be? I don't know if they're trying for art nouveau or art deco, but whichever it is, it always just says one thing
to me, and that's Sir John Fitzgerald Ltd, 1988. There's pretend
books on pretend cases, an inlaid clock above the bar that ticks
off all the seconds you'll never get back and, as well as the usual

ad-hoc picture collection of chocolate-box scenes your gran would love, there's stuff by Toulouse-Lautrec, Rossetti and many others who'd be clawing their way out of their graves if they knew what their hard graft had amounted to. Yes, you get a decent pint here, and yes it's a million miles away from the snooty lounge or the sweltering theme pub, but I've continually bypassed this place over the years and, considering it's the style of pub I'm always hankering for, that's not much in the way of a recommendation, is it?

For: There's a verdigris peacock on a ledge just before you enter the bar's lower main area. I think it may well disappear just before the next Mother's Day. You'll not tell them, though, will you?
Against: Years and years ago, I was served a pint of line-cleaning fluid in here, an incident that has remained imprinted on my brain ever since. I still haven't forgiven them.

The missus pointed out that the walkway from the upper to the lower levels is like a catwalk. She's right. I sat facing out towards the door watching the semi-naked lasses strolling in - and scurrying back out again - while I made her look other way. 'Er, just keep looking at the decor, love, I really want this review to be accurate...' What a fucking rotter.

Fusion
31 New Bridge Street West, NE1 8AN
'Naked arse-kicking'

There's a standard technique popular with lazy writers where, if you've got nothing to say about a given topic, then you write about how you've got nothing to say, and make your struggles with your mental block fill up half the word count. I'm sorely tempted to do that with this here review of Fusion. There really isn't much that I can write about the place that hasn't already been said - albeit with a lot more vitriol - in countless other reviews. It's not like I have a bone to pick with them, but there's just so little to really get animated over. Basically Fusion is one little room with a bar in it, the sort of place where you actually want them to turn the music UP so the chumps at the next table - and the staff - can't hear every word you're saying, especially when you're bouncing ideas around as to whether to give the place a critical mauling. I've only ever been in straight after work, when there's been next to nobody there, and I've always felt too embarrassed to make much of a racket by, y'know, talking and that. Even looking around to clock the decor makes me feel a bit paranoid, but what you get is this: the usual purple paint everywhere, plus a huge painting over by the bogs of a bloke with a perm doing what I can only imagine is some sort of naked arse-kicking dance, and a cod-lesbian 'Mirror? Or dykes?' picture by the door. And there's seats and, erm, tables, and... have I said there's a bar yet? You get the picture? It's not exactly unpleasant, but it doesn't float my boat either. We left as a couple of pensioners came in and started poking the sandwiches, something that seemed to speak volumes to me. About what, I'm not really sure, though. You'll have to use your imagination. Like I say, I have no axe to grind with them, but I really can't imagine becoming a regular. Sorry.

For: It's open from eight in the morning.
Against: Apparently it's the 'Official Envy Pre-clubbing bar'. Do NOT get me started on the concept of 'official' product tie-ins. See when you're watching the Champions' League? The official websites, I can handle. Official lager, less so.

Fusion might be canny in the summer, sitting out next to the Blue Carpet with a beer and watching whatever local pride there once was at being a (failed) City of Culture contender slowly decaying away. I see that 300 grand staircase next to the carpet has been trashed already.

Hoko-10

16 Dean Street, NE1 1PG
'Sleeping rough'

Once the city's latest razor-cut style venue, Hoko-10 used to pull off the trick of being so ridiculously over the top that it transcended its own wankiness. Now, despite still having the same pretensions, it looks like it's been found sleeping rough under a bridge and given a good fucking hiding. Hoko-10 is still a mix of split levels, dark browns, muted lighting and all the usual posh-bar bollocks, but you don't have to look too hard to see that this is scuffed, that's broken and there's a bit hanging off over there. I remember thinking when this place first opened that the cushion-stuffed wooden booths that you had to clamber into to get all, like, intimate with your companions were quite a nice, daft little touch. That was when the bar had only been open for a matter of days; I'd imagine they'll be somewhat less appealing these days, after years of being showered with tab ash, broken glass and used condoms, and I'm certainly not prepared to hop in and check unless you're stumping up for protective clothing an extra-strength Marigolds. They've still got the tanks full of piranhas, all swimming about looking as fearsome as nature intended, but with an extra cockiness now that they've scared off the sushi chefs who used to stand next to them and pull 'you're next' faces through the sides of the tanks. Chefs? Fucking pussies. Anyone can be a tough guy when they've got a carving knife in their hand; try stripping a man's arm to the bone in under ten seconds and then you'll know tough, you pair of split-crotch panties. Trying to flog sushi in a bar was a foolhardy plan anyway; it doesn't matter how elaborate the concept or how forcefully a bar rams a gimmick down the punters' throats, they all eventually realise that nobody in this town gives two feeble fucks about anything but getting ratted. And while it's clearly on the slide, I'm not going to pretend that this place has turned into the Blackett Arms. It's not a dump yet, by any means. But it's definitely a lesson in what happens when you allow drunken people anywhere near your fancy design statement.

For: Luxury roped-off VIP area.
Against: If you're stupid and insecure enough to spend a week's wages on a bottle of Krug to validate your social standing, then the rope needs to be there to keep you in, not us out.

Beer prices are a crime. But as long as one bar can make people pay them, then others will follow suit simply because they can, because that's the marketplace we're in. This is one of the few things I learned about business whilst working for a multinational company. You see when your joke managers are off to London for the day on 'business'? They're not building for the company's future. They're not strengthening the brand. They're not even arguing over how much money to piss away on IT systems that will never work. What they're doing is drawing lots to see which one of the greedy cunts will stand up and defend his 400% pay rise and buckshee share options, just so all the rest of the parasites can say 'Market forces. It's the going rate' when they get the same obscene deal three months later.

Idols

Newgate Shopping Centre, Newgate Street, NE1 5RS
'Honest incompetence in the act of love'

We're getting old. There's no denying it. It's tricky enough these days to even get up the stairs at the match, never mind add any more unnecessary climbing to our Saturday afternoons. And it is for that reason, and that reason alone that we've been giving the subterranean Idols a wide berth for the past few years. But, y'know, to celebrate the mackems' relegation we thought we'd hobble down for a swift, raucous pint watching the strippers, and maybe write the review in the process. Ye bugger, this place has changed. Although the tatty stairwell remains the same, gone is the '80s throwback decor of industrial tat and springs and bits of tubas, and in their place is a minimal, empty shed so beloved of lazy bastard designers the nation over. And while they're still advertising exotic dancers, in their upmarket semi-refurbished state they actually mean dancing and nowt else. It's a tragedy to see the comedy strippers (two stone overweight, cellulite-ridden, knockers like beagles' lugs on our last visit) replaced by uninterested bunny girls and over-rehearsed, over-choreographed dancers in leg-warmers, especially when one of them is a fucking BLOKE. Dancing girls are really starting to lose their attraction these days, an' all. Bearing in mind that the inference of all the grinding and thrusting is the thought of what they'd do to you beneath the duvet, I just find your average under-dressed turn on the podium so utterly sexless; with all that left hand UP, swing hips ROUND, slap arse HERE business, it's all as regimented and as procedural as a fucking MOT-check. It's like in The Man With Two Brains, when Steve Martin finally gets to consummate his sham marriage to gold-digger Kathleen Turner and pronounces it 'so... so... professional'. What's wrong with a bit of honest incompetence in the act of love? Does there have to be a fucking British Standard for it? I've given too much away again, haven't I? Better get back to the review, by saying stuff like... And to make matters worse, it looks like when the previous DJ moved out, headhunted by the Sports Café round the corner, he not only took the strippers, the atmosphere and the legendary banter with him, but he even took his ladder, judging by the way some poor lass had to clamber up the optics and onto the shelf to do her act. Yeah, I know they're pumping out the dry ice for a bit of a show-biz feel, and bringing on fire jugglers to compensate for the lack of bristols, but it all seems a bit desperate and, more importantly, anything but a money-spinner. I only stood nursing my pint to see if the girl in the nylon mini-skirt with her hair all over the shop was actually going to set herself aflame; once she'd got to the end of the song with only a few soot marks and a splash of lighter fuel on her skimpy T-shirt, we were off, headed for somewhere more interesting.

For: The 'tits' will be back 'oot' sooner or later, you can guarantee it.
Against: Why can't toilet attendants just fuck off once and for all? Next time I see one, I'm going to cack in my hands, piss down my trousers, and puke all over my Toon shirt. Then I'm going to

ask THEM, 'Alright, mate?' and see if they can work miracles with a bottle of Blue Stratos and a paper towel.

I've never understood the appeal of being a dancer. Fair enough, with all that exercise you get to be trim and toned and fit as fuck, even if you've got a face like a German helmet. But for the ratio of effort to reward, it's pretty depressing, if all your big break will ever amount to is being third grinning nobody from the left behind the latest clueless fuckpuppet RealityPop! winner. Still, it could be worse. They could spend every hungover Sunday morning hunched over a keyboard, hammering out witless pub reviews that nobody will ever even read, let alone enjoy. Now that would be a waste of a life.

Intermezzo

10 Pilgrim Street, NE1 6QG
'A dachshund in a deepfreeze'

Squeezed into the dead space under the Tyneside Cinema that used to be the shop until they realised they'd never be able to flog off all the Betty Blue posters left over from the '80s, Intermezzo is the closest Newcastle has yet come to the genuine Euro café-bar article. I've often popped in for an overpriced Peroni in a grubby glass before going upstairs to watch subtitled porn masquerading as art house cinema. If it wasn't for the absolute tossers who get in here, this would be quite a decent bar. It's not *you* I'm getting at here, obviously, but the rest of the sad fuckers. Come rain or shine there'll be a specky twat in a black polo neck sitting plotting out his gallery re-hang on his palm-top Bluebottle or whatever they're called. Or you'll see some dizzy bint in trousers made out of curtains supping knackaccino outside, kissing her mates on the cheek and going 'Like, ciao!' while shivering like a dachshund in a deepfreeze. Go inside, you dopey mare. There's another reason why I hate the punters; they remind me of what I'm in grave danger of becoming if I'm not careful. Every time I nip into the cinema foyer for a programme I have to make sure I haven't accidentally grown one of those chinny twat-beards or developed a penchant for flowery language. Penchant? Just shoot me now, will you? On the plus side though, the cocktails here are class, and made with a bit of skill and jiggery-pokery an' all - none of your slop + mixer here. Quality. As for décor, it's just a narrow room with red leather seating and a long counter stretching the entire length of the window wall where you get to watch the alkies raising Cain in the back alley. Which reminds me: whatever happened to that drunken old get with the beard that used to push that six-foot high trolley about collecting cans and swearing at the passers-by? I guess my mother makes him stay in of an evening nowadays. Huh huh huh.

For: When I'm on a promise, I like to bring the missus here for a few cocktails before a mucky film. It avoids any of that tedious foreplay nonsense when we get home.
Against: Brown corduroys. And the wastes of chromosomes that wear them.

Tom Waits has got a lot to answer for. I only like his later stuff - from Swordfishtrombones onwards - but, against my better judgment, I borrowed one of his early CDs from the local library. Stuck it in the Walkman one morning, listened on the way to work, thought no more about it. Later that day, Dog co-founder Egdell and I were having a few after-workers and, already the worse for wear, we headed for Intermezzo for a couple of cocktails to see us on our journey home. Unfortunately, we picked a quiet night where, not only was there just one barmaid and us in, but she was in her last week before trekking off round the globe. And in her devil-may-care way, she was more than liberal with the measures. Oh, Christ, was she. And Egdell, not being the greatest fan of spirits, kept passing his drinks to me in favour of a Peroni spacer. I remember thinking at the time, Fair enough. But a couple of hours in, I suddenly turned into Tom Waits, in his grizzled, sozzled, counter-banging barfly days, before he sobered up enough to actually sell some records. What a state. Stuck Waits on the Walkman again on the way home, and even before the bus stopped I was mumbling, 'Step raaaaaat urp!' And by the time I got home I was roaring drunk, biting a hole in my shirt for reasons I've never understood, before howling round the garden in just my underkegs like one of Waits' chain-rattling later creations. I have no idea what happened after that. Our lass still won't tell me. I didn't make it into work the next day. Or the day after, for that matter.

The Lane
41-51 High Bridge, NE1 1NE
'Ignorant swine'

Formerly, and probably still known to most people as Turks, The Lane wins the Dog award for most-passed-least-visited bar in the whole of the town. It's not that we felt any sort of nostalgia for the old place, or a sense of betrayal that one of the city's more historical pubs had been changed, but more that, frankly, it's not much cop. Just look at the decor for a start. It appears that they've tried to fool a few customers into thinking it's one of those new-fangled lounge bars, what with all the splashes of cream and purple and the exposed wood. The trouble is, it also looks as though when they were doing it, they asked, 'Shall we refurbish this place properly? Or should we just fucking slap this paint on top of all the old shite and hope nobody notices?' And the rest of the stuff, the things that make a bar a pleasant place in which to while away the hours? Let's have a pop at that, too. In no particular order... 1) They need to get the speaker system sorted out so you can hear it properly: a guitar-free Ramones was surely never the idea. 2) The quiz machine is in the window, so you can't see the questions for the glare on the screen. 3) The no-smoking area: good idea, aye, but while we're no experts on convection, it looks to us ignorant swine like the air conditioning vents above it suck up all the smoke from the rest of the pub and into your face on the way into the ceiling. 4) The beer ain't up to much, either. Plus, on the review visit we thought for a while that the legendarily disgusting toilets had been sorted out; putting aside the choking stink of bleach – like early morning in the municipal baths - they did seem a little less evil than expected. Unfortunately, it was all a con. In the time it took to watch the match on Sky the toilets ended up swimming in piss again. Obviously we don't go to bars to spend all our time loitering in the crappers, like, but decent amenities never ruined anyone's afternoon. So how would you sum The Lane up? Shabby is a good word. Neglected would just about cover it, an' all. Desperate, too. We've got it on good authority that they once tried to cash in on the tittypub 'craze' by having exotic dancers on the bar. Still, times change fast in the drinking world, and we're sure there'll be another bandwagon along soon for The Lane to clamber aboard. Or maybe they'd be better off being Turks again. Don't fuck with tradition.

For: Those balmy afternoons in summer when the big windows at the front are open.
Against: This is England. We don't get balmy afternoons in summer.

I hate being lied to by the council and the media. What the hell happened to the rumoured gentrification of High Bridge? Where's the café society and the cosmopolitan buzz? Where is the mix of history and new business? Half a street of dereliction and a brand-new tattoo parlour. Is that what they meant?

Lennon's
63 Newgate Street, NE1 5RF
'This week's meat draw'

If Lennon's is not a close relative of the appalling Sgt Pepper's at the Haymarket, then I fully expect to see some tear-stained, separated-at-birth Chronicle feature any time now. This place calls itself a nostalgic music bar and, like that festering scab up the road, it's less of a theme pub, and more of a bar where time has actually stopped, round about the time when the specky Scouse twat got plugged. The punters are exactly what you'd expect in this type of boozer. Strictly pot-bellied geezers in un-tucked shirts, and leather cleavaged divorcees who can do 'The Bump' and all the moves to 'Tiger Feet' without spilling their lager and lime. And this is the sort of bar where the DJ is more like a bingo caller than a Gilles Peterson: 'If you take your seats, ladies and gents, we'll do this week's meat draw.' The music is always wedding reception material, and though we didn't stick around, you can guarantee that, come eleven o'clock, there'll be some lachrymose old boiler mouthing the words to the trite self-help anthem that sums up the tragedy of her life. Despite a heavy-duty refit and peer pressure from The Gate's pubs, the whole bar now looks tatty as fuck again, and no amount of bat-tered drinks promotion posters is ever going to change that. Someone's kicked half the plaster off the walls in a drunken tizzy, and the laminate flooring - this year's Artex, all you DIY sheep - is in a right state, despite the tacky (in both senses) Ab-bey Road zebra crossing leading to the bar. Other Lennon-related stuff includes the piano key motif around the bar - from the Imag-ine video, where everything was, uh, purple - and four Beatles jigsaw pieces on the wall. Really, to even mention the decor in passing would be to miss the whole point of Lennon's, which is a last chance saloon for old growlers who just haven't got the time to be fussy any more. Straight up. Much as I like to think of my-self as a good looking lad who could pull wherever he wanted, I'm appalled to have to write that I got more eye in here than any-where, on account of being the only bloke under forty in the place. Try it yourself. You won't need even your fifth best lines. Just ask for a light and you'll have some desiccated old steg with a rum and Coke and a never-ending sob story sucking your face until your eyeballs meet your tonsils. I know I did.

For: This place proves that there are people who find the shoddy Gate leisure mall too classy.
Against: You come in feeling all superior - 'let's chortle at the old timers' - but you soon realise they're having a better time than you.

Writing this review made me wonder: how long before we get a '90s music bar, where the son of the Burglar's Dog comes in to laugh at all the sad indie losers getting nostalgic over the likes of Oasis and Radiohead? Mere months is how long; that was the time between my rhetorical question and the opening of that abysmal Boom! '90s Bar down the road.

The Living Room
12 Grey Street, NE1 6AE
'Swearing, nudity, incest'

Anyone remember Oliver's, the sandwich bar next to Burger King on Northumberland Street? The one that disappeared when Greggs decided to move in there and ensure a trail of pastry and litter from one end of the street to the other? Ah, it was grand; four quid for a sarnie - and that's when four quid was four quid - served on a paper plate with a few stale crisps and some 'luxury' coleslaw, sitting at a Formica table, watching yourself get onions all over your face in a hundred different mirrors. I'll tell you what, mind; I thought someone had been pissing about with my space/time continuum again, because the downstairs bar of the Living Room is exactly like that. *Exactly.* That's what happens when you go for a wazz as soon as you go in to a pub. The ground floor - the bit you'd come to first unless you were looking for a contrived intro to a review - is more full of creams and browns and exposed brickwork, all the usual stuff, and while the decor is par for the course for a bar these days, it did feel quite pleasant and bright. The whole wall of sepia prints of Christ-knows-who wasn't too much like an Athena closing down sale, I didn't instantly want to take a Stanley knife to the painting in the hall-way, and the cocktail glasses with their wonky stems seemed well worth pinching. Top marks also for the coat hooks under the bar. It's the little things like that - plus the acknowledgment that some people in Newcastle do actually wear coats in January - that make an old bastard like me happy. Fair enough, the place is pricey, it's part of a chain, and there's a restaurant attached that just sneers, 'I'm too flashy for scum like you.' And who cares if the punters are a little on the mature side? What's wrong with happy couples out for a nice pint after shopping? And who but a curmudgeon would carp at a couple of well-spoken ladies chatting up the barman, getting off their Agent Provocateur-clad tits on expensive cocktails and bunging them on the plastic? That barman was a complete tosser though. How come TV watchdogs waste all their time trying to ban swearing, nudity, incest and trivia like that, when they should really be clamping down on adverts for spirits? Bacardi is the name that immediately springs to mind. You know the ones I'm ranting about, the ones that try to portray bars as happy, exciting venues and not the centres for misery and sorrow-drowning that they so obviously are; the ones with bottle-spinning, shape-throwing, lime-kicking party scenes; the ones that give dickheads behind the bar the idea that it's perfectly acceptable to make me wait half an hour for my pint. I go to pubs to get drunk, and fast, and not to watch some grinning twat mucking about. And don't turn around to make wisecracks to your mate when I'm ordering, either, you berk.

For: It's actually alright, to be honest. Well, when it's quiet and you can feel a bit relaxed and decadent, anyway. Later on, when it's packed and people keep whacking into you, it's an overpriced pain in the arse.
Against: I can't believe some places are still doing this, but when we first tried to get in - the week it opened – I was knocked back for wearing trainers. What fucking difference does a pair of shoes make? What is it, a boozer or a bowling alley?

Cocktails on the plastic: a cautionary tale. The missus and I ran out of cash in one of Newcastle's flashier bars a while back. Normally when you run out of readies, you think, 'Hmm, time to go home.' Not us. No, we decided it'd be a wheeze to work our way through the cocktail menu and stick the bill on the credit card. Sitting on the bus on the way home, I turned back from gawping out of the window and thought, 'Wait a minute. I'm covered in puke.' Just like that. No warning, no squeaks or grunts or mm-mmnn-mms; she'd just opened her gob and fetched up her dinner in my lap. She's got the whole bus to aim at and I'm the one with a pocket full of mint leaves and olives? Disgraceful.

The Lodge
26 Mosley Street, NE1 1DE
'A terrible idea'

Despite the fact that loveable cheeky chappie TV presenters Ant & Dec had apparently ploughed quarter of a million quid into the refit and rename of the old Jonny Ringo's, and despite our quite liking the previous incarnation of the place, the few times we'd been in since the change left us thoroughly nonplussed. In fact, we hated it. A magnet for stag parties, hen nights, and general arseheads, the place seemed to hold all our least favourite types of social groups, coupled with a dark, depressing atmosphere, with the overwhelming brownness of it being lifted only by spirit-strangling orange lighting. We went back again on a Saturday night to review it seriously and, sadly, found it just the same, only scruffier. Sat in one of the booths on the mezzanine level (the one with the broken telly, typically), we listened to a disembodied voice telling the punters how great the bar was and how the two-for-one offer was a bargain. What they're not telling you are the normal prices which, for a bar of this quality, are an absolute crime. This place has no business whatsoever charging three quid for a pint of cooking lager, unless Ant & Dec are trying to claw back some capital before bailing out of the whole sorry venture. Bloody Popolo doesn't even charge that much, man. The surroundings, the prices, the punters and the general unpleasantness of it all sapping our conversational abilities, we just had time to clock the massive light shades full of straws and tabs and other amusing projectiles that people have launched from the balcony bar, before draining our pints and leaving, never to return. So why is it so damned popular, then? Is it the celebrity link, the vague hope of seeing the co-owners downing an off-duty Beck's between reality TV shows? Must be, but for all their 'proper Geordie, me' protestations, I don't think Ant & Dec would wipe their off-duty feet in the place, to be honest. Yeah, call me a sour bastard, and yeah, it's probably much nicer during the day with a bit of light coming in but, frankly, I'd sooner crap in my pants than even nip in to use their toilets. Horrific.

For: The fact that there's often a queue of one-born-every-minute fools lined up outside, making you much more likely to go somewhere else.

Against: If you have done any work - paid or unpaid - during in the last seven days, your colleagues will want you to drink in here on their big night out.

I'm a pedantic little fucker and I'm in a right bad mood, so I'm going to say this: the big, illuminated orange menu thing on the right-hand wall as you go in is littered with mistakes, most notably my favourite bugbear, the misused apostrophe. Fair enough, if it was handwritten on a blackboard by some divvy earning a quid an hour I could almost tolerate it, but this retina-ruining monstrosity was done by a professional. What the hell is the world coming to when 'experience of words' is not an essential qualification for a sign-writing position?

Lord Collingwood

12 Clayton Street, NE1 5PU
'Chelsie - get here NOW afore ah fuck'n bray ye'

Lord Cuthbert Collingwood was the second in command at the Battle of Trafalgar to Horatio Nelson, who once famously said, 'Now, gentlemen, let us do something today which the world may talk of hereafter.' That was easy for him to say, with his musket and his sextant and his big bastard boat. He never had to stare death in the face by reviewing this bloody dump. Let's get one thing straight from the start: if a man called Cuthbert had dared to show his pampered face in here he'd have been torn apart and eaten with a dollop of Daddies. 'Fuckin' rear admiral, are ye, y'puff...?' Collingwood first sailed into the drink at the age of 12, which, by bizarre coincidence is around the same age the bairns start trying to sneak in here, under the neglectful eye of their mam and dad. You know the type of unfit parents I'm talking about: fat fucking twat in pie-stained Toon top and his whey-faced missus, mouth wrinkled like a cat's arse from her 20-an-hour Lambert & Butler addiction. They'll be joined by their pre-GCSE daughter with her Fred Perry sweatshirt and trackie bottoms, whose busy teaching the finer points of English to her baby, father unknown. 'Chelsie - get here NOW afore ah fuck'n bray ye.' They'll be outside the doors at eleven, rat-arsed by noon and stabbing each other in the kidneys before five, only to bond in A&E over the brutal beating of a hospital porter, before returning to do it all again the next day. And they will look at you like YOU'RE the pile of shite, just because your face hasn't been seen in the Chronicle with a line underneath saying 'Preyed on pensioners' or, simply, '15 years'. Right, that's my anthropology degree sorted out; now for the pub review. It's horseshoe-shaped, it's got absolutely fuck all in it, it has karaoke in the afternoon and it sells beer. Any questions?

For: It closes early - 8pm - during the week.
Against: I don't know what the hell the decor - and I use the term sarcastically - is playing at. Taking a wild guess, I'd say that the pipes in the upstairs crappers burst one night and filled the entire place from top to bottom with raw sewage, the bobbing turds a cruel play on this pub's alternative name of the Fish Bar. And instead of pumping the insurance money back into repairing the damage, it looks like they've just shoved every penny into the bandit, left the shit-stained walls to dry out and then called the resulting mess a colour scheme.

I know sod all about drugs. I have no vices, other than a nice few pints and maybe a bit of schadenfreude at the weekend. So maybe it's just my imagination that leads me to believe the reason all the tiled surfaces in the Gents are covered in fucking Vaseline is to stop the dirty bastard punters from hoovering up the cocaine while they're having a slash. Maybe.

Market Lane

72 Pilgrim Street, NE1 6SG
'I cried salt tears'

Nobody I know refers to this pub as the Market Lane; it's always been known as the Monkey Bar, and here, just to prove we do things properly, is why. The blokes who built the Tyne Bridge, which starts just down the road, used to leave their hods, or 'monkeys', behind the bar in exchange for beer, and would only get them back after they'd settled their bar bills. So now you know. Don't be put off by the tatty outside; this is a decent little pub, with reasonable beer, although you do get the feeling it belongs more on a high street than in the city centre, especially with the over-studied cool of Popolo being right next door. The pub is basically two rooms and a soft toy monkey-covered bar in the middle, with the punter types being split between the rooms. You've got your old gadgies scanning the racing pages in the front, and ageing rockers in the back, though you do get the occasional office crowd in the no-man's land in between. And that's about it for the Monkey Bar; to be perfectly honest, it's a bit of a tip these days, but I reckon any sort of refit or even a new roll of wallpaper would somehow detract from the grotty charm of the place. I know I cried salt tears the last time they gave it a once-over, back in the late '80s. Incidentally, and for the last flaming time, I'm going to spell this out for all you jellied eel-slurping, 4x4 driving, Bluewater-bound, M25-stuck Southern fools. It wasn't the Geordies who, in the 18th Century found a shipwrecked monkey dressed in a captain's uniform and assumed that, because it couldn't speak English, it was a French spy and hanged it. That was the inbred bumpkins down the coast in Hartlepool, and it's a tale of which they're particularly proud. Better to be a monkey-hanger from Hartlepool than a sex case from Middlesbrough.

For: Cheese, nuts, pickled onions and crackers on the bar early evening. Perfect for a stomach liner, at least until the statistically proven 200 types of man-wee end up in the dishes.

Against: I am responsible for putting the wee there, thanks to the contents of my ever-present briefcase. Would you care to see a sample?

And while we're on the subject of regional stereotypes, people often ask why Newcastle and Sunderland hate each other. The simple answer is we don't: they hate us, but we just find them amusing. Have you ever witnessed such an embarrassing display of inferiority complex? We have a world-famous bridge; they get themselves a crappy fun-size version of it. We're a famous city - with the mandatory fucking cathedral - so they mewl and whine their way to city status, whether they're entitled to it or not. We sack a shit manager mid-season and they follow suit, only too stupidly late to make any sort of difference to their doom. Just the fact that it's Tyne and Wear and not the other way round is enough to turn them apoplectic, the poor, downtrodden, vowel-mangling oafs. And - despite the fact that we're geographically north of Wearside, you'll never hear of a mackem going UP to Newcastle - always 'through'. Or is that thrayeew? Let's all laugh at Sunderland indeed.

themushroom

82 Grainger Street, NE1 5JQ
'Piss-on-their-heads-and-tell-'em-it's-raining'

Hidden away downstairs under TJ Hughes' redevelopment of the former Binns store, themushroom manages to combine the very worst bits of Bar 42 and the city's most horrendous nightclub, Madisons (ask your dad, if your mother's sobered up long enough to remember who he is). It's dark, dingy, depressing, and with its computer controlled lighting that fades from pink to orange to purple, it still never quite manages to be bright enough to let you see who the hell you're talking to. I assume the management are worried about overspill from the scum pubs around the Grainger Market straying into their exclusive Grainger Town address, and that's why the bar is only open from five bells onwards on a weekday, long after the radgies have either passed out or booked an evening at Her Majesty's Pleasure. Now, I'm not going to suggest that they have a policy here of piss-on-their-heads-and-tell-'em-it's-raining; that would be ridiculous. But I'm struggling to come up with any other reason why they would ask their surly, obnoxious barmaids to inflict their special deals on you, like the chance to have a lager of similar strength, taste and quality to the one you ordered for exactly the same price. Uh, no thanks, love, I'll have what I asked you for in the first place. There's a dancefloor down the far end, with barely enough room to swing a fat lass, but I've never seen anyone take much interest in it. In fact I've barely seen anyone at all, to be perfectly honest. The only punters this bar seems to attract are people who've chanced upon the place, gone 'Ooh! Pub!', and then stopped for a swift pint simply because they were too embarrassed to turn round and walk straight back out. So, with its average beer, average cocktails, and average atmosphere, I'd stick this place down for an average lifespan. It'll be history by Christmas, you mark my words. Just don't ask which Christmas.

For: Probably a good place to spend an evening if you've got something to hide. Like your ugly fucking face, for example.
Against: Descending that staircase from street level makes you feel you're letting yourself in for something far, far better than this.

Hey, wait a minute. Maybe I'm having a pharmaceutical flashback, or something, but I've just remembered the last time I was in Madisons, in what must have been, like, 1989. All I can recall is a sense of really strong, pure, white light, and a feeling of real love and joy towards the people I was out with. Bearing in mind this is fucking Madisons we're talking about, and the crowd I was with were the cunt's cunts, I have this vague feeling that someone might have, you know, slipped me an E. Would anyone care to enlighten me?

Northumberland Arms

Prudhoe Chare, NE1 7AT
'Drunken, puking, disco dancing fools'

The Northumberland Arms has survived longer than any pub blighted by a shopping centre location deserves, mainly thanks to the delights of the bargain cruise break. Supping your pint in here on any given afternoon, you'd soon notice that this bar is part of some bizarre three-way European cultural exchange programme: Amsterdam gets our drunken, puking, disco dancing fools, and we get moustached shoppers hot off the Scandinavian ferries, all with matching carrier bags and a sense of deflation. And where do the Dutch go? I dunno, man. Do I sound to you like I've researched this crap? So aye, there's Helga and Sven, launching a couple of cheap Carlings after their citywide tour of the Baltic, the Sage, the bridges and Northumberland Street, proudly clutching their Marks & Spencer bags full of cut-price undergarments and easy-care suits before heading for the bus back to North Shields. Christ only knows why they end up in here, apart from the obvious proximity to M&S. Because this place, as any local will tell you, is a dump. Subterranean, down a flight of gloomy stairs, the Northumberland Arms is a relic from the days before it was realised that daylight is not a luxury extra in a non-haircut bar, and it's as grim as it's possible to be without crossing the line into menacing. As compensation for the basement setting, the lights in here are always too bright for my sensitive eyes, but I'm of the opinion that the billion watt bulbs and the strategically placed mirrors are there to stop any nefarious activities or sleights of hand. That's how suspicious I am. I can't even point to the food as a recommending factor, since it comes across like prison standard catering to me, ladled out with as much attention to presentation as you'd use to bin one of your dog's turds. I say the grub looks poor but you don't honestly expect me to have tasted it, do you? The sole logical conclusion I can come up with for this place's continued even-breaking is that, since this is the only 'public' bogs for miles around - despite the increasingly furious signs to the contrary on the toilet doors - people are guilt-tripped into buying a beer when they nip in for a slash, shortly before vowing never to return. That was certainly the case with me.

For: No kids allowed.
Against: Seeing people queuing up in an orderly fashion for their pints makes me think there's something shifty going on. And when I find out what it is, you'll be the first to know.

Stood watching the match on the Northy Arms' new plasma screen telly, I couldn't help but marvel at the advances in technology. HD, HHD, SuperHHD, the whole kit and caboodle. And maybe, in a few years' time, with the advent of AAAAA TV - that's Almost As Accurate As Analogue - we'll be able to see a striker bearing down on goal without his blur of a shirt trailing three seconds behind him. I'm being a little sarcastic, just in case you needed me to point it out. The great analogue switch-off? Why? To make way for something no better but expensive enough to line the pockets of industry, and foreign industry at that? Fucking disgraceful. Life's shit enough just following the route of birth, buy things, death, without being told that perfectly good stuff you've bought is now obsolete and has to be hoyed out on some greasy politician's say-so.

The Old George
Old George Yard, Cloth Market, NE1 1EE
'Like turds from a sewage outlet'

One of Newcastle's oldest drinking places, historically sited down a urine- drenched alley, the Old George is reputedly - and inevitably - haunted. Not by any restless spirit, you understand, but by buck-toothed, bearded, boring bastards on ghost hunting nights, pretending to search for spooks and spectres while trying to get their calloused hands under the cagoule of the nearest specky spinster. This is a dismal bar, I can tell you that for nothing. It's hardly surprising they're trying to pull in the sensible rainwear crowd, since if you're young and even half-alive, it's doubtful whether you'd make it fully through the doors without turning tail and legging it. Here's the historical connection, as accurately as we can remember it. Way back in 1646, King Charles I was held captive in Newcastle by the Scots over some petty gripe or other. Being an affable race, they let him nip out for a round of golf in Shieldfield before the regally inbred goon scuppered it, whacking his monogrammed balls through the windows of the tower blocks of his subjects. And loyal as those subjects may have been, they certainly weren't loyal enough to hoy the fuckers back. To cheer the berk up, it seems they then allowed him to pop in the Old George for a swift pint and a Pukka pie from the hotplate behind the bar. And this landmark in history, this wondrous occasion, led to a room in the pub being named in his honour, with the chair in which he sat given pride of place and - clearly to retain some traces of regal DNA - the bogs where he shook his royal drops off remaining seemingly uncleaned ever since. That's how it happened. You see? We have been known to do our research, even if that amounts to no more than taking sneaky, blurred snaps of the pub's menu spiel so we can make asinine comments about it later. And if all that isn't enough to hammer home the historical notion, we can tell you that virtually every surface in here is stripped and stained wood, and the bits they couldn't be arsed to give what-for with the chemicals and sandpaper, they've just daubed in wood-effect paint. For fuck's sake, even the bloody radiators are 'antique pine'. They've got low ceilings with beams, creaky old furniture, an open fire and a whole host of stiffly grand settees upstairs, only one of which has anything even approaching a decent view of the big screen telly. It's not all clock-watchingly dull, though. For all that it gets the respectable, clean-living, courteous dickdrips from the Duke round the corner and the ghost hunters we invented earlier, the Bigg Market feeds straight into the other end of the alley, so at least you get the chance to ridicule and feel superior to the yobs bobbing around the doorway like turds from a sewage outlet. Aye, let's give the Old George their due: at least they're not pretending to be old and traditional, which in our book is a far greater crime than being merely dull. Be thankful it's not a King Charles I theme bar, with cardboard walls and plastic ornaments, but instead is a genuine split-level mess of knocking through and adding on; nobody but a lunatic would build a bar like this nowadays. Which reminds me: I'd better warn you now that if nature comes a-calling, you'd be strongly advised to head for the toilets before you're bursting, or you'll piss your pants in the maze to get there. That's experience talking, an' all.

For: It's alright, man. Nowt to start throwing a tantrum over.
Against: I dare say it was a hell of a lot better when His Highness turned up for a half of Carling and a shot on the bandit.

When I was made redundant from my last job – on a Christmas Eve, charmingly enough – the room to the left of the main entrance looked just like Yuletide would have done in 1646 i.e. barren as fuck, with nary a sprig of holly or a shitwit in a Santa hat. Matched my mood perfectly, I'll tell you that much. I shall remember them in my will.

Popolo
82-84 Pilgrim Street, NE1 6SG
'Half a million to live above a roundabout'

Popolo is a bar that divides opinion. And, after changing my drinking habits and my laborious route round the town, I've discovered why. There seems to be a cut off point where the relaxed, airy cafe-bar that produces nothing more than those hitherto elusive chilled vibes becomes a thumping hellhole provoking blistering fury in normally placid individuals. So, to try and keep this balanced, I'm going to first review Popolo through the haze of a few late afternoon scoops, and then rant about what I've since found the night times to be like. Long ago this place was Don Vito's, a cheap, no-frills Italian restaurant. When the owner passed it on to his kids, they almost immediately closed it and turned it into a bar-lounge-kitchen, probably in anticipation of the wankers who'd be shelling out half a million to live above a roundabout when the Swan House office block was converted into flats. And while I wasn't exactly delighted, I didn't see that change as being the biggest crime in history, since a) I'm clearly turning into a wanker myself, and b) Popolo looked just like the sort of place where I like to prop up the bar at last orders, albeit in somewhere like Paris or Berlin or wherever greasyJet are flying to this year. With crimson and pastel shades and clanking metal barstools, Popolo boasts the city's least irritating design-conscious interior, and has the added bonus of the front windows being tinted red to cut out the sight of the dereliction over the road. It's never heaving and never dead, and at least you get pre-mium beer for the premium prices, unlike in some other bars with foreign names I could mention. And it's tremendous, up to, say, half seven, the cut-off point I mentioned earlier. But when it starts filling up, everything goes to shit. It's easy to see how it happens. It doesn't matter how much effort you've put into your stupid outfit, or how much you blew at the hairdresser, if you're promised luxury and don't immediately get the service you think you're paying for, you're going to feel pissed off. Take, for ex-ample, the drinks menu – there's no denying that the cocktails in here are good, but I won't order them simply through deep shame at holding up the queue. The thing is, here I am definitely in the minority, since every other smug twat with the Aviator shades or elaborate ponytail seems to see it as a badge of honour that their drink is taking a fucking lifetime to mix. They had to wait, so other people can wait for them. Don't know about you, but I'd find it difficult to remain unflustered when there are a dozen people behind me wanting to knife me between the shoulder blades. Of course, when bars are getting busy and people are getting angry, they're going to need security, and it's no secret that Popolo's doorstaff make Tiger Tiger's look liberal, kicking off at the slightest indiscretion. I can remember seeing one old bloke being forcibly ejected, picked up by the arms and knees, carried out and thrown in the lane, obviously for not being pretty enough. And the poor old bastard was – to my eyes – the least offensive punter there. He was only having a bit of a nap, man. It was the rest of the cunts they should have turfed out. Look at them, preening and pouting and sitting with their tabs in YOUR face to keep the smoke out of theirs. Those arseholes only came here because some style mag from That London told them to, like this is the only establishment worth bothering with in this shitty town of ours. And, inevitably, they have to seen to be seen, even if it's only by jackasses as vacuous and stupid as they are.

For: Strictly no stag or hen nights.
Against: Simple undeniable fact – drink in Popolo and you will stink of grease for the rest of the night.

Popolo is Italian for 'people'. I've been thinking about the use of all things foreign as a marketing gimmick, and the idea that un-familiar = exotic. I've often wondered if, deep in the foothills of Patagonia, there's a band of Geordie buskers playing execrable versions of The Blaydon Races and Home Newcastle ('Ye can keep ya London wine') as a payback for those fuckers with the pan-pipes on Grey's monument.

Rose & Crown

5-7 Newgate Street, NE1 5RE
'Badger's Arse of the Year Awards'

We at the Dog like a proper, down-to-earth boozer with a bit of history, and would cheerfully bypass any haircut bar you care to name for a portion of spit and sawdust. Oh, we like our old timers grumbling in the corner, our battered furniture and our authentic local grit, we do. Call us boring, call us inverted snobs, fit us with a frock and call us Fiona if you want, but that's just what we like to see in a town blighted by anonymous chain pubs and beige luxebars. But this place, it has to be said, is a fucking dump. With its prehistoric flock wallpaper, broken windows, tatty seating and general air of unpleasantness, the Rose & Crown would beat all comers in the Badger's Arse of the Year Awards and, to make it worse, it looks like it's doing it on purpose. This is where our Bill-tainted imaginations find city-drinking villains planning their blags; where they spend their time before they take one kicking too many off Plod and end up dribbling and confused and slumped over the racing pages in the Clock round the corner. Spill their pint? I'd apologise and offer them a tenner and a free punch any-where except my knackers if I so much as stepped on their shadow. And if you see a whole pub full of blokes with Phil Mitchell's head but wearing Noel Edmonds' shirt, are you going to take the piss out of them? Are you prepared to tell them their bar's a tip and that you'd prefer it if they didn't use the c-word in front of your lass? Like shite, are you. You're going to sup up quick, back the hell out and pretend you were never there. And if you have to change your name, your address and book yourself in for a session under the surgeon's knife, then that's just the price you'll have to pay.

For: The bay window at the front and its line-up of grizzlers guarantee that you'll never wander in by accident.
Against: It bathes the atrocious Boom! The '90s Bar over the road in a positive, glowing light.

Don't be giving us any crap about 'salt of the earth', either. You show me salt of the earth and I'll show you a string of convic-tions as long as my face. And posing with a picture of your bairns is no fucking let off. As if people are really going to see you in the Chronicle, complete with a babe in arms, and think, 'Aaah! He might have kneecapped three and slashed the throats of an-other two, but he loves his kiddies so he can't be all bad.'

Secco
86 Pilgrim Street, NE1 6SG
'Don't make me draw you a picture'

If you've ever heard anything at all about Secco and its custom-ers, and have persevered thus far with this book, you'll probably be expecting me to rip the arse out of it. But I'm not going to, and this is why: it's because I'm the only one in the place, at least in the upper bit by the tastefully shaded windows. The lads are at the bar – obscured by that laughable CD mixing deck – and the lasses are in the bogs discussing, no doubt, whether my lithium is really helping. I'm sitting here in my swivel chair, seeing the place as the designer's blueprint intended, and I'm free to put in my own fantasy clientele instead of the trend-felching morons I suspect will form this bar's target market. Even the staff are nigh on invisible, their uniforms blending into the dark walls like that kid in that shirt in that Garden State film (don't make me draw you a picture). Things I can see: a colour scheme that is possibly the most revolutionary in Newcastle's drinking scene for five long years. Meaning? It's blue. And it isn't purple. I can also see the door to the Blue Room, which differs from the blue room I'm in now in ways I'm clearly not hip enough to comprehend. At either side of the step down to the main bar there's a curtain, like the divider on a plane. In first class – down there – you get to look towards the rooftop terrace with its views of the glowing embers of the western sky; in economy – up here – I'm stuck with the ruin of Pilgrim Street. The elaborately framed mirrors reflect tasteful (and blue) lighting, while the ebony furniture makes me blissfully less aware of the sodding black napkin attached to my pint. And all around are huge monochrome prints and orange backlit posters, their tableaux of bar life captioned by scribes who've managed one solitary shag and then written endless reams of embarrassing, stilted prose about the experience. But this, for all its astonishing pretensions, is not a bad bar. So why is it empty? I think it's because when Secco first opened at the back end of 2005 it billed itself, quite outrageously, as being absolutely exclusive, for members and guests only. And now they've decided to throw the doors open to any old scumbag like me, I get the feeling they're reaping what they've sown; some bored girl has handed me the same advert leaflet on Northumberland Street fourteen times this month already. It's like they expected people to beg to be allowed in, and when the punters just went, 'We can't come in? OK, fine, we'll go somewhere else,' they've ended up being the ones doing the begging. Mind you, having said that, it is idiot o'clock in the afternoon, so maybe that's why there's not a soul around. Trust me to realise that right at the end.

For: No bar with a rooftop beer terrace can ever be shite, even if it overlooks the back of Grey Street, the unwiped bottom to the pretty made-up face of Grainger Town.

Against: How frigging narrow are those booths up the top end? Sit up straight? You've practically got to STAND up straight to get into them. And there's no possibility of the lasses being ladylike when they're in there; unless they're sitting sidesaddle it's practically cross-ply girl-on-girl. Perhaps I should have made this the 'For'.

Who makes that bloody music, the endless Bossa Nova they play in places like this? Apart from the money, what's the motivation to play a tune with as much care and attention as I'd put into, I dunno, filing, or something? Are they really as bored with it as they sound? Is the grass always greener? Maybe that's it. Maybe they're thinking, 'I'm sick of sitting at this piano. I just want to stare out of the window and answer phones all day.' If they fucking want to swap they know where to find me.

Trillians

Princess Square, NE1 6AQ
'Relentless, joyless, friendless'

It's not something I like to boast about, but I went to Trillians on its opening night, way, way back in 1986, when poodle metal was as popular with the kids on the street as smart-arse indie pop is now. A mirthsome mess of spandex and lace, and hair backtatted until it squealed, the bar resembled nothing so much as a no-budget Whitesnake video, one in which I was an all-too-willing extra. Man, I was a foxy fucker in them days. Nipping in for a re-review in 2006, pot-bellied and rapidly greying, it saddens me to report that the comedy flamboyance of Trillians has been toned down over the years, echoing in its own way the relentless, joyless, friendless grind of modern metal. Gone are most of the laughable devil masks, the knackered instruments, and cod-satanic paraphernalia, and in their place is a nasty collage of Kerrang!-approved rock heroes. And the beautiful people, those punters for whom every trip to get the round in was a sashay along Sunset Boulevard, are long departed; it's all grunting porkers with tribal tattoos and mini-Mohawks these days, each of them no doubt in a grindcore act that's as serious as testicular cancer. There's a gig-guide calendar above the bar, listing the attractions for the weeks ahead; while I'm fully aware that they'll probably have split and gone back to their meek call centre monkey jobs by the time you read this, the idea of a band called – and you need to adopt that rumbling movie-trailer voice to even utter their name – Nails of Christ playing on a, quote, 'Party Night' is something that'll make me chuckle 'til I'm dead in my grave. I shouldn't take the piss, really; I'm sure their hearts are in the right place. Maybe I should just concentrate less on the sarcasm and more on Trillians' reputation for showcasing up-and-coming bands, as well as the next-stop-CIU-clubland balding former legends. It's not a bad venue, with a good view of the stage from most vantage points – more than can be said for a lot of the hipster places – and if you're the sort of punter who can keep a straight face through the nightly dose of paddywack rock, then you'll be in your element here. Me, I could quite happily live the rest of my life without seeing another pair of knee-length black shorts or fuck-hard goatee. But overall, Trillians isn't all bad – in fact it's friendly enough, and the beer's alright – but, I'm sorry, I have to say I preferred it when it knew it was ridiculous.

For: The hand dryer in the bogs is absolutely roaring. Attach some wheels to it and you'd shatter the land speed record, no problem.
Against: Jeremy, take that eyeliner off and go and tidy your room.

Facial piercing: can there be a clearer signifier of self-esteem problems than an iron bar stuck through the forehead? It's tantamount to saying, 'Yes, I am a pig ugly fucker and I don't care who knows it. Dieting is for pussies. I am an individual and I am the truth. Now if you'll excuse me, I'm off for a cry and a wank.'

Vineyard

1 Grey Street, NE1 6EE
'Some daft bastard gets kneecapped'

We'll be honest here – we've always purposefully ignored the Vineyard, suspecting it to be just a poncy wine bar (maybe the words 'Wine Bar' above the door were a bit of a hint, though), but sheer boredom with the rest of the town's boozers prompted us to go and investigate properly. The good news is that, yes, it does serve beer. And the other good news – putting aside the obvious ruin of your wallet at seven quid a pair – is that it only serves Duvel. You've got to admire their bloody mindedness; not only serving just one beer, but having that one beer as the most deceptively lethal known to man. For the uninitiated, here's a brief guide to the Belgian elixir in the comedy glass: first one = 'Mmm, this is really tasty'. Fourth one = 'Oh, fuck, help me. I can't see properly'. As far as decor goes, the Vineyard is small and rustic looking, with all manner of clutter flicking the Vs in the general direction of the sleek minimalist bars in the surrounding area. There's plenty of designer dust and grime, knackered old marionettes (can't spell pupetts, me) strung up on hooks together with glittery stars hanging from the ceiling, and what looks like a grubby old basque draped over the wine barrels by the window. Top marks also for having the Christmas tree up all year round, too. From my vantage point I can see a full wine rack of empty bottles under the smashed-tile tables. I'd like to think that some daft bastard gets kneecapped by the bottle ends at least once a night. Even the bogs show a bit of imagination. Wandering down the rope-lit stairs and through the King and Queen playing card bog doors you'll find crazy-paved walls and lion's head fountains instead of taps. I must admit I wasn't really sure where the trough was, mind, so I just pissed in the nearest empty corner. Apologies to the poor sod who had to clean my mess up if that grating bit wasn't actually where I should have emptied my bladder. And I suppose that only leaves the customers to discuss. I have no idea what the typical Vineyard punter is like, mainly because we were the only ones in, but I can't imagine it being chock full of half-witted Geordie Boys at those prices. So, aye, if you've got money to burn and fancy acting all snooty, we'd recommend it. I'm far too much of a miser to make it a regular haunt myself, like, but if you're buying...

For: In the age of the chain superpub and the associated misery that usually follows, being a tiny bar with a bit of character is a definite plus point in its favour.

Against: Constantly being told, 'You went to the Vineyard? You fucking wanker' takes its toll after a while.

Our lass, who's forever got her beak in those fancy, four-eyed reading books, says the whole bar is a bit like Miss Haversham's decaying wedding feast in Dickens' Great Expectations, only transferred to a Christmas bash in Newcastle. Our lass is a blithering idiot.

6

Hang The DJ

George Orwell once famously wrote that, 'If you want a vision of the future, imagine a boot stamping on a human face – forever.' Had he, however, been forced to suffer what passes for entertainment – and unsolicited entertainment at that – in your average city centre bar, then we're sure his pronouncements would have ended something like this:

'... imagine all human communication drowned out by some po-faced fuckwit behind a turntable.'

Now, before some cock whines at us for our blanket contempt for dance music and for being fifteen years behind the times with our griping, we'd like to set a few things straight from the outset.

First of all, we don't subscribe to the tedious notion that dance music is all theft and that anything that's not white boy whining over guitar, bass and drums is somehow invalid. Fuck knows we've endured far too many terrible bands in our time to support that laughable notion. Plus, any so-called muso who thinks their noodling is superior just because they've spent half a lifetime learning their craft is an arsehole. We all know that for a fact.

Secondly, we're not so bloody miserable that we want to rid the world of DJs full stop; we fully comprehend that people are so stressed by even the thought of getting on the bus in the morning – never mind doing a day's graft in some India-bound call centre – that they have an obvious human need to unwind. We understand that there is a place for clubbing. And while we'll never quite grasp how folk can escape from the nightmarish cacophony of endlessly ringing phones by listening to what sounds like a million of those same phones set to a thumping four-to-the-floor with some ickle gurl panting on about nowt, that's probably just down to our age, our hearing loss and our general resentment at our vanished youth. We'd never be so churlish as to deny the benefits of chucking yourself about and getting a few endorphins pumping through the system. Of course we wouldn't.

No, for us the culture of the DJ is fine in clubs, catering for people who've actively sought it out and who've paid for the (dubious) privilege. We really don't mind what goes on behind closed doors, as long as it doesn't involve children, livestock or poetry, but please, for the love of Jesus and all his little disciples, will someone please listen to us as we ask:

WHY THE FUCK DO WE HAVE TO SUFFER IT IN THE PUB TOO?

Why? Obviously the promises of untold riches and endless flap have left the market so crowded they're effectively trying to piss a pint into a pen top, plus the downturn in the popularity of clubs has left DJs seeking asylum in any place that'll have them. But why do we always get stuck with the really, really shit ones? Why should we be swamped by the bandwagon jumping scrotes? And why should we subsidise their poor investment in Technics separates?

Is their presence in the bar supposed to be a taster, a little dimebag intended to whet the appetite and make you want to schmoove on down to the nearest superclub queue to boost their flagging profits? Sod that. Being subjected to that incessant bollocks is no more likely to get us to move on to a club than an inbox full of Viagra spam is going to make us reach for the Visa card when we've got the droop. If we want something, we'll pester *them*, not the other way round.

It's really quite simple. Music in the pub should be background noise, pitched just above the air conditioning. Why can these idiots not hear what's happening? How man, fucko. Take off your cans and listen for once. You are not the most important sound in the building. If people are making more noise than your tunes, it's because they want to hear what is being said. It's because talking whilst drinking is what pubs are for. The fact that they are trying hear each other is not a valid reason for you to turn your shite up even further to compensate. The joint is not jumping, you prick; it's just plain fucking angry.

As we said earlier, we have no overbearing hatred of dance music; in the right hands, that is. What we find so abhorrent is the yawning chasm between the bar DJ's claims of 'cutting edge' and the formulaic slop that gets pumped in our ears when we're trying to have a pint and a natter. The sheer ineptitude of the average headphoned twat in the corner astounds us. If music is played at an inescapable volume, then surely it should emphasise the highs and lows, the dynamics and emotions? We're pretty certain that those qualities are something the original artist had in mind, at any rate. So how then, can some fucking arse be allowed to get away with half an evening's worth of musical murder, bludgeoning innocent 'choons' to death with impunity?

We wouldn't mind so much if there weren't so many outright lies printed on the promo materials. Maybe if they put as much effort into ideas for their acts as they do into their litany of mendacious adjectives, we'd feel a bit more appreciative. Uplifting, you're saying? Sexy? Joyous? Funny, 'cause all we can hear is the usual monotonous shite, with every tune at the same tempo to cover up a complete lack of mixing skill.

We really fail to see how these self-serving dicks can still consider themselves to be some kind of radical underground scene. After all, isn't there a maxim that states, if you can spot a movement, it's already dead? So where's the glory for these gravy train-chasing chumps who actively queue up to fuck its decaying corpse? If DJing got anymore mainstream you could sail a bloody yacht down it, man. Wasn't it Frosties who did that 'jun-

ior DJ kit' giveaway a few years back? How can something be re-
bellious and 'street' when it's been co-opted by The Man, tidied
up, repackaged and sold back to you with your fucking breakfast
cereal? When you've had the piss taken out of you to that extent
then no amount of glossy flyers is going to give you back your
credibility.

On top of that, the arrogance of these chumps is really
shocking. 'Featuring DJ sets from...' say the posters. DJ set? A
fucking SET? How pretentious can you get? How much of a 'performance' can there be - and it won't hurt to repeat this for the
billionth time – in playing some other fucker's records in a pub?
It's like a station announcer laying claim to a 'timetable recital'
for crying out loud. And get a load of the witless 'star' pseudonyms of the ones who think they've tried, and the sheer lack of
imagination of the ones who haven't bothered. 'Excuse me, is
there already a DJ Decks? There is? Oh, I suppose I'd better stick
with Dave Smith, then.' Christ, those aliases boil our piss. In the
'70s they'd have been Donnie Spangle; in the '80s, Bolshoi Beneath; Snoozer in the '90s. That's about the stamp of your typical
bar DJ. And why? Because they're all fucking cunts, that's why.

Where's the honesty with these arseholes? Why can't they
spin some stuff they might actually LIKE instead of either studied
cool or ironic cheesiness? For all their claims of musical freedom
and barrier smashing, with their self-imposed boundaries and
rigid format fitting they end up as evil as daytime radio. And
where's the sense of joy? Why do we see them moping in, night
after night, sullenly dragging their discs and equipment behind
them? Cheer up, you knacker. Give us a fucking grin. Nobody
forced you to pay £300 for that deleted 12-inch on eBay.

You know us, we hate to be negative. But we also hate anything that hints at the emperor's new clothes. We hate the hideous grasping of otherwise-decent bars, with their blind allegiance
to this shite. 'Ooh, THAT bar's got a DJ, so we have to have one
or we might lose a few quid.' Fuck off, will you? Ever thought you
might actually get more punters if it wasn't for the nipple behind
the decks? Christ knows, we'd certainly pay a bit extra if we
could avoid feeling so beaten and depressed at the end of the
night. 'Well, you could always drink elsewhere,' goes the tired

argument. Yeah? Why should people who like to talk be forced to do so in shitty bars surrounded by shoplifters and heed-the-baals? Why does the ability to string a sentence together preclude a bit of decent decor? Why does the smell of fresh paint have to be accompanied by the din of utter cretins?

Look, we understand that everyone needs a hobby. We know that, to hit the heights in any sphere you care to name, you've got to practice, but is there just an inkling of a chance you could you do it elsewhere, eh? Look at us. We're on our creaking knees in desperation. We are literally at the end of our ropes. Please, could you do it in your bedrooms, do it in a rehearsal space, do it on the bloody moon if you must but, we're begging you, keep it the fuck out of the pub.

We'll buy you a pint if you do.

Haymarket & Gallowgate

'As well as being home to the whole city's administration at the Civic Centre, the Haymarket is the transport hub for its northern outskirts. Two excellent universities fill the streets with a colourful student population and the Playhouse theatre has undergone extensive refurbishment and modernisation. Adjacent to the Haymarket area, the Gallowgate district houses Newcastle's Chinatown with its breathtaking gate, and of course the city's beloved underachieving football club, Newcastle United.' - Norman Undercroft, Historian.

Crow's Nest

137 Percy Street, NE1 7RY
'A blight on the Haymarket'

I walk past this place four times a day on my way to and from work, and it was only about three weeks after the refit that I even noticed that anything had changed. The Crow's Nest has quietly, and with the minimum of fuss, replaced the appalling Australian theme pub Bar Oz, and done away with the surfboards, the crocodiles and the rest of the woeful tat that has been a blight on the Haymarket for what seems like an eternity. In an attempt to recapture a bit of the building's original history (the sign above the door says 'Crow's Nest Hotel 1902'. That's as much research as I can be bothered to do) they've tried to make it look – and this'll kill ya – like a pub. Nowt flashy, no 'leisure experience', no shit-itching gimmicks, just a new carpet and a wipe down with a dishrag, something that Bar Oz needed for at least the last three years of its existence. The woodwork's all been buffed up and revarnished, the walls have been painted – badly, I'll grant you, as if under protest or a Community Service Order – in traditional pub shades of grubby red and burnt orange, and the emphasis seems to be, not on posing or networking or designing your next ridiculous haircut, but on beer and conversation. It'll never catch on. They've even taken the trouble to sort out the basement area, with a new roll of wallpaper on the staircase and an attempt at basic hygiene, and if the bogs haven't been completely refurbished, they've at least been cleaned. There's still a stench of day-old mashed turnip down there, though, as a reminder of the bad old days. So aye, ale, chat, maybe a bit of no nonsense grub and a gawp at the telly to see which superstar that fool Shepherd is refusing to speculate on this week. That'll do me just fine. Like I say, there's nothing revolutionary, and nothing to make you shout from the rooftops, but there's nothing that demands that you pay through the nose for style mag wankery, and even if it still is and will always be full of fucking students, it's decent enough for a quiet afternoon pint. If we gave marks out of ten, we'd give it five, maybe six on a good day. High praise indeed.

For: One less theme bar is always cause for a celebration.
Against: They've still got a DJ booth, which can only spell trouble.

Crow's Nest? I'm surprised such a thing exists. Crows really are the stupidest birds of all time. Even the fucking dodo had more gumption than those raaaacking little idiots. Look at them, bouncing along the side of the motorway, hunting for a bite to eat. 'Mmm,' they think, 'Roadkill. I wonder how that got

there...' Next thing you hear? The thunderous roar of an eight-
een-wheeler. And the next thing you see? A splatter of innards
and feathers, with a shattered wing flapping forlornly in the
back draft. Extinction's too good for the likes of them.

Fluid

17-25 Gallowgate, NE1 4SG
'Sorry lads, you can't come in'

Let's say there's a lass who's been out shopping for clothes who
comes home with a new top. It's nothing flash but looks alright,
and though it wasn't really what she wanted, she had to buy
something and that style was all the shop was stocking this season. And besides, it was only £12.99. That, to me, is what has
happened in Fluid. There's bits of this bar that seem to have
been taken from every bar that's opened in the city over the past
few years, all cheaply cobbled together in a 'please love me, I
look the same as everyone else' way. Fluid bills itself as a 'Bar &
Kitchen', leading us to expect some sort of Barluga-like wank-
fest, with pints pushing the four quid mark, but turns out to be an
average-price, nothing special, yeah-go-on-then city centre
boozer. It's not that the place is offensive or anything, just so
utterly indescribable without referencing at least a dozen other
bars in the city. Just off the top of our heads, we can point out
the colour scheme from the Long Bar, the exposed air conditioning from Destination, and the brickwork from Clear. We could
also mention the general clumsy attempt at a cosy-stroke-stylish
hybrid atmosphere of the Bacchus, but we're feeling generous
today. There's a collection of sporting stuff nailed onto the walls
suggesting that they're attempting to cash in on the bar's proximity to St James' Park on match days, and it's good to see that
they've got their licence restrictions sorted out and haven't
fallen foul of the, 'Sorry lads, you can't come in this sports bar
wearing a football shirt' fiasco that befell Jonny Ringo's. And
while it's a pain in the arse getting served, Fluid is still a place
near to the ground where you can go and, like, talk about foot-

ball rather than a) having the breath squeezed out of you by the crush in the Strawberry, or b) having your senses pounded by the d-d-don't-stop-the-beat aural assault of other bars in the area that will remain nameless. And while we're on about that, a quick note to the staff at Madisons (shit, named them): we all love a party and a bit of a rowdy vibe, but not at half eleven in the bloody morning. Back at Fluid, two floors with plenty of standing-around space mean that nobody gets too pissed off before the match but it's a pity that the happy hours in here are only on weekdays and not Saturday afternoons. Finally, as we seem to have spent most of this review talking about other bars, we'll just say that if you enjoyed the pre-refit Bourgognes, then this is the place for you. Us? We'll be standing in the car park with a few cans.

For: You can squeeze in another pint before kick off.
Against: As if to underline that they could see straight through the Burglar's Dog's anonymous, mystery shopper facade, they played Mustang fucking Sally when we were walking out, purely to piss us off.

Post-work happy hours break the spirit and crush the imagination. There's a clique in my office who, whenever there's a night out, stamp on the suggestion that there may be life in other parts of the city, and complain and wheedle their way into making everyone sit in the same dismal bar for half the night, just because a pint is 10p cheaper than up the road. And you can see that attitude creeping into the rest of their blinkered worldview. You could say to them, 'Right! We've won the lottery! Where shall we go? Pony trekking in Thailand? Surfing on Bondi Beach? Hang-gliding from the top of the Eiffel Tower?' The response? Wetherspoon's.

The Goose
Eldon Garden, NE1 7RA
'A quality, traditional pub'

We believe that small is beautiful when it comes to pubs. It's a viewpoint that has held us in good stead over the years, and provides a yardstick with which to batter this gargantuan hellhole about the face and neck. Once the merely massive Filament & Firkin – a tacky chain bar that was good for watching sport, if nowt else – they then knocked through and annexed the smaller but no less grim Scruffy Murphy's next door to create this, the insufferable idiot's idea of a proper bar. Throughout all ten million cubic feet The Goose occupies, you'll find weak imitations of a quality, traditional pub, served up in that horrible atmosphere vacuum typical of Goose 'outlets' throughout the nation. You ask anyone, at least anyone with the tiniest bit of sense, and the best thing they could ever say about The Goose is that it's there, handy, by the bus station. Well, that and the fact that it's cheap. Everyone I know is convinced that the beer in places like this is only cheap because it's within touching distance of its sell-by date by the time it hits your glass; people regurgitate this 'fact' endlessly, as if it's everyone else's pint they're talking about. So how can they still fucking drink the stuff? Jesus, man, what the hell is wrong with people today? The berks who drink in The Goose are living, breathing, gibbering proof that you could sell people shit on a shovel and call it all-day breakfast if they thought they were getting a special offer. Everyone who comes in here out of choice - you're partway excused if you're heading to the match and you're only here because it's near the ground - should have their right to vote rescinded. They are clearly not of sound mind. Students, dickheads, misers, psychopaths; they're all here. There's embarrassing Uncle Jimmy, and mad Auntie Joan, who's a lovely lady, at least until she starts twatting people after fifteen trebles and a Smirnoff Ice. And look at them over there: the pudgy, on-the-shelf moos drinking wine to show a bit of class, and then, after downing four cut-price bottles of Blossom Hill, they'll be wondering why, instead of in the arms of bliss, they're lying in the wet patch from some bloke they'll never see again. Oh, fuck it. I could sit and rant about the sort of knackers who are prepared to give this place the time of day until my spine fuses to the chair and my fingers are typed down to bloodied knuckles. But what good would it do? Pubs like this are successful because human beings are, by nature, thick as absolute fuck. I can count on the legs of the former Heather Mills-McCartney how many times I've been in this godawful place. Take it from me; The Goose is a damned disgrace, a cavernous leather-bound shed, and a fool's paradise. And any so-called mate of yours who has the temerity to suggest you go there just to save themselves a couple of bob on their round should be ditched or beaten or thrown in the road. Hit 'em, and hit 'em hard. You'll thank us later.

For: Ample space to cram in the very worst of Newcastle's drinkers and keep them the hell away from us. Or so you'd think...
Against: ...since I've seen people actually lining up to get in. Where are these people coming from? Why has there not been a cull?

What the hell is the matter with bar chains? Why do they persist in wrecking everything they touch? You name any once-outstanding pub that's been bulldozed by corporate blandness and meal-deal homogeneity; name any innocent drinking venue that's been tricked and sullied, and you can bet your dimpled arse that a chain have had their dirty fingers in its crisp, white, schoolgirl panties somewhere down the fucking line.

The Hancock
Hancock Street, NE2 4PU
'Quietly, and with dignity'

The Hancock is a bar I absolutely despise. There. Got that out of the way. Why? I've got my reasons. Number one, I'm still sore that they did away with Bierrex, the relaxed European-style cafe bar with surprisingly few pretensions, and replaced it with this, a fucking Scream Fun Pub. You'd expect after all these years that I'd find some way to come to terms with it, but every sunny afternoon when I'm up near the Haymarket, I think of coming in here for one of the extensive range of comedy beers that Bierrex used to boast, and then remember there's now a choice of, like, one lager. But it isn't even the lack of variety that gets my goat. The real pisser for me is, number two, the students. Why do I hate students? Just look at them, man. Isn't that enough? No? Then picture them bouncing up to you on rag week, legs tied together and greasepaint all over their faces, shaking their fucking charity tins in your face like you haven't already - quietly, and with dignity - given enough. Imagine their braying, bucktoothed faces spouting their gobshite, over-rehearsed opinions on any topic they think they won't be pulled up on. Just listen to that berk over there, for instance. He thinks he's fucking Wittgenstein, trumpeting his received wisdom and borrowed philosophy into that specky bint's lug. Why didn't the sexually over-exuberant tit just marker-pen it on his damn T-shirt? 'Ooh! Can I try my cock out on you, yeah?' Look, I understand that if a bar is near to the university, it's going to be full of academics. Hang on while I stop chuckling at the last word in the previous sentence. It's bound to attract students like dog's eggs attract dragonflies. But why this one? Why shun the bar on campus and then head straight for a pub that's little more than a college refectory, complete with a chip-strewn sticky floor? And it's not even as if the Hancock has the decency to simply wring its hands at the good fortune of just being in the way. This place is actively encouraging the loathsome little shites to part with their - or rather the taxpayers' - hard-earned cash with their patronising, it's-your-first-time-away-from-home-kiddies, come-and-join-in-our-wacky-promotions ethos. You'd think the future rocket scientists of our nation would be wise to it by now, but no. The irritating twats fall for it term after term, and sit there monopolising the beer garden - the one that's MINE by rights - whining on and on and on about having no money whilst scraping the scarf fluff off their £80 shirt with their platinum iPod Mini. And they've got the nerve to stare at me like I'M the cunt? Looks like Professors Fists and Toecaps will be taking the lectures next semester.

For: It's a joy to hear over-confident student wankers gawping at the Civic Centre across the car park and sneeringly pontificating about how they'd never end up there, safe in the knowledge that, in three years' time, with their useless degrees, the council is exactly who they'll be begging for some menial office job.
Against: Hancock's Half Hour? Fuck that. Nine and a half minutes of this place and we had to get the hell out.

When I was a kid the Jesmond area of Newcastle was a desirable place to live. Look at it now; with all its student boxrooms it's now nothing so much as a frigging ghetto. All the affluent locals have left, becoming ever richer by subdividing their subdivisions and hawking them out to gullible saps with far too much student loan money for their own good. I hate to break it to you, Ben or Tim or Jessica or Hannah, but when I worked for the leccy board, your fancy NE2 address was known to us as the fucking meter cupboard.

The Hotspur

103 Percy Street, NE1 7RY
'It doesn't take much to be knowledgeable about Foster's'

Situated in the middle of the Haymarket no-nonsense line of pubs, The Hotspur remains a proper boozer serving a proper pint to proper people who've got no time for any of that Tizer-flavoured fashion shite. What it has got? frequent beer festivals, a healthy smattering of terrible beards, and big bastard bellies that'd stop you in your tracks. And what it hasn't; kids, expensive haircuts, and certainly no bloody DJ. Owned by one of the more respectful and least contemptible chains, T&J Bernard - whose values come from a time when 'chain pub' just meant creaming off the profits from an established boozer, and not destroying everything that was good about them in a desperate attempt to enforce the brand - The Hotspur is renowned for its choice of real ales, and also for being fucking heaving when there's a Toon match on telly. It's also notable for having an alley down the side that has seating, a telly and heaters, and for being down-to-earth enough to call it an alley and not a service pavilion, or some other such cobblers. I've never known the staff be anything but friendly, and while it doesn't take much to be knowledgeable about Foster's, they're always there with a smile and a word of advice for the discerning drinker, as opposed to the scowl and the dismissive shrug you get while the staff in more pretentious places piss about chopping up dandelions for £8 cocktails. I still recall the day when I witnessed a French lad in there who, when asking for 'blonde beer', was offered a sample from the pump to see if it was to his taste. If he'd tried that elsewhere, they'd have broken his fucking jaw. The punters, like the bar, are worn around the edges and comfortable with it, the music's palatable but not in the least bit trendy, and you're almost always guaranteed to get in a strange conversation with some lovable mentalist, whether you want to or not. Class. And if it wasn't for the students, it'd be perfect.

For: Beer, sport, conversation, atmosphere, staff. And the memory of the previous landlord, all three foot six of the lecherous little get.
Against: The bogs are rank, and I still haven't recovered from nearly standing in that discarded pair of heavily shat underpants three years back.

They say your best Christmases are when you're a kid. Bollocks, I say. Just before Christmas 2001 came a winter wonderland that'll stay with me forever. We arrived outside the Hotspur on a Saturday just before Final Score to find the inside absolutely jam-packed and the Leeds v Newcastle match on the big screen. So we're standing out there in the perishing cold, wiping our breath off the windows with our cuffs so we can see the game, when it starts to snow; gently at first, then steadily, then a blizzard. There's snow on our heads, down our collars, in our pockets, and we're tapping on the glass like some Victorian urchins, with expectant faces that say, 'Please guv'nor, let us in by the fire. It's perishing out here and no mistake.' And then, with the last kick of the match, Nobby cracks the winner in for 4-3 from the right. The bar erupts, we're dancing in the road, dodging the snow-blind traffic and, suddenly, finally, there's peace on Earth and goodwill to all men. Oh, man: what a moment. Our lass got me fuck all that year, by the way. And I've hated Christmas ever since.

Luckies

14 St Mary's Place, NE1 7PG
'Pasties with cack'

Newcastle City Council's environmental department have got some strange ideas about the upkeep of the town's streets. While we wholeheartedly encourage the bloke in the little muck-spreading van who drives up and down Northumberland Street every day, trailing a wash of filth behind him and spraying the kids' pasties with cack, we find it a little bit depressing that the pavements have gone to rack and ruin. Every time it rains you have to pretend you're Harrison Ford in *Indiana Jones and the Last Crusade* just to get from A to B without getting your trousers drenched by the puddles under the rickety flagstones: 'In Latin, Jehovah starts with an 'I''. Not Luckies' fault, I grant you, but it's enough to set me up for another round of tenuous linkage. Everyone's first choice bar for a guaranteed summer beers disappointment, this pub in the shadow of the Civic Centre has finally been refurbished after a geological age of neglect and rot. And some - The Chronicle probably, since they're always sticking the boot in - might say that the refit has been done to a standard that would make the council proud. Undoubted vast expense has been frittered away with very little to show for it, as if they were so busy box-ticking and taking care not to offend anyone that the idea of producing anything of any merit has gone straight out of the window. So where there once was a determinedly scruffy little boozer with an American diner theme, the corridors of power and their unnecessary consultants have decided that this is what the public want; an eyesore of gift wrap wallpaper, beige ceilings and tasteful objets d'art, together with 'that' fucking shade of purple paint on any surface without an armed guard. Look over there; they've even got a terrible picture of the Civic Centre to reflect its lofty position looming over Luckies' corner location in a way that I would describe as Kafkaesque, if I'd ever been arsed to read any of his impenetrable, paranoid gobbledegook. The punters, as they've always been up this end of town, are students you can't help but detest, and office drones from the ten floors of '60s ugliness with the crown and seahorses on over the road. That's the indoor customers, at least. Outside you're stuck with anyone and everyone with a dead-eyed scowl and a rottweiler on a rope, whose sworn duty is just to ruin your alfresco pints. And that brings me finally to the bar's real pisser, the insulting, arcane policy of glass glasses inside but plastic pint pots out on the terrace, as if that's somehow safer and more civilised. I suspect the Council's licensing department to be behind that, too. I don't know about you, but being trusted so little that I have to drink out of a plastic glass would make me more violent, if anything. Aye, stupid beakers and breathing in bus fumes: guaranteed to turn you into a murderer.

For: Grabbing a seat on the terrace on a sunny day, leering at the student babes sashaying past on their way from their hour a week of hard study, safe in the knowledge that you'll never get or want the opportunity to talk to the tedious titwitches.
Against: Even if you camp out from seven in the morning, you will never get to grab that seat.

Second most depressing part of the student year: freshers' week, when fancy-dressed gimps hand out endless reams of bar adverts and drinks promotion leaflets, practically begging people to part with their cash in some shoddy fun pub. First most depressing? The way they look straight through me, as if I simply do not exist. Maybe my defeated, underpaid, style-free, hopeless, suicidal wage slave disguise is a little TOO good these days.

Mr Lynch
Archbold Terrace, Jesmond, NE2 1DB
'This year's must-have'

I hadn't been to the Archer in over a hundred years so when I heard that the place had suffered a refit I must admit I didn't have same sense of betrayal and dislocation as some of my mates. The scruffy-but-with-good-music dump has been replaced by a 'neighbourhood lounge bar', with more emphasis on DJ culture and all that depressing crap, and although they're plugging live music I have no fucking idea what 'too cool for school' entails. It sounds absolutely terrible. I really can't imagine the new layout being that popular with the bands who used to play here, what with the stage design being somewhere between bad cabaret and Punch & Judy, and the tacky audience area seating giving it that woeful chicken in a basket atmosphere. When are designers going to understand that it's not necessary to be 'ironic' every hour of every day? As for the rest of the bar, they've tried hard with the deliberately godawful '70s furniture, lamps, wall hangings and sit-in hairdryer, but I felt I was drinking in an installation at the Baltic rather than a relaxing bar. I dunno, maybe it's because I'm so ancient that I actually remember all that furniture from when I was a kid (golden rule of ironic kitsch: never get involved with anything you recall from the first time round), but it didn't make me smile knowingly; it just made me sad. Why? Perhaps in my mortgaged misery I don't like being reminded that this year's must-have is tomorrow's cheese. I saw no evidence of the advertised soul food when we were in, but you can bet your arse that they just mean the usual pub grub with a picture of some knacker with an afro on the menu instead of any rice & peas concoctions. And if you've seen any of their promotional stuff and are wondering what 'genuine people' they attract, it's this lot: uprooted ex-Archer indie kids, bored office workers from upstairs and tedious Jesmond fashionistas (that's Italian for wankers, by the way). Oh, and yes, yes, we understand the reasoning behind the pub's moniker, taken from the mysterious artist J H Lynch, copies of whose work adorn the walls, but it has to be said that Mr Lynch is a bloody dreadful name for a bar.

For: I hope to God that the presence of sockless haircut victims outside dribbling into their phones means you can't get a signal inside under all those tons of brutalist concrete.
Against: Although the happy hour beer was alright and reasonably priced, some fucker's got to pay for this hubris and you can safely say it'll be you.

No flashing machines or rigged shooting games for Mr Lynch's happy hours. Here you get a choice of Flip A Coin, Which Hand Is The Bottle Top In?, or Paper Scissors Stone. I, naturally, opted for the latter. The barmaid gave me stone; I gave her the finger and got charged double. Well, it seemed like a good idea at the time.

Madisons
Leazes Lane, NE1 4PF
'Novel'

Ah here, this is getting beyond the joke. You're telling me they've rebranded this bloody place again? I really don't understand why they keep pissing about with it and, to be quite honest, I fail to see why I should have to re-re-review the place when next to nothing has changed. It's not like I've ever liked coming here in the first place; if it wasn't stuck right between St James' and my bus stop there's no way on earth I'd even cross the threshold. But no, here I am again, scooped up and dragged in like a dolphin in a trawl net. What's the point in even trying to capture it in words, since it'll probably have changed yet again by the time you read this? If you care that much, you can always click on our website for the original review when we hated it as Sanctuary Bar or check out the shite we wrote when it was Bar 2XS before that. You may find a few positives in there, something we're not even going to try when we're forced to come up with a review for the nth time of asking. It's still a shed and the beer's still rubbish to my jaded tastebuds. Every time I go it's still full of glum faces after the match, and it still has the same under-dressed and over-cocky kids lurking in the corners. Aye, fair enough I might be getting older, to the point where everyone under twenty-five is a child to me, but it still looks like this place has abandoned the idea of a lower age limit; I'd dearly love to see what the fucking rozzers make of it. If reports on the decor are that frigging important to you, I can tell you about the pictures of jazz legends that adorn the walls: quite ironic, really, since every time I've been in I've been subjected to some dick with a turntable telling me how he's 'got so much love to give' over and over and over again. This incarnation is no better or worse than the last one, and I can't imagine the refits they'll attempt at Christmas, Easter and August Bank Holiday will make the slightest difference. Fuck it: the review ends here. I've got enough on my plate with thinking of novel ways to pan the brand new bars, without the heartache of rehashing this place every six weeks.

For: Subdued UV lighting in the bogs, so you can't see what you're wading about in. Sadly it also means you can't even spike a vein to relieve at least some of the misery.

Against: I see enough expensive tinkering for tinkering's sake in my working life. I really do not need to see it in the pub, too.

The original Madisons in Newcastle was a dire 'niteclub' over by New Bridge Street, the sort of moustache, tie and white socks establishment that gave Newcastle its terrible reputation. Fuck knows what's there now. I think it was a gym the last time I was brave enough to head that way, but I tend to avoid that area now it's become a training ground for serial killers and general dickheads who think it's only fair to slash the faces of total strangers and throw them on the central motorway just because they've wasted all their taxi money trying to pull some slobbering hound.

Newcastle Arms

57 St Andrews Street, NE1 5SF
'Faceless McLoungebar'

There's a bar that represents the absolute pinnacle of a pub designer's dreams, a bar they're sure that the whole wide world
can't live without for another second. It combines the very latest
in Contemporary Retro furniture with an air of sophistication,
adding just a soupcon of chilled beats for that essential leisure
experience. Thankfully, the Newcastle Arms isn't it. Traditional
and historic, and looking like a proper boozer to boot, the Newcastle Arms is the complete opposite of the vapid, overpriced
cackholes that are beginning to have a worrying stranglehold on
the rest of the city. And considering it's on what is essentially the
same block as the horrifying Gate complex, the fact that they've
resisted the temptation to go for the big bucks and turn it into
something that looks like a bloody furniture store deserves some
kind of award. With a name that actually contains the town it's
in, and pictures of Newcastle all over the walls, it makes a
change to have a pub that underlines its own heritage and is not
trying to hoodwink you into believing you're in some ambitiously
faraway destination, or a faceless McLoungebar that could be
anywhere and nowhere. The beer's award-winningly good, the
staff treat you like a human being and not some fleeceable com-
modity, and even if it is a first pint pub for West End radgies hot
off the bus at the Gallowgate, plus a claustrophobic push-and-
shove fest on a match day, there's still more to recommend here
than in a hundred haircut bars. What more could you want? A DJ?
Hadaway and shite.

For: If I was ever put under house arrest, I'd like my house to be
the sandwich shop between here and no-frills eatery Chinatown
Express, with a sneaky side door into each. I'd back any tin pot
military junta you care to name if there was so much as a whiff of
that happening.

Against: Bloody global warming means I'll probably never get the chance to sit by the fire, warming my glass of port like a proper sad old bastard.

The Newcastle coat of arms is the one with the daft seahorses either side of a shield, with a lion atop a castle above that, and it's the one Newcastle United simplified for their club crest. How am I so sure about this? Because I had it on my living room wall when I was a kid. And why was it on the wall? Because my family are hereditary Freemen of the City. Oh yes; generation after generation of villains, lunatics, nursery school drop-outs and Chronicle salesmen, all charged with a musket in the defence of the City. And when I scrape together enough pennies for a silver coin for the investiture, I'll be on the list with them. The cows on the Town Moor won't know what's hit 'em.

Old Orleans
Haymarket, NE1 7PF
'Above sea-level'

Quietly choking in the fumes of the Haymarket bus station, Old Orleans has been providing an unnecessary Deep South theme bar for people with no imagination for a good while now. With mound upon mound of desperately poor tat, whether you're upstairs in the restaurant or downstairs in the bar, you're virtually guaranteed an astonishingly bad time. You could say that Old Orleans has become the baton-carrier for knackered trombones, Moon Over Bourbon Street signs and all-that-jazz since the Jerry-built 'New' version in the States blew over last time there was a bit of a light breeze. I suppose you could claim that the dreck in this bar can be considered 'new authentic' now that the genuine article is caked in mud and buried under an overturned station wagon. You could also point out that, if nothing else, someone at least had the wisdom to build this place above sea-level. But, speaking personally and from my little Cajun heart, I think I'd rather have taken my chances with the looters and disease in

Baton Rouge than have suffered the spectacle in here. Look, there's no point in sugaring the pill by telling you about when it's quiet; you need to get in at the critical moment and see it at its most potent, just to underline why you should never, ever be so stupid as to come in again. Best time? I'd say a Thursday evening, just after the corporations shake the winnits from their open-plan orifices. See them waddle past the windows and through the doors, thirteen stone piglets with flabby arms aloft, in true dancing ant formation. 'Hee hee heeeee! Looka mee! Eeh Shelly, I'm ganna get pissed!' Watch in disgust as they order the most difficult-to-mix cocktails, with their hilarious, innuendo-ridden names. 'Can I have a Finger Up The Shitter With A Twist?' No, but you can have a smack in the fucking fat mouth if you want. Look at him, the contemptible prick behind the bar - yes, YOU, dickhead - shovelling in the ice with the ineptitude that shows why he failed the exam to shovel cowshit. Keep looking at him, since it'll be an eternity before he's ready to pour your pint. His sticky dreams of glamour are a distant memory and, because he simply can't be trusted in a decent bar, he's going to over-compensate by lobbing the bottles around in here, acting like Tom Cruise and that miscellaneous bloke out of Cocktail, even though it's been nigh on twenty years since anyone was even remotely impressed by such twattery. Did I say anyone? I meant except for the - and I hate to use the word - sluts at the bar, that is. With a chuck-chuck-chuck, a slop-slop-slop, a ho-ho-ladies and a tee-hee-hee; on and on it goes. The patter's getting filthier, while you're just getting thirstier. And angrier. You could piss off for a spacer to the Hotspur, or the Percy, or to fucking Azerbaijan if you wanted, and they'd still be there giggling when you got back. See when I finally get to Heaven? I'm having words with the Lord and I'm cleaning out His cloth ears. And the next time He's dishing out the hurricanes and the 'Acts of', He'll send them where I fucking well tell Him to, make no mistake.

For: The huge windows at the front open out on a sunny day, so if you grab the right seat you can howl with laughter as the bus station roof falls in. Again.

Against: They had better fucking NOT have 'live saxophone nights'.

I remember when they were building the extension to Marks & Spencer next door. Midway through the lunchtime nacho session, a whopping great rat came in from the site, did a soft shoe shuffle across the tiles and then fucked off back out again, to the shrieking, chair-mounting horror of the diners and shoppers. It made the front page, as I recall. Disgrace! Vermin! What About The Kiddies?! Me, I'd have had the cunt on Mastermind for having the sense to scarper before the happy hour.

Pacific Bar Cafe

12-22 Northumberland Road, NE1 8JF
'The socially inept and the recently divorced'

Pacific is a theme bar in denial. It likes to think of itself as a luxurious leisure venue catering to a discerning, upmarket clientele, but it's really just the worst kind of chrome and sparkle and desperation you could ever imagine. And we imagine a lot. This is an '80s bar that doesn't even realise it's an '80s bar. It's a relic rather than an ironic refit, and to step inside it's as if time has stood stubbornly still, with the same defeated customers from the same offices having the same conversations as they've done every night since 1985, with only bulging bellies and sagging scrota measuring out the years. How, though? The bloody bar's only been there for, like, half a dozen years: maybe they just built it around the punters. This is the sort of place the socially inept and the recently divorced from Sgt Pepper's go to when they really want to push the boat out. This is the bar where they still play Whitney Houston, for crying out loud. You get the same squealing and hollering as you've always done, the same boob tubes and spray on glitter, and the same insulting notion that horrific expense = good time. There's a coloured lamp to suit every bad mood, a pointless glittery artefact in every nook and cranny, and a whole host of soundless TVs to comfort the lonely and conversationless. The big staircase in the middle confirms that there's definitely two floors, maybe even three, but I don't think I could have got more than five steps up without bursting into tears at the wasted effort and absolute futility of it all. Oh, man: I'm so depressed. What a terrible, terrible bar this is. And even after all this time, I still fail to see how the fact that it cost £9 million to build can justify serving up rubbish beer at astronomical prices. For all the carping and pussy whining we've done about haircut bars, I'd still rather drink in Apartment than here, and that's tantamount to saying, 'Yes, I think I'd prefer babies for tea tonight.' You need this bar like you need an amputation.

For: Posh bogs.

Against: The mid-pub, mid-life crisis that prompted me to rant about the faults of the punters when I know in my heart that I'm really just describing my own decaying self.

Best bit about the entire visit? Watching that fucking Dr Gillian woman on 'How Fat Is Your House?' or whatever it's called, with the sound off. I'd never normally give her the time of day but, y'knaa, presented with a choice of that or listening to anecdotes about mail merges, I know which one I'd go for. How the hell does she get away with it, though? 'Right, Sally, you know you're fat because you eat cream buns all day?' Eeh, really, Dr Gillian! I didn't know. 'Mmm, yes. Right, let's have a look at yer shite.' I'd love to go on that show, just to say, 'Aye, I'm a bit tubby round the waist, I'll grant you. But look at the bloody clip of you, pet. Which is your favourite shoulder; the left, the right or the one in the middle?'

Percy Arms

83 Percy Street, NE1 7RW
'A fitting tribute'

When I was a skinny little teenage twat with a studded belt that weighed more than I did, I used to drink in this bona fide, fuck-rough biker hang out, where the city's Mad Dogs, Spiders, Lone Wolves and Laurences gathered to compare sump oil stains before riding their hogs into the sunset and never lookin' back. Now it just looks as though it's been reduced to a biker apology pub, with an embarrassing plastic TT-bike stuck on the wall, a blinding Easy Rider sign above the bar, and not the least sign of WD40 let alone a Hell's Angel. There's plenty of pierced metal kids and old buzzards and tramps, but no real bikers to speak of. Even the die-hards with the Mam-bought Doors T-shirts under their leathers look like they need stabilisers to keep them upright, since they've clearly grown far Fonda (Christ!) of Burger King than the Lizard King over the years. What a tragedy. My disgust at the half-arsed theme tempts me to follow suit with this review; I can't be bothered to blather on about the beer (decent enough), the atmosphere (fine if you like a bit of Zeppelin) or the bogs (wait until you get home). What I will say is this: I was last here on 27th April 2000 and remember a bloke with a fucking huge Afro was propping up the bar. Standing here in mid-2006, I see, right in front of me, that same bloke with that same Afro still propping up that same bar. Now I come to think of it, he was here when I was a nipper, too. Maybe he's just been waiting all these years for Bat Out Of Hell to finish; three more choruses and a couple of false endings and he'll have finally got his money's worth. That would make perfect sense to me. Take the singer out of the MC5, and take Columbian football legend Carlos Valder-rama; add them together and square them, you're still not even close. This man's 'fro is by far the most remarkable thing about the Percy, and when it all falls out they should glue it to a dummy and have it standing at the bar like that plastic cunt in the Drizabone who used to trip me up in Bar Oz along the road. That would be a fitting tribute to one of the town's last remain-ing characters. And it'd be the about the only real reason to come here again.

For: The biker motif means I can dedicate this review to the amusingly goateed little shit who used to get on my bus, com-plete with full regalia championing his Chapter, and wipe his oily kecks all over the seats. Being a tolerant sort of chap, I reasoned, hmm, takes all sorts; it was only after I'd got off I thought, 'Eh? If you're that much of a biker, what the hell are you doing on the fucking bus, you odious turd?'

Against: Half a review on a bloke's haircut? That's just pathetic.

I feel I have to mention that the (possibly ex-) live-in manager of the Percy is a personal friend of Burglar's Dog 'Does what, exactly?' John Egdell. In the interests of anonymity and protecting the innocent, we'll call the unfortunate manager Derek, on account of it being his real name. Egdell likes to recount the tale of how Derek and the lads went off on a summer jaunt to, I dunno, fucking Torremolinos or some other place where daft lads go to get smashed and take photos of each other's nads. At the time, Derek (still his real name) was working in a bar in Gateshead. One morning that bar received a postcard from the lads on holiday. It had four words: 'Derek shat the bed'. Two days later came another postcard, this time less conversational than the first. This one said simply, 'Again'. Just try to remember that when you're in the Percy. And make sure you ask for a clean glass.

Rosie's

2 Stowell Street, NE1 4XQ

'Tattooed, pickled and rough as a nympho's knees'

Rosie's Bar is a Newcastle institution, and has long been regarded as the best place to kick off a night stuffing your face in Chinatown. Or at least it was, until the horrible, horrible Gate complex round the corner opened. But as long as The Gate continues to filter off all the fucking idiots wittering on about 'flied lice' then I'm a happy man. I can't imagine Rosie's giving a shit, like. It's not as if they're going to miss the trade: this place is busy at the best of times, and to describe it as even chockablock before the match would be to water down the truth for the faint of heart. If I had to pin a label on the customer base here, I'd say Rosie's probably attracts the crowd from the West End - tattooed, pickled and rough as a nympho's knees - especially now that the Newcastle Arms across the road has pulled its socks up. But I've never seen any trouble. In fact, some match days you get just as many away fans here as Toon ones, even if they are meek little real ale merchants following teams we expect to take a pasting. The decor in Rosie's is just the right side of tatty, with old sports equipment on the walls, a broken one-string guitar on the shelves and a clock that runs backwards behind one of the pillars. Anything you like as long as it's knackered and looks like it's been dredged up from the bottom of the Tyne seems to be the order of the day. And, above the bar, there's a row of dummy's heads with wigs on - Uncle Toboggan and Aunt Nebraska or whoever - that rotate and blink and tell you the tricky answers on the quiz machine. I think. Other than that, there's a ton of NUFC stuff on the walls - they could hardly not - plus massive windows with a head-on view of the Chinatown arch, and St James' Park framed beautifully through that. Of course, I'm just rambling and rambling about the decor to tease you, and make you wait for the best bit, which is – and this is no exaggeration – the pint prices that make you think you're in dreamland, or at least back in 1983. No shit. Sixteen pints and you still get change out of a fiver? No wonder I can't breathe before kick-off.

For: Dedicated customers, keeping the makeover mafia the hell away.
Against: The Gents, and the door that opens up to give the far end of the bar a good view of things they'd probably rather not see. You might as well just lob your pecker out and walk through the pub for all the privacy you get in the bogs.

Those dummy's heads above the bar have given me a cracking idea. Why not use real severed heads, starting with those can-clutching scumbags who hang around Grey's Monument and harass you at the cash point? I'd pay over the odds to see their stupid fucking heads mounted on spikes, that's for certain.

Sgt Pepper's

Vine Lane, NE1 7PW
'Grim inevitability'

Sgt Pepper's is a bit like Lennon's across the other side of town in that it's a '60s theme bar stuck firmly and inescapably in the 1980s. And, like Lennon's, it hasn't got a bloody clue. Call me a stickler, a pedant or an elongated teat, but it struck me as being a bit strange that, in a bar named after a Beatles album, the most visible picture is of Mick Jagger. Nice one. We arrived when the evening session was in full flow, which meant that we got to see first hand the stunning effect of the glitter balls and pathetic geezer-with-a-torch disco lighting, and to listen in astonishment to the Butlins Redcoat pretending to be a DJ. This bar is very popular with flabby blokes plagued by excess sweating and blubbery, sow-faced women, and while there was plenty of excited shrieking, the hacky looks being dished out between groups guarantee that one spilt drink would see lasses clubbing each other with their heels at eight o'clock at night. Sgt Pepper's, with a certain grim inevitability, is also a mandatory stop on the hen night tour for those too old and too crippled to make it down to the Quayside, so don't say you haven't been warned when you get molested. The speakers outside blaring shite like Dire Straits into the alleyway let you know before you enter what kind of music they play here; there's a constant barrage of late '80s golden oldies, giving the punters the chance to sing along to stuff before realising that they don't know more than the first line of a single bastard song. That's the night-time experience then; during the day you're stuck with the beer-stained Sgt Pepper's brand carpet and the gimme-two-glass-eyes-and-make-it-snappy tangerine and lime colour scheme. If you've ever wondered what the leisure centre bar in Hades is like, then wonder no more. This is it, and it wants you as a member.

For: The spanking new relief Union Jack design on the far wall must've kept some toerag on an Asbo occupied for at least a week. I hope to fuck they counted the damn woodwork tools afterwards, though.

Against: If you score in here you're in for a rude awakening the next day. Your conquest will be sporting a hairpiece, a corset and someone else's teeth, and will probably have gone to school with your dad. And humped him. You might as well top yourself to save the embarrassment of seeing them again. Go on. You know it makes sense.

This little shithole hasn't progressed at all over the years. Fair enough, we like a bit of untouched tradition, but this place remaining intact is like leaving your vomit on the hallway carpet as a reminder of a good night out.

Shearer's

St James' Park, NE1 4ST
'Insipid, gutless slop'

Opened at the arse end of 2004, Shearer's Sports Bar and Lounge underneath the Gallowgate End at St. James' Park quickly proved itself to be to Newcastle's drinking scene what Titus Bramble was to the team: huge, overpriced and utter, utter shite. But while eventually, with the right guidance and as half of a strong defensive partnership, poor old Titus will clearly live up to his early promise, this bar is beyond help. If you've ever had the misfortune to attend a function in one of the many suites inside the ground, you'd know that Shearer's is more or less an extension of that depressing rat shit. And for those who've yet to witness the corridors of power, let's just put that the bar is on a par with, say, Chester-le-Street's third best nightclub. Why not pop along, dig deep in your pockets to buy an insultingly priced drink served on a stupid fucking club crest doily, and then try to find a spot to relax in the cavernous shed that is Newcastle's biggest bar? You won't, like, but at least you can feast your eyes on one of the many plasma screens showing DVDs of Newcastle's glory days i.e. when we still won fuck all, but at least it was entertaining to watch, unlike some of the insipid, gutless slop we've been served up since Shearer's opened. The blurb on the Toon's official site says something along the lines of the place being laid out in three distinct areas: ground floor, mezzanine and first floor. The fucking new-look Homebase DIY on the Team Valley has much the same design, but it wouldn't entice me to part with my hard-earned, not even if they were showing Matchpot of the Day on the big screen. Shearer's apparently cost £2.5 million to build, which is roughly a quarter of what we'll end up paying the next panic-buy European import to fall over his own feet on the rare occasions he feels like being fit from now until the end of his contract. What a fucking waste of money. Ever the diplomat, Mr Shearer himself was asked for a few words the monstrosity that bears his name. 'It goes without saying I am very proud that part of St. James' Park will bear my name,' he said. At gunpoint. His chairman, thankfully, was unavailable for comment.

For: At least it makes the ground look finished.
Against: I have no problem with the angry youth of our city expressing themselves in biro on toilet cubicle walls, just as long as they make an effort to spell it correctly. I think you'll find it's 'Freddy ShepHERD is a cunt,' actually.

When European and domestic cup games are half full of miserable fuckers and burger-munching kids, when the atmosphere is like a mausoleum and all you see around you are once-a-season whingeing part-timers claiming to be the 'loyal-est football supporters the wooooorld has ever had', what is the point of sticking the match on in the stadium bar as well? Where's the fucking sense in having an empty ground and a full boozer? (Penny drops: three pints in the bar costs about the same as a match ticket. Nice one, Freddy.)

The Strawberry

Strawberry Place, NE1 4SF
'Broken bones and asphyxiation'

Have you got the number 8 on the back of your Newcastle top with 'WE' above and 'MACKEMS' underneath? Do you queue all night outside the club shop to get your new replica shirt literally hours before the rest of the world? Do you have to be THERE, where it's AT? Are you, in short, a Toon lunatic? Then this is the bar for you. Get yourself along here on match days with all the other lovers of broken bones and asphyxiation who pack every square millimetre of available space, and you'll be laughing (as least as hard as your ribcage will allow). I've scratched my head for an hour and a half, but I still can't find a sensible reason for the match day popularity. What's the point in being in a bar a season ticket's throw from the ground if the crush means it takes you an hour and a half to get served? It's not like Freddy Shepherd's going to present you with a bloody loyalty card if you risk life and limb squeezing in here, is it? Beats me. But here, don't get me wrong: this isn't going to end up as the usual Dog panning. In fact, there's absolutely nothing wrong with the bar itself, or the punters for that matter. It's just that it's always so jam-bastard-packed of a Saturday (or sodding pay-per-view Sunday) afternoon. If you go on non-match days, when there's space to breathe, you'll see it's a cracking traditional brown pub with a bit of history, awash with pictures of Toon legends new and old. You're guaranteed a good pint and friendly staff, there's better-than-average chance of a nice bit of setting sun blazing through the windows - and the atmosphere is always relaxed; that's the old-time meaning of relaxed as opposed to fucking 'chilled'. But for the sake of the Lord, why the desperate squeeze on match days? Yes, it's a really good bar with a ton of Toon stuff and a raucous shouty atmosphere, but it's hardly the last lifeboat off the Titanic, is it?

For: I'd still sooner have the lifeblood pressed out of me in here than ever set foot in that bloody shed Shearer's over the road.

Against: Did I mention that it gets quite busy from time to time?

It's a good sign for a bar if all you can find to really gripe about is the hand dryers in the bogs. When are those fuckers going to stop lying to us? How much longer are they going to insult us with their dynamic names like Cyclone and Jetstream and their promises of instant drying comfort? You whack them and you hoof them, you dance beside them like St Vitus, you turn their stupid nozzles until they come off in your hands, and what do you get, if you're lucky? Two seconds of freezing ferret fart, that's what.

The Tavern

10 Northumberland Rd, NE1 7RY
'A daring foray into the world of open-plan design'

This place has never really been somewhere we've given much thought to, and if I hadn't started working at the Haymarket end of town it's doubtful whether I would ever have noticed the latest alteration to the name. The pub has finally completed a full circle of name changes from the Tavern to Steppes to Huxters to Stepps (no second 'e') and back to the Tavern again, displaying a terrible dearth of imagination if nothing else. There's a sizeable chunk of me that thinks it'd be nice if I could apply this to my own life and get back the twenty years I've wasted in the meantime, especially all the time spent typing idiot reviews about dull little pubs like this. The name aside, there's been no real change to the inside of the bar, just the same old stuff painted milky-tea beige. If you liked it before - and I didn't, to be honest - you'll still like it now. I don't remember seeing the chessboards inlaid into the tables the last time I was in, so they might be part of the refit; then again, all I did the last time I was here was look at my watch, so I might be wrong. I don't really know why I'm not that keen. Maybe it's because the place always seems a bit grubby to me; the tables in the booths were covered with ash and salt and smears of ketchup, and that's no bloody good when you're out in your Saturday best. The sports bar idea looks to have survived the name change, with the huge screen upstairs still blaring out minority sports to over-enthusiastic knuckleheads, though the individual tellies in the booths have had their control panels boarded up behind a few tatty off-cuts. And that seems to be a bit of a theme running through the bar: if it's broke, just nail a plank over it and paint it brown. A final quick nip to the Gents before moving on revealed a daring foray into the world of open-plan design, with an airy, taboo-busting approach to the toilet layout. Well, either that or some cunt had nicked the bog door.

For: There's a taxi rank outside.
Against: I think it speaks volumes about this pub that the last time we came here was only because the Northumberland Arms was temporarily closed for repairs.

I had my first ever city pint in the original Tavern, bright-eyed, slim, and clearly underage. I remember it like it was yesterday, and could probably do a more accurate review of that incarnation than I ever could of the new one. It should be illegal to try to trade on former glories: this bar is no more the Tavern than a Whitley Bay sandcastle is Krakatoa.

Three Bulls Heads
57 Percy Street, NE1 7RN
'Something sticky underfoot'

Apart from the fact that the Three Bulls Heads could do with a bit of a spring clean, there's really bugger all to say about the place. It remains a typical city centre bar - well, what typical city centre bars used to be before they all became pitch-black luxury establishments - and it could really do with a lick of paint, or at least someone with a bucket of paste to clag the wallpaper back up. It's not that it's a complete dive, or anything, but there always seems to be something sticky underfoot on the rare occasions I go in these days. The decor, like you care, consists mostly of old pictures of the town and the Toon, with plenty of big mirrors and tellies and what have you to brighten the place up. No problem with that, I say. And it's always useful in a pub like this that's a million miles past heaving on match days to have the bar in the middle, making it a bit easier to get served without any of that hey-man-how-man pushing and shoving. Match days are when you'd probably feel safest here: on non-match days, it just tends to be populated by punters who just don't give a fuck any more. Unless you're starting, like, ye twat. I've personally never had any bother here; it's a place that's good for a few afternoon pints talking bollocks about nothing, and then leaving before the hardcore radgies turn up. But aye, overall, I suppose it's the sort of boozer that I always campaign for and then continually ignore. Just goes to prove what a whingey little cunt I am.

For: Sensible prices and no bloody kids allowed.
Against: I still wouldn't recommend it as a first date pub.

I've already confessed to being a metaller when I was a kid. One of the places you were duty-bound to loiter in and get mugged by glue-sniffing skins back then was the old Handyside Arcade. The Handyside, in roughly the area where the Three Bulls is now just in case you don't remember it, was a run-down (only slightly) Victorian shopping arcade full of period charm, and was exactly the sort of place that the Council (and shitehawks like Starbucks) are begging to redevelop and preserve. What's there now? Eldon Garden - yet to see its 500th shopper after ten years of business - and a half-arsed, in-name-only recreation of the original Three Bulls Heads. All this forces me to muse on what exactly it is about human nature that leads people to adopt the mentality of 'MUST. DESTROY.' only to end up a few years later trying vainly to recreate what was there in the first place. Everyone does it, sure as eggs is eggs. Trouble is, if you stick your paw up and say, 'Excuse me; this is alright, this here. Can we keep it?' people look at you like you're having a wank at a wedding. Makes no sense to me.

211

The Trent House

1-2 Leazes Lane, NE1 4QT
'The first sign of dickdom'

The Trent House is, if not actually as World Famous as they claim, definitely a Newcastle institution. In a poky little building off the beaten track up by the RVI, The Trent has miraculously survived the appalling makeover craze that has swamped virtually every other bar in the city, and yet is still free of squalor or psychos. In fact, they have a cast-iron policy of refusing to serve any sort of charver. Class. This place is a Soul Bar, a description that makes you fear the worst, but here it's one that's evolved naturally rather than fallen out of a crate like the abortions we could mention by using the words Mr and Lynch. It's a little bit tatty, but in a good way. Yes, they do refits every now and then, but they do them like you'd do up your own house - change a few colours, move this here and that there, maybe throw up a few new pictures - and they always manage to keep some semblance of their personality instead of desperately grasping at a fashionable, shop-bought identity. After all this time they've still got the foreign currency pasted on the walls, and the African masks and that, but there's not a whiff of tackiness, not even in the prophylactic - that's blobs to you - display cabinet. Actually, I don't remember seeing that the last time I was in, but that's just because I was so busy gawping at the original table-height Space Invaders or, to be more exact, down the top of the lass playing on it. There's two floors, with the upstairs room usually full of squabbling students hogging the pool table - in a laid-back way, obviously - and while you'll have to juggle your pints up the stairs until the upper bar opens, it's a good place to just slump yourself down and listen to the fantastic free jukebox, the one that's never yet played what I told it to. Now we're not saying The Trent is without its faults; constantly claiming to be cool is the first sign of dickdom, and for all that their promo stuff trumpets a twat-free environment, using the expression 'v' popular (our quotation marks) does let the side down a little. Still, for every negative there's a positive and a half, and even if the wall of the downstairs bar heralds the embarrassing slogan 'drink beer be sincere', there's always the tremendous 'be nice to people, don't be a twat' halfway up the stairs: that's long been our mantra at the Dog, as any fucker will tell you. So aye, they can be a bit up themselves, and they attract a lot of idiots, but they can't really be held responsible for this term's intake, and I'd still rather be irked by a bit of individuality than be numbed by any more chain bar mush.

For: I once got indirectly barred from here despite being out of the country at the time, thanks to a dispute between the management and one of their former staff and the subsequent banning of 'everyone you know'. Top work.
Against: Comic Sans. On every bit of tabletop blurb. Simply evil.

Alongside the toy farmyard animals that sit behind the optics on a little ledge behind the bar, is a half empty tube of KY and six packets of Extra Strong Durex - I stayed seated.

8

Ouseburn & City East

'Learning from the mistakes of the past whilst both embracing sympathetic redevelopment and retaining history, the Ouseburn and east of the city are home to Newcastle's art spaces and its emerging music venues, as well as its educational city farm and stables. Funny we should mention stables, because I feel like I'm flogging a dead horse with this introductory banter. Are we done yet?' – Norman Undercroft, Historian.

The Cluny
36 Lime Street, Ouseburn, NE1 2PQ
'The usual vulgarity'

This is going to be a bit tricky for me. It's not very often that I come to review a boozer that I actually really like, so the chances of this being full of the usual vulgarity are looking pretty slim. Let's see how I get on. I am, by all accounts, a bit of a tosser and a stuck-up twat. I'd say I can't help it, but the truth is I do it on purpose just to get on people's tits. I also have a reputation for spending more on a holiday than most sensible people would spend on a trip to the moon, and when I'm off on one of my la-di-dah European capital jaunts, this is exactly the sort of bar I seem to end up in. It's in an old whisky bottling plant and still has an industrial look about it. It's huge and bright, has a band on every other night, and it even has an art gallery on the upstairs level. The beer's decent and varied enough, they've got a better range of spirits than my drunken ex-next-door neighbour, and our lass, who's a right bloody whinger when it comes to food, says the grub is pretty good. Alright, fair enough, I might have spent half the night after eating in here puking thick, brown vomit up my bathroom walls, but I blame that on the dodgy pint I had in the Stout Fiddler afterwards. Putting aside the minor quibble about the pub being an absolute bugger to get to, and conveniently ignoring the fact that ninety percent of the punters whenever you go are manbag-swinging knobheads, I'd go so far as to say that this place deserves the near-legendary status it seems to have in every two-bit 'alternative' style mag you pick up. I love it, but then it's not every boozer where you get to sit out in a beer garden between a big chimneystack and derelict warehouses; if they'd put a few more seats out there I'd be in heaven. Oh dear. This is becoming rather dry, isn't it? Shit. Piss. Arse. Nipples. There: that's much better.

For: They've finally sorted out the pillars in the venue bit, so you get to see the bands for your £12.50, and not the bloody speaker stacks.

Against: To paraphrase Mark E Smith from The Fall, people from Byker are alright; it's the people IN Byker who are twats.

I take back what I said about the food. I'm no Ainsley Harriott: any old junk will do me when it comes to soaking up the ale. But even I know that it's not on to charge a fiver for nachos and then serve up fucking cheesy Doritos, you robbing bastards.

The Cumberland Arms

Ouseburn, Byker, NE6 1LD
'No talent required'

According to the pub's own website, the Cumberland Arms, 'established in the 1850s, is truly traditional, with real ale, folk sessions, live music, storytelling...' Normally we'd rip the piss something rotten out of stuff like that, shatter a few illusions and generally stick the boot in, but after trying to rewrite the same slagging a hundred times for all the identikit designer bars in the town, it fills us with joy to see a place as unique as this. It really is as good as they say. Notable as a live music venue, eclectic doesn't even begin to describe the range of acts they have on upstairs. For every sonic laptop terrorist there's a round of lavenders-blue-dilly-dilly on a homemade banjo; and for each fey, shy indie strummer there's some over-confident loon who thinks reciting his wince-inducing poetry constitutes entertainment. And that's just for the paying customer; if you're crackers enough to favour a more hands-on approach, then we can guarantee you'll be up for the 'sessions', where every bearded deviant for miles around comes to throttle the bejesus out of their comedy instrument, blocking the sitting room and playing a G chord non-stop for three and a half hours. No talent required, just a nine-pint grin and an alarming sweater. Still not enough for you? How about cookery classes? Humorous improv? A sewing circle, then? Maybe you just want to relax with a pint, or sup as much mead as you can neck before the diabetic coma kicks in. Or perhaps you're after a bench outside with views over the Ouseburn Valley right the way over to Dallas Carpets and the Gateshead tower blocks in the distance. It doesn't really matter what fondles your nadbag; if you're the sort of lunkhead who thinks any bar without a thirty grand paint job (beige and purple, naturally) is beneath you then you won't even have got this far down the page. But if you're prepared to unleash the inner honey nut loop then rub some Lurpak in your hair, grab a paperback for the Bring One Borrow One Library, stick on your favourite anorak and get yourself along.

For: I think this is the first review ever by the Dog that's been entirely based on FACTS and not the usual space-filling nonsense. Blimey.

Against: If you're coming from the top (i.e. non-Cluny) end, getting off the bus at the arse end of Shields Road, we'd advise that you carry a spare pair of shoes to replace the ones that'll be robbed before you even hit the roundabout.

If the Cumberland does have a downside, it's their traditional outdoor-but-indoor bogs, with what look like bullet holes for ventilation and bare brick walls. And that's brick walls where the plaster has fallen off through centuries of neglect and widdle fumes, and not some New York loft space design statement. Nobody's going to mind slumming it when they're wazzing out the odd jar, but if you're planning on hunkering down for a fireside winter pint marathon then it could get to be a bit off-putting. Just saying, like.

Free Trade Inn

St Lawrence Road, Byker, NE6 1AP
'Sleek contemporary design classic'

Two things that will strike you when you go to the Free Trade Inn: 1) It's an absolute dump, and 2) it's fantastic. Struggling along the nettle-strewn path up from Quayside, you find that what looks from a distance to have been derelict for thirty years is actually one of the best, scruffiest bars in the town. From the dirty brown walls with huge holes in the plaster to the boarded up fireplaces, there's been no attempt made whatsoever to smarten the place up or to impose any sort of diabolical theme. In the age of the sleek contemporary design classic and polished stone furniture, it's good to still be able to spot a few Formica tables with S&N Breweries blue star in them, an' all. There's not really much in the way of decor to speak of: just art-for-sale and gig adverts on the walls. And I like that approach. Even the punters seem like a friendly bunch, with barely a trace of Bigg Market idiots or lounge bar style-victims, though what we will have to point out is that the Free Trade attracts a lot of students; the prick who wrote 'you're my wife now' on the otherwise magnificently vandalised bog walls should be barred for life. Get your own personality, you sad twat. The standard of the pint's good, and there's a choice of two beer gardens - one overlooking the Tyne (both the river and the pub of that name) - to park your arse in and watch dogs chomping on wine corks and gravel. Fuck it, man: what's not to like about the place? Especially since its very existence is one in the eye for all the greedy developers who want to stick another unoccupied office block right in front of the bar and ruin the view. There's always some battle or other with skyscraper-obsessed fools, and it'll be a sorry day if those wankers finally come up with a big enough backhander to get the go-ahead. Whoever coined the phrase 'the banality of evil' clearly had the gentrification of the east quayside in mind. Clearly.

For: We've been on to UNESCO and they're quite happy for the Free Trade Inn to go on their list of protected World Heritage Sites. Well, maybe not.
Against: It's always woefully understaffed when we go.

Guinness drinkers: what is their fucking problem? How come I always seem to get stuck at the bar behind the sort of dickhead who orders his mate's Foster's in an Australian accent (it's brewed in Manchester, you tit) and then waits until the very end of his massive round order to say, after a lengthy dramatic pause, '...and a pint of Guinness'? It takes about a month to pour, and you KNOW that, you obnoxious shites. Stop making such a fucking spectacle of your tastes, stop making me wait forever for my pint and start ordering the damned tarmac at the beginning in future. Jesus, man.

Logic

Argyle Street, NE1 6PN
'A throat cut from ear to ear'

The Quay Point development to the east of Newcastle - a building site at time of writing, but completed enough for us to make wild assumptions - is a triumph of low-rent box room flats with inadequate soundproofing, and looks specifically designed to deprive its student tenants of any sleep for the entire duration of their course, turning them into the nippy little Nazis their business management qualifications require them to be. Located at the western end of this lab-rat maze is Logic, or Bar Logic, or Logic Bar, a potluck lounge pub with an ersatz Moroccan theme tacked onto it. (Ersatz is a great word for shitty sham; I wish I'd looked it up earlier). The wooden slatted exterior hides a scatter cushioned boothfest, with garish flock wallpaper reflected in whole walls of mirrors, and lamps from a junior school version of Ali Baba casting greens and yellows and blues on the ceiling. And, once again, the sinister emulsion brotherhood has offered the choice of their purple paint or a throat cut from ear to ear. There's wickerwork bar stools, wooden blinds and a full range of exotic potions behind the bar, like Carling. And Stones. And the ingredients for a cocktail called a Wibble. I see there's also an upstairs bar, with more of the same, but locked away from my prying late afternoon eyes. I have no idea how long Logic has been here: it looks new enough to still be full of its own self importance, but old enough for every single item of table-top promotional literature to have been through the boil wash. Twice. I'm not going to pan Logic today, mainly because I don't care enough about it. But I won't be back unless I really want to waste a companion's time and leave them as unimpressed as I was. This is a student bar or, to be more exact, a warm up bar for the knobs who go to the Foundation club down the hill and round the corner. If that's what pokes your prostate, then good luck to you. It looks alright at the minute but it WILL be wrecked in the near future, and there's no point in pretending otherwise. Why? The evidence is on the toilet walls, where the bogey retrospective exhibition is already being installed. And who's responsible? It has to be him, the prick in the corner in the festival T-shirt, since anyone prepared to root about for a weekend in mud and shit in a hole in the ground can't possibly be bothered about hygiene. It's the fucking logistics of the wiping that confuse me, though. You need one hand to keep your flies from mangling your chopper, and the other hand to point it in the right direction. How the hell can you get a finger up your sneck, too?

For: The fun-size plasma screens, taking you right back to when a 14" portable was big enough for an average bedroom, instead of the mile-wide bastard no one can be without these days.
Against: Widescreen. Wide. WIDE. W-I-D-E. See the next development in TV technology? Tallscreen, the revolutionary 'new' system that restores the picture to the proportions it had before Sony convinced you to part with three grand for the lopsided shit you've got now.

The small print at the bottom of the menus says that the photos are for guidance only and should not be taken as a literal representation of the food advertised thereupon. Too true. It's like that when you see protesters outside McDonald's, with their placards showing a crudely drawn sketch of a cow in a bun, all sad eyes and blood-dripping limbs. The fucking burgers NEVER look as good as that when you get them. And do animal rights activists never stop to think they might be taken more seriously if they didn't look quite so much like animal rights activists? Put it this way: I'm a vegetarian and I still hate the scruffy cunts.

New Bridge Inn
2 Argyle Street, NE1 6PF
'Saggy tattooed tits'

The New Bridge is owned by the Sir John Fitzgerald chain and, if the night we finally got round to doing the review visit was anything to go by, is populated with the exact post-work crowd that used to monopolise the pubs around Grey Street in the centre of town. That's really the best way to describe it: from the cracked coving down to the tatty carpet, it's along the same lines as Fitzgeralds (visits in the last three years: one) and the pre-rebuild-masquerading-under-legend Bacchus, and is the sort of bar we used to gripe about as being bog standard but now, in our stubborn, nostalgic way, worship, revere and avoid at all costs. Why? Because nowt pleases us more than being deliberately miserable. There are wooden booths with leather seating. They've got old pictures and books, and ceiling lights shaped like saggy tattooed tits. There's endless nooks and crannies in which to sip your half of Dogslobber (ABV 1.2%) or your glass of medium dry white, plus chest high dividers at the back that are just crying out for a game of bar volleyball. And if the telly's boring, you can always take your life in your hands and stare at the odd indigenous grumpy charvers in the corner who are wondering where the fuck all these wankers have come from. It's a fine old bar, with a relaxed atmosphere and a place that we really should get to more often, if only in the hopes that we might wake up there and realise the last twenty years have just been a bad, bad dream. Finally, in the interests of common sense and word count, we'd like to pose an open question to the clientele based on prejudice, bitterness and a seven-pint-slanted viewpoint. If, as you claim, you're high-powered, super-intelligent executives making decisions for the good of the people then how come a) you're always leaving your coats and baggage all over the place so nobody else can sit down and b) you're then genuinely startled to find your laptop missing and your briefcase covered in hockle?

For: We'd highly recommend this place...
Against: ...if it wasn't for the soul-sapping, fearful trudge across the motorway bridge that divides New Bridge Street, not to mention the Manors Metro smackheads

I've got a bad feeling about bars along this way and the sort of punters they're beginning to chase. The Cluny: exclusively for hipsters. The Ship: desecrated and wine-listed. Tanners: DJ-courting. I blame all the new, expensive, shoebox apartments springing up all along the banks of the Tyne. You know, the ones with the commanding views of all the other new, expensive, shoebox apartments springing up all along the banks of the Tyne.

The Ship Inn
Stepney Bank, NE1 2PW
'An ill-tempered stray dog with a balloon'

It's like this: you get out the serious guidebooks and you look under 'pubs'; you find an entry for a traditional old bar, usually 'dating back to the early 1800s', and full of 'untouched history'; you trek out there, because pubs like that are always, always miles from anywhere, and you find that it's, to put not too fine a point on it, a shite hole. But, there's always something about it that makes the hike worthwhile. That's The Ship for you. I'd be surprised if this place has seen a lick of paint in the last hundred years, a cleaner ever, and it'd be no exaggeration to state that the pictures on the wall of the Tyne Bridge being built and trams running along the Quayside represent the future as far as this place is concerned. The bandit and jukebox are the only things to have been brought in since the invention of electricity, and as far as I can remember, this is one of the only bars I've seen with a dartboard that's used for the sport and not as an 'ironic' decoration in some rotten old-time theme. Top marks for that, I reckon. The punters are a grim old bunch; old codgers in the main bar and, sprawled outside, the sort of people who wake up one morning, realise they've got NAILS tattooed across their foreheads, and need somewhere out of the way to repent for their past stupidity while waiting for the ink to fade. And what better way to whittle away an afternoon than watching a small child hit an ill-tempered stray dog with a balloon, and guessing what time the first blood will spill? Certainly kept me entertained, I'll tell you that. The Ship shares a beer garden with the Cluny bar-café-venue over the way and... hmm, better scrap that... The Ship has a beer garden where you sit and realise that what looks like the Byker Farm souvenir shop over the way is actually the Cluny, and you've just missed the first three songs of the band you were going to see. But what the hell: better off sitting in here with a few nice pints than listening to some indie strummer bleating about his girlfriend problems, eh?

For: It's heartening to see that a knackered old hovel like this can still exist in the age of the caviar-café.

Against: If anyone from a pub development company takes so much as a Dulux colour chart in here, they should be hung, drawn, and quartered. And buried. And dug up again. And barbecued. And you can say we gave you permission.

Stop press: Some fucking idiot has ruined The Ship. Some contemptible little cunt has given the go-ahead for all the period detail to be hoyed in the skip and replaced by artsy prints and bare planks that look like they've been salvaged from warehouse pallets. And some utter buffoon has failed to grasp that this bar can never again be historic; even if they change it back to how it was, it can only ever be historically themed. It's little short of criminal, and that's before we even consider the wine list. Pass us that fucking Kleenex Man-Size, will you?

Stepney's

3 Bridge View, Stepney Lane, NE1 6PN
'I was THIS fucking close'

I've got a bee in my bonnet about the typeface known as Comic Sans. I may have mentioned it. I hate it and everything it says about the institutionalised morons who use it to display their balls-aching wackiness. In my working life I am constantly subjected to its amusing curves and friendly lines, and I have reached the point where I simply refuse to deal with it any longer. Any documents in it passed my way go straight in the bin, and e-mails - especially the ones saying 'forward this to ten people or you'll die of plague' - are deleted immediately. I'd go so far as to say that if I was presented with a cheque for a million quid written in Comic Sans, I'd burn it - uncashed - rather than stand and look at it while I was doing the paying-in slip at the bank. I tell you, having seen advance pictures of the front of Stepney's, I was THIS fucking close to just ranting for an entire review about Comic Sans instead of writing a review. I'd even printed off the pub's name - double sided to save paper, naturally - in several mixed cases just to make sure. It turns out that the Stepney's sign is in some other font, one that's as close as it's possible to be to Comic Sans without actually making me boil with fury, so I suppose I'll have to do a proper review. Situated in a warehouse unit between those fugly new Quay Point flats and the thundering Metro line, Stepney's ticks all the boxes a student could ever want, with cheap beer, floppy striped seating and a pool table that's virtually impossible to use unless you angle your cue down from chin height. It's got the usual pale stone, bad carpet and shipwreck wood, plus a line of what look from here to be orange pastel pictures of naked blokes. Their hearts seem to be in the right place with their trusting bring-one-take-one book swap shelf; me, I'd ditch that straightaway, since your average little cunt from Yoo-neh can't even be trusted to do a simple thesis without stealing it from the internet and claiming it as their own graft. They also do a 'Sing for your Supper' night, which is essentially an open mic for aspiring musicians, poets, performers and jackasses who think they're comedians to make a tit of themselves and get paid in roast dinners. That's what their Myspace page says, anyway. Bearing in mind I go on holiday more times than I wander down these back streets, I feel almost as if this bar is in someone else's town, a town that can do its own raging about pubs. I just remain indifferent to the whole lot; I don't like it much, but I can't be arsed to pan it. I'm fairly sure that if I took the trouble to make it one of my regular bars I'd have a different student wanker pissing me off for a different reason every single night of the year, but for one-off for review purposes I have no complaints. That's almost a complaint in itself.

For: Pubs in warehouse units: not a bad idea. At least I'd be able to say, 'Aye, love, whatever you want' when our lass is dragging me round carpet stores, and nip next door for a jar while she's filling in the paperwork.

Against: How the fuck do you get to the bogs? I can see the sign says 'Toilets upstairs', but how do I get there? The stairs are chained off and the disabled lift goes nowhere I want to be. I suppose I could have, like, asked.

Call it coincidence, synchronicity, kismet or fluke, but the day we came to do the review and saw Stephen Hawking's A Brief History of Time on the bring-one-take-one shelf was the exact same day as I had Hawking on the phone to me at work. I swear it was him. Certainly sounded like the fucker, anyway. I could hear all this whirring and clacking and I'm thinking, 'Eh? Is this a prank call? Hello?' Eventually his computerised patter comes out, and it's in the most miserable, monotonous voice I've ever heard. Friday afternoon, an' all; you'd think he could have cracked a smile. And he's banging on and on and on, never once sounding remotely interested. I said to him, 'Don't you fucking adopt that tone with me...'

The Stout Fiddler

132-140 New Bridge Street, NE1 2SZ
'Never lend a banjo to a man named Seamus'

Situated across the road from whatever the fuck they're building on the old Warner's Cinema site - something boot-ugly for students, I'm told - the Stout Fiddler is an Irish theme bar, but one that's nowhere near as repugnant as Callaghans at yon end of the motorway bridge. You don't need me to tell you that this means Guinness ads on the walls, Shillelagh sticks behind the bar, Father Ted font wherever it'll fit, and broken instruments on the shelves. What the hell is the fascination with bust things in Irish bars? Is there some sort of maxim I'm missing, one that says never lend a banjo to a man named Seamus 'cause he'll only knack it? Or is it just bone-idle themesmanship, something to tick off on the checklist along with old mincers and pisspots and other Bargain Hunt reject crap? The Stout Fiddler does, however, have enough character to hold its own although, as you know, characters have their ups and downs. Yes, I like the quaint little pub with old fireplaces and dark brickwork, but no, I'm not particularly struck on the pinky-red rag-rolled walls in the back room; it looks more like it was fucking jam-rag rolled from where I'm sitting. Whose eejit idea was it to do it to the radiators too? I've always had this down as a quiet boozer, with the background music just loud enough to cover the din of the live bands downstairs, but as I'm duty bound to speak as I find, I have to comment on the earth-shaking racket that greeted us. For some reason I will never fully grasp, the pub was rocking to hardcore Fucker House, more suited to 11pm in the Bigg Market than the 4pm on a nothing Friday afternoon when we turned up. The only thing I can suggest is that the barmaid - your gran, but with a footballer's haircut - was doing requests; besides us, there was only Mr & Mrs Ben Sherman in, and once they'd necked their ales and pissed off, the volume went down to an acceptable level, although sadly too late for my tinnitus. That aside, the Stout Fiddler has all the things I like in a bar; it's a music venue, serves a good pint, has a pool table and a bit of atmosphere. And even if their beer garden is no more than a wonky picnic table facing the Metro station, the pub's still full of character, and its only down side is when it allows itself to be spoilt by tits.

For: 10% discount...
Against: ...for students only, which means - quite obviously - they're actively trying to cater for the twats.

There was an owld fella I used to see in the shop every Sunday morning. I'd stand next to him at the counter with my arm full of papers and my bags of Monster Munch, and his voice, while not quite top o' the morning to ye, still had enough of an Irish accent to make an impression. He'd buy his baccy and leave, untie his dog from the bollards outside and head home to somewhere up past the park. The trouble with the old boy was - and he was either too embarrassed to admit it or too addled to realise - that he had a tic. A BAD one. And whenever the tremors took hold of him, he used to blame it all on the dog. The poor, docile mutt would be padding merrily along, tongue lolling out, thinking of his Bonio, when whoOOP-ah, there'd be a yank on the leash and a good, hard skelp across the muzzle. Every thirty or forty yards this happened, up to and beyond my street, and sometimes I couldn't get the key in the door for laughing. What a crap dog that was. Why it didn't just rip his fucking arm off, I'll never know.

Tanners

1 Byker Bridge, NE1 2SW
'Frothy piss'

Sometimes being well off the beaten track can be a blessing for a bar. Practically in Byker, and therefore outside the hideous grasp of today's bar designers - who, let's face it, would have christened it t@nners, blacked out all the windows, and dished out branded miners' helmets at the door - Tanners has been given a bit of a refit recently, and a refit like they used to be, where they keep the same name, the same character, and just give the place a fresh lick of paint. And it's class. The beer's good, the atmosphere's not far behind, and the punters are a mix of growling old timers - always a plus point in our book - and younger folk who look like they might actually have something to talk about other than their phones. Y'know, the sort of people that you used to see in bars before they became catwalk dressing rooms or playpens for overgrown kids. The refit, for the record, has gone as far as some tasteful green paint, a few candles on the way to the bogs and a lick and a promise on the outside walls, and most of the decor is provided by art-for-sale: I wouldn't buy the damned stuff, like, but that's because I'm a tight-fisted wee shite and not any reflection on the quality. And even if they are advertising bloody DJ nights, at least they've had the decency to keep the live bands on too, even going so far as to remove at least one of the panels obscuring the performance area. It'd be nice if they got shot of the other one an' all, but I suppose I'm not that desperate to see the bloody bassist's feet tapping away. The only problem that I'm having, to tell the truth, is trying to pad this review out. It's a piece of frothy piss to give a bar a deserved savaging, but not so simple to wax lyrical on somewhere halfway decent. So, aye, I liked it a lot, and even though at five bells on a sunny Friday night I'd enjoy a pint in Baghdad, I'm prepared to stick my neck out and recommend it. Watch it be a bucket of wank when you go, though.

For: Decent surroundings and no bloody wankers.
Against: I'm frightened of Byker.

Of course, all our lavish praise might just be the usual blinkered nonsense, coupling nostalgia with half a dozen post-work pints and no tea. If you've been sworn at, kicked, punched or gouged in the Tanners long after we've skipped off merrily into the sunset, then don't blame us.

The Tyne

1 Maling Street, NE6 1LP
'The Burglar's Dog's shite'

This is weird. At least half a dozen times we'd wandered right along the east Quayside trying to find this legendary 'Tyne' boozer without once coming anywhere near it. And then, one Sunday afternoon, it appeared before us like some low-budget Brigadoon, and our prayers were answered. Thank Christ we persevered. A quick history lesson: many years ago, the owners of The Tyne were turfed out of the Barley Mow on City Road by that awful Firkin chain, so they basically took everything from the old pub - the management, the atmosphere, even the bloody pub sign - and lugged it lock, stock and barrel along the river to what used to be the Ship Tavern under Glasshouse Bridge. And there it remains today. The thing is, there's very little in the way of a tacky '80s 'theme' here, some criminal mullets notwithstanding. It's not so much that time has stood still, more that it's proof that pubs can thrive and have a bit of character without being sub-jected to the whims of arsehole developers every few years. In case you're worried, though, I swear I'm not going to start telling you that this is some sort of primitive dive that I'm praising to the skies on account of its embarrassingly Luddite quirks. They know their way around the wonders of technology, alright; at least enough to have that rarest of things, a website that's updated with upcoming events when they're upcoming, and not when their techie consultants get round to changing the site. Have a look at www.thetyne.com, and you'll see for yourself. It's obvi-ously not fit to pick the sweetcorn out of the Burglar's Dog's shite, but it's worth a visit nonetheless. Even the stuff on the free jukebox is bang up to date, though you have to be an expert in gynaecology to fiddle with the insides and get the damn thing working. The decor's nowt to write home about - some Gaudi-style bust crockery on one wall, a church pew outside, a big sun-flower mural in the beer garden under the bridge, band posters everywhere else, but none of it seems forced in the way that your average refit does. I'll reserve judgment on the live music in the beer garden, since I've got no idea what playing under a bridge does for the acoustics, but 10/10 for effort regardless. All this, and the beer's spot on, too. And just to show you how good this place made me feel, I didn't even mind seeing bairns in here, since they looked more like hippified children of the revolution than the usual charver kids trying to nick your wallet. If only I wasn't such a bone-idle bastard I'd be along here every week.

For: This place just underlines what a complete cock-up the Fir-kin chain made when they gutted the Barley Mow. They wrecked a perfectly good boozer with their laughable dreams of the fu-ture, and then bailed out when they got bored, leaving it free for the debacle of Stereo.
Against: Do not, under any circumstances, use the hot tap in the Gents. You will lose your skin, your bones and possibly your life. You have been warned.

This pub's previous incarnation, The Ship Tavern, was apparently a whorehouse long, long ago. A brothel? On the edge of Byker?

Jesus, how low would you have to stoop to satisfy your urges there? Have people never heard of the chopped-liver-in-a-jam-jar trick? Though, on reflection, the liver probably cost more.

The Dog In The Bog

MAXIMISE YOUR BAR'S EARNING POTENTIAL! ENFORCE THE BLAD-
DER TAX!

Landlords! Do you feel that your licensed premises are not being
utilised to their fullest? Are you convinced that your customers'
disposable income would be better off in your pockets rather
than those of the next sucker on the vine? Do you - quite rightly -
despise your paying public? You should. After all, the ungrateful
bastards are wiping their expensively shod muddy feet all over
your floors and are clearly making no contribution to the thrup-
pence a week it costs you to power your state-of-the-art lighting
system. True, you've already forced these vermin to pay over the
odds for your vile, gassy lager, but what about when they feel the
urge to answer nature's call? Are there no further opportunities
for pocket picking? Can you be sure that the potential for ripping
the piss out of your clientele until they squeak is maximised? The
Dog in the Bog has the answer.

We firmly believe that the average customer is completely
incapable of even the rudiments of cleanliness, and requires as-
sistance, guidance and necessary force to wash, dry, buff, scent
and massage their hands, body and face to your exacting stan-

dards before re-entering your drinking area. We will not hear of the lower orders of society spreading harmful bacteria throughout your lavish establishment, of these heathens traipsing through your corridors unfragranced, or of their having passed water without experiencing the wildest of beatings with a scrubbing brush.

With The Dog in the Bog, you can be sure that your tipsy and bewildered customers will be so intimidated by the over-attentive, leering, presumptuous berks we will subcontract to pounce on them the very second they've shaken the drops off, that they'll willingly part with their hard-earned cash simply to avoid further embarrassment. Allow us to carefully select your perfect toilet attendant from our register of lapsed-conviction offenders, with the guarantee that all will be proficient in both the half- and full-Nelson. Why not sign up for our obligation-free demonstration and watch amazed as our representatives indiscriminately splash around the very latest genuine fragrances - like Brut, Kouros, Denim and Creosote - purchased fresh from the Quayside market each Sunday morning and forced upon your resentful customers before the hooky labels peel off. Marvel at just how much pointless shite and how many half-empty bottles of dubious content can be unloaded from a single tatty Head bag and spread along your designer fittings.

All our agents receive special training in financial processing, and are willing to accept most recognised forms of payment for their unsolicited manhandling, such as cash, cheque, Visa, and punch in the fucking mouth. We guarantee that our employees have zero understanding of the word 'no', and will have the agility to trap even the most determined of dodgers. Their knowledge of perfumery will know no beginning, and their reluctance to get out of the bloody way will remain unsurpassed in the industry. And for that extra-personal touch, every day each of our attendants will lovingly attach a fresh, hand-picked pubic hair to the nasty white soap of your choosing for no extra charge.

Contact us now for your free* quotation.
Tel: 08457 5554716211
E-mail: thedoginthebog@theburglarsdog.co.uk

The Dog in the Bog is a subsidiary of Burglar's Dog Racketeering Services Plc.

Should you wish not to utilise our services at this point then don't worry: we will simply send some div along to set up shop in your crappers regardless. Take your cut or fuck right off: there's money to be made and dignity, privacy and human rights mean nothing to us. Oh, and we don't do cleaning, so you'd better get some fucking old wifey in to sort that. You think we're going to mop up piss and go hunting for bog roll on your say-so, you joker? What the hell do you think this is?

* An administrative charge of £19.50 is payable, to be offset against your first purchase of suspect Paco Rabanne.

10

Gay Scene

'Based around the Centre for Life scientific museum and the Times Square plaza, this area is home to winter events such as skating on the outdoor ice rink, and summer celebrations like the huge TV screens erected for the major football events. That's about it, really. There's a what? A thriving gay scene, with numerous cafés, pubs and clubs? You're shitting me, right? Really? You want me to say a few words about them, I take it. And you're saying you'll dock my fee if I use the word "sodomite"? Get me my agent, will you?' - Norman Undercroft, Historian.

@NE
1 Marlborough Crescent, NE1 4EE
'Wait-for-me'

The gay scene's newest bar at the time of writing, @ne (At One) has a uniquely chilled atmosphere that's buzzing with happy funky house anthems, live vocalists, musicians and free internet access. Well, that's the official line, anyway. What it actually is - from where I'm sitting, at least - is a bog standard, wait-for-me! lounge bar, only one with an eye on the pink pound. From the embarrassing use of the @ sign - now as fashionable as your dad in Evisu jeans - to the grand piano and bongos on the stage area, this shameless cash-in is a welcome as Marmite in the Vaseline. A limping excuse of exposed brickwork, red chairs, parquet flooring and the usual twig-in-a-pot crap, @ne is no more and no less a haven for the gay equivalent of the rent-a-cunt punters who give that fucking abominable Perdu a reason to open its doors. Is this what they meant by Equal Opportunities? The minimal and taste-ful decor runs as far as huge '60s chandeliers, fuck-me wallpaper as artwork - that's fuck-me as in gorblimey, as in trousers, rather than any sort of invitation - and a big red painting of a bovine-looking eye, one that's crying out for a razor blade through it in the manner of Buñuel's *Un Chien Andalou*. And you don't need me to tell you there's also a DJ, plus the ubiquitous Ophelia Balls drag act wheeled out one more time. Look, I'm sorry if this isn't what you expected to read; trust me, there's no homophobia involved in our dismissal of this place, just a contempt for the insipidness of today's lucky dip bars. And this is alphabetically first on our trawl to the 'other side'? I fear the worst.

For: If you set your stall out to be fashionable, you've got to keep on changing or suffer the consequences. Roll on the next style mag issue date.
Against: I dread to think what's next.

Whether you're gay, straight, or just not fussy when you're soz-zled, bars that strew around tea lights in arty little glass jars are an absolute nightmare. And this is why: imagine it's nearing the end of the night and you're a bit the worse for drink. You're not mortal by any means, but you've switched from the lager to the spirits, if only to stop yourself from bursting for the bogs. You're gassing to someone you really fancy across your designer bar ta-ble, and you're maintaining eye contact, imagining yourself to be charming, debonair and intimidatingly handsome. Still with that penetrating gaze, you reach down for your tumbler of single malt or imported vodka, raise it to your lips... and singe the end of your fucking hooter on the damned candle you've picked up by mistake. It hurts like hell, take it from me.

Baron & Baroness

Times Square, NE1 4EP
'Burning poo'

Our lass is mental. She looks at the 17th Century roof beams in the Baron & Baroness, then looks at me and says, 'Do you think they're the originals?' Sorry to report, dear, that this bar has been here for, like, a month, and the building itself less than five years, so it's a little unlikely that that condescending git off Grand Designs will be tugging himself into a frenzy at the sight of these heritage features. Dopey mare. I never thought I'd use this expression in a review, but the Baron & Baroness is like a poor man's Gotham Town. Yes, really. Chandeliers, pulpit, ornate carvings, you name it, it's all large as life and twice as cheesy. Obviously I'm not that much of an arse that I'd complain about the lack of authenticity of the place, but I still can't say I'm a fan of this bar, or, for that matter, any of the other bars in the Centre for Life development. Having them all crammed together in adjoining units makes the place feel like the Mediterranean Village at the Metro Centre at best; at worst it's like a row of Butlins chalets, and the crap they were playing on the jukebox would certainly be more suited to some dispiriting seaside holiday camp. The Baron & Baroness is right in the middle of the gay village, but as it was practically empty when we were in - hardly surprising at six bells on a Saturday night - I can't really tell you about the state of the punters. There were a couple of podgy dykes looking pretty pissed off in one of the nooks upstairs, if that's any help. We left after a solitary pint to escape from the geezer standing outside who seemed to be burning poo and wafting the stench into the pub; the sign next to his performance said 'Barbecue', but I remain unconvinced. I can't really stick the boot into the pub, though, since I know I'll never drink there again, but I'll end by saying that if a place like this opened on my usual drinking route, there'd be merry hell on.

For: They served the best pint we'd had all night.

Against: Some old doll sitting outside looked and sounded exactly like my drunken former next door neighbour. Just for a second, mind, but long enough to have me hunting in the haversack for the claw hammer.

It's not exclusively a gay phenomenon, I grant you, but I saw it here and I'm stuck for a wildcard so I'm going to whinge about it now. I want to ask, What the FUCK is wrong with mobile phone users today? Are none of them educated enough to realise that a mobile is a device you talk into and through which - via the miracle of science - your voice is transmitted over the airwaves? It is NOT something you place beside your head while you fucking SHOUT in the vague direction of your mate in the next town. Man, I hope those mutation scare-stories are true.

Camp David

8-10 Westmorland Road, NE1 4EJ
'Irrational hatred'

With the Burglar's Dog only being a bit bi-bar-curious after eight pints, and my hastily typed post-visit notes containing just the lines 'said a thoutasbaNSD TIEMS begf0perfe' and 'blankdf is blanbd nowe mytatter wherre it loveces a bvit cock', I think we can safely say this review will be a struggle. But here goes. Run by the people behind North along the road, Camp David aims to combine beautiful decor with an exquisite cocktail list. With a brand new bar and staff with a great attitude, a mixed clientele of straights and gays are guaranteed to want to return again and again. Camp David has a superb music policy and the nicest spiral staircase ever... You can tell I'm cribbing this, can't you? Ah, sod it. This is impossible. I've even tried plodging through the internet to find some other reviews of the place to plagiarise and they're all saying the same thing: it's quite nice but it's nothing special. It's almost like it's been designed to be piss-take proof. Even the simple facts are a bit hazy, and bearing in mind it's never a good idea to have a crateful of beer instead of your tea, these are the things I can recall: it's a sock-shaped room with lots of exposed brickwork; there are pretty natty cross-shaped lights above the bar; at the arse end of the room they've got some soft, squishy and positively hazardous stools. That's it. That's the sum total of my recollection. No grumbling about the beer quality, no irrational hatred of the bar staff, no ridiculing of the toilet facilities. And I can't even remember any punters at all, let alone anyone to make low-quality stereotypical quips about, so that's that line of mockery screwed, too. Buggery buggery bollocks, this is hopeless. Oh, I know: Camp David is really expensive, apparently. I could gripe about that, but since it wasn't my round I neither know nor care whether that's true, and I'd feel like an utter fraud and an ungrateful little twat if I started complaining. Forget it. Christ, I was smashed. There's a lesson to be learned somewhere.

For: Watching some daft cunt trying to sit on those marshmallow stools and falling arse over tit onto the floor with their pint all over them. Twice.
Against: When that daft cunt is me.

It says here that Camp David have had Scissor Sisters Tour DJ Sammy Jo gracing their decks. Don't know about you, but my idea of heaven is to have one, just one day where I don't have to hear the bloody Scissor Sisters. And the same goes for Shakira, Pink and all the other bearable-once-but-not-all-flaming-day merchants. It's not so much their songs I object to, but the fact that the fucking wankers in charge of radio playlists seem to pull their heads out of the charlie dish on a Monday morning, say 'Bollocks to the 200 new singles out this week, let's just stick the same old stuff on hour after hour because it fits the format'. Bone idle bastards.

The Dog

5 Marlborough Crescent, NE1 4EE
'Sugar my arsehole and call it a doughnut'

Imagine the lesbian bar of your dreams. Picture trim, toned, beautiful girls sipping superlative cocktails on leather sofas, and exchanging meaningful glances by flickering candlelight. And conjure up the mental image of soft girl-on-girl smooching giving way to full-on Sapphic lust in a secluded back room. In our pathetic, dim-witted, misogynistic way, we like to imagine something along those lines. Do anything for you, too? Yes? Sorry to plop on your pizza here, but this place is nothing like that, nothing whatsoever. What The Dog, the scene's most prominent lesbian pub, actually has, is a ghastly crowd of bootfaced dykes scrumming and mauling amongst decor to shame the very worst of the Bigg Market. I'd stick with the fantasy if I were you. Formerly known as the Barking Dog, this bar was where I cut my gay review teeth, and where I was convinced some bloke was trying to tap me up. Well sugar my arsehole and call it a doughnut - but maybe it was only my paranoia that made me think the cunt was after me; perhaps our lass was the real prize and he was just breaking the ice for his charming, buzzcut lady friends. I'm sure she would have loved to take a trip upstairs with them to The Dog's legendary how-how-hoooowlingly bad karaoke, where the horridest, squattest, punchingest lezzas take a real delight in a bit of tuneless bellowing, like doomed Friesians in an abattoir. She'd have been right up for hoying herself around to cheesy '80s hits spun with no real care by a school disco DJ. You'd have been in your element, wouldn't you, love? No? Ah, she's just being shy. Wait a minute; dirt-cheap beer, you're saying? Get yourself in, pet.

For: Proper plug-ugly, humourless, militant, angry stereotypes.
I've never been convinced by the we-do-naughty-things-together posing of her with the tits and her mate - with the tits - in the Daily Star.
Against: This pub is called the Dog; we are often referred to as the Dog. Potential for confusion, huh? Not, however, as much

confusion as when I once wanted to know the football scores from the Chronicle's internet-usurped sports offshoot and asked the geezer in the newsagents over the road for a copy of The Pink Paper. Hmm. You can tell I made this bit up, can't you? There's no fooling you.

Do you frequent bars such as The Dog? Can you spell? How would you like to earn no extra money writing for the Burglar's Dog? Applications must be received before Armageddon. If you have not heard from us within six weeks of that date, you must assume that you have been unsuccessful.

The Eagle
42 Scotswood Road, NE4 7JE
'The return of capital punishment'

Every genre of pub and its associated demographic has its archetype, its epitome, its handy hook for lazy fuckers to hang their prejudices on. If you hate giggling checkout girls running wild, then a trip to Buffalo Joe's will reinforce every stereotype you could ever have; if you've got a grudge against shoplifters, a swift pint in the Black Garter will have you campaigning for the return of capital punishment. And if butch, leather-clad queers writhing about in the darkness turn your sensitive stomach, you'd be advised to stay well clear of The Eagle. Even their website tells you to keep the hell out of it if easily offended. The Eagle is, almost down to the last dotted i, the gay bar of your very worst nightmare, only with more of an intimidating industrial vibe. And when even the bar's biggest champions warn you it's not recommended for anyone who is weak of body, mind or spirit - that's me on all three counts - you know it's not exactly the venue for tea and scones. Factually speaking, The Eagle plays host to regular live entertainment including top male strippers, and the basement area of the building is billed as being men only at all times, including, I would suppose, the jizzmoppers. Christ, I thought my job was bad. Go on, amuse yourself; try to imagine my face on the review visit. Think of my expression, my jaw-dropping, pint-slopping, eye-popping astonishment, followed by my hasty retreat and subsequent therapy. And then whack yourself upside the fucking head for imagining that I'd even go there in the first place. What the fuck do you take me for? Duty only goes so far you know.

For: The reflex action and involuntary movement that lifts my hands to squeeze my head to prevent me from even picturing it. Ugh.
Against: If a straight bar carried on like this, how long do you think it would last? Serious question.

Hang on. This all seems far too ridiculous to be true. I suspect that it's all just a great prank, and that the basement bar is full of nothing so much as the gay scene's chin-stroking intellectuals, having a quiet pint and a bash at the crossword, safely cocooned behind their elaborate subterfuge. Or maybe it's the hide-out for the world's most wanted terrorists, luxuriating in uphol-stered comfort and chuckling to themselves about that div Sad-dam being dug out of the camel shit without so much as his Just For Men. I'm not planning to test any of this out, like.

Eclipse

48 Clayton Street West, NE1 4EX
'Fat, stupid, paranoid'

'No more heroes anymore', sang that grizzly twat out of The Stranglers when I was kid, back in the days when you could have a face like a turd and still get on Top Of The Pops. I can't recall him being as overjoyed as I was when I found out what had hap-pened here, though. A nation celebrates and calls for a public holiday now that Eclipse has taken over, gutted, and completely refurbished what was the shittiest bar the city has ever known, the dog's toilet that was Heroes. In terms of comparison with its predecessor, Eclipse can hardly fail to impress but, set against all the other modern bars in the town... well, that's the problem: it's virtually identical to all the other modern bars in the town, albeit firmly aimed at the gay community. We only witnessed the downstairs area: lots of wood, lots of blinds, lots of tellies, but very few things that struck me as being out of the ordinary, except maybe that smokers are shunted to the back corner, forcibly if need be. The punters seemed friendly enough, especially when it dawned on me that the bull-dykes at the bar were staring, not at me, but at the screen above my fat, stupid, paranoid head. As for the beer, I didn't notice gay Foster's tasting any worse than straight Foster's, but we'd been out for hours by this point so I can't be absolutely certain. And that's about all I can remember, to be honest: can't say I'll ever go back, but that's only because it's a gay bar, and not because it's in any way unpleasant.

For: The refit here will have at least a dozen other pubs in the town shitting themselves for fear of being labelled the new Newcastle's Worst Bar.

Against: I'm sure there'll be some arsewit who'll bemoan the disappearance of another traditional bar. Listen: getting nostalgic over Heroes is like getting nostalgic over the time you stood in dog shit.

I took it as a measure of how placid and tolerant I've become lately that, even in my twitching, uneasy, homophobic state, I still managed to maintain more dignity than the complete arseholes that were gathered outside at the time of the review visit. There were half a dozen charvers in full Rockport regalia leering through the windows and trying to look menacing, like in Assault on Precinct 13. What the fuck for? Did they take it as a personal insult that these 'porvorts' could set up another bar? Or were they just wrestling with the uncomfortable fact that they really fancied a piece of the 'action' themselves? I wish they'd kicked off, though. It'd have been hilarious to watch them getting stomped by a handful of nancy boys.

The End

78 Scotswood Road, NE4 7JH
'The witness-protection scheme'

I've hit a bit of a stumbling block with this one. There's this song that some weirdo at my school used to sing, and that has stayed with me ever since, tattooed indelibly on my juvenile, snickering brain. It goes a little something like this: 'Oh Rocky, stick your cocky next to mi-ine'. And even though the gay bar that was Rockies has had, not so much a makeover as the full effects of the witness-protection scheme, and is now called The End, I just KNOW that if I went in to try to do a serious review, that that song, egged on by the nine pints of Dutch courage I'd need beforehand, would come tumbling out at the most inopportune moment, and would guarantee me the biggest fucking kicking the world has ever seen. So that's why I'm going to do some proper research and put this review together with hard, concrete FACTS instead of the usual bollocks, prejudice and supposition. Let's see how far I get... Once a riot of sound and spectacle, The End has ditched Rockies' kitsch for the feel of a homely lounge, where mocha leather sofas surround low level occasional tables and cube stools, and where soft warm lights and colours surround your senses. With an eclectic mix of everything from soulful jazz to the very best in vocal house, this bar promises something a little different from the hedonistic overkill of its previous incarnation. A vast array of cocktails is available for you to sip while you relax and unwind with the 'Sunday Night Live' sessions, featuring No.1 Sinatra tribute act Paul Martin. And the customers? Well, as my gay mate so succinctly puts it, it's full of fucking puffs. Ha ha ha! So near, yet so far...

For: Free wi-fi internet access all week long, if that means anything to you.
Against: Come on, it's a designer-haircut-luxebar-lounge. And as such it can fuck off.

I still can't remember the name of that kid who sang that damn

243

'Rocky' song. I tried looking it up on that Friends Reunited site, but gave up in disgust when I saw the patter of some of the idiots I used to go to school with. They're either shambling mammy's boy cretins or the sort of wankers who've just gone on to brag about how they're 'pulling down' forty-five 'K' a year and have a personalised reg-plate (one that reads KN03 HED, if there's any justice). Ever wonder WHY people lost touch with you, you tedious fucking cunts? See if you can work it out.

Switch

4-10 Scotswood Road, NE4 7JB
'Extortionate ponce-bar'

Regardless of the sexual persuasion of its clientele, the thought of spending time and money in any boozer describing itself as Newcastle's trendiest bar is about as appealing to me as a night on the hoy with the catchiest leper. Fair enough, with its big red sign and its windows that open onto the street, Switch looks alright from across the street, but that's only if you're on the way to somewhere else, in a hurry, with no intention of stopping. When you get closer to Switch, however, you'll see the reality, which is a shuddering fun pub priding itself on hardcore cheese and head splitting DJ sounds. Catering for the evil young-and-noisy crowd, Switch is run by Pure Leisure and, because they also own The Bank next door and luxe club The Loft upstairs, we're excused from doing anything more by way of a review of those places than acknowledging their existence. Switch has a curved bar and a floor that's partly carpeted, wooden and tiled - no bet-hedging there, then - and they've got custom-made carpets, which is no sign of greatness, as anyone who's ever endured Sergeant Pepper's will tell you. The paintjob features everyone's favourite pairing of mustard and maroon, and I suppose makes the place sort of like a gay Tilleys, but with shit, shit, shitty shit music, of the type that only a 'lively disco bar' could tolerate. Switch's standing as the official warm up bar for Shag Tag! (their exclamation mark: it's certainly not mine) means absolutely noth-

ing to me, but it sounds appalling. If, however, you have a burning desire to go and see the Shag Tag Queen and get your sticker,
then step the fuck up: I'm sure you'll get exactly what you deserve. Let me get this straight: they're actively encouraging the
worst sort of Bank Holiday Blackpool tackiness, yet they've still
got the nerve to charge extortionate ponce-bar prices for the
drinks? I'd like to think there's a gay equivalent of the Burglar's
Dog somewhere, sitting in the corner and becoming more and
more furious that every fucking bar is pandering to the biggest
imbecile in it. Surely there's someone whose heart sinks like jism
down the pan at the thought of yet another cabaret night, and
who finds the idea of 'fun' with Miss Thunder Pussy as wearisome
as weeding. Is there nobody who'll say, Listen for once: what if I
don't fucking WANT to get in the party mood in every single pub I
go to? Come on man, make yourself known. Quit letting these
fuckers tell you what you enjoy. You plucked up the courage to
tell your folks when you came out, so you could at least have the
bottle to let these cunts know that their number is up.

For: I'm a massive fan of typos, so the unintentional honesty and
simplicity of their website's 'Why not take a look at our oneline
menu?' question makes me a happy man.

Against: You're still smarting about the way that I've lumped the
Bank and the Loft in with Switch, aren't you? I am not doing
them, and that's final. Put it this way: if you went to the estate
agents and someone was selling a house with an attic and a garage, would you demand a separate print out for each? No, you
wouldn't, so quit whingeing.

*I'd be surprised if I'm the first fool to pose this question, but I
haven't yet so much as eavesdropped on a satisfactory answer, so
I'm going to ask it here: why are all the gay bars traditionally
down this end of town? Is it because the Blaydon Races 'gan along
the Scotswood Road' and right past all the pubs' doors and windows? I'm asking because the night of the review 'visit' was the
same night that the Bigg Market was stowed out with people in
running gear, what with it being the 9th of June and everything.*

Is that the reason for the location, though? Is it so the punters can lean out or stand on the steps and yell, 'Yoo hoo!' at all the participants, before marvelling at the athleticism and the flolloping cocks? Bearing in mind that researching this chapter has ticked off every possible gay stereotype (I made a list), I'm going to say it here and you can quote me: Yes, THAT is the reason.

Twist

Times Square, NE1 4EP
'Endless to-do'

It's time to face the fact that I'm getting old, and that my memory is not quite what it used to be. It's now, what, the dog days of summer, and it was only when I was on my way to the Arena to embarrass myself in the name of rock watching some band I'm too ashamed to mention that I remembered that, far from Twist being just a name on the endless to-do list, I actually had a few unseasonably alfresco beers there earlier this year. Stupid bastard. I wasn't even drunk that day, either. Playing Tetris with my recollections, I've come up with a picture of having an average pint in a boxed-in beer terrace amongst foul-mouthed, hissing shitwits; the gay counterparts of the Bigg Market's 'tits oot' squad. Other than that, I'm screwed. And, because I'm a closet homophobe with the emphasis on the phobia part, a second visit is out of the question, so the rest of this review will have to be full of the usual waffle and space filling. But what I can tell you, from the one and only sideways glance I made when I was getting served, is that this place looked exactly like the Jolly Miller in Gateshead's Low Fell - along from the Angel of the North, and passed by many / visited by few - so I'm just going to describe that and pray that nobody can spot the join. It's a huge place with no pretensions of cosiness, with drab green walls and job-lot furniture, the odd bandit and even odder punters. In one corner sits a tapioca-faced youth in a Bench hoody; in another sits your gran, wondering where that smell is coming from. Outside are a few tables, and you're asking yourself, are these people the bar's typical radgies, or are they just passing through? And why does it have to be Carling every frigging time? I think what I'm trying to get at is this; for all the flashing lights and the regeneration-area location, this place feels like the sort of housing estate hellhole I fear I'm going to end up wasting my twilight years in. And I doubt they'd thank me for saying so.

For: The ice rink outside the Centre for Life from mid-November onwards.
Against: If you ever have an ear infection, like the one I've got today while I'm typing this, keep your ear-dabbing hanky far, far away from your regular nose-blowing hanky. Jesus, what a fucking stench. It's like pigeon shite.

Gay blokes do get an unnecessarily hard time, though. I once went to see the stationery lads at work to scrounge a box of A4 paper. 'Alreet mate? Got a big job on, then?' they said. But when I mentioned that a gay colleague was involved then it turned into, 'WHAT? He wants to stick the fucking paper up his ARSE, does he? EH?' Funnily enough, he did, too.

The Yard
2 Scotswood Road, NE4 7JB
'Popular with coffin-dodgers'

Never let it be said that we don't personally visit every bar in the town, even if it was just once, for one pint, in 1989, when it was called something else. On the, ahem, review visit this place looked exactly like Moulin Rouge at its campest with what research tells me was the performers from Greta the barmaid's drag show milling about. I couldn't help but stare: not out of freak-show value, but since I thought I was Robert Smith out of The Cure at the time, I was only jealous that the geezers in there had better makeup than me. Old queens, as I believe I can get away with calling them without a hoof in the nads, will remember this place as the dark and depressing Courtyard, which was so popular with coffin-dodgers that it had the nickname The Grave-yard, but a revamp has transformed it into a cosmopolitan bar complete with street tables in summer. All ages converge on what is now a very open and airy bar, with plenty of pastel shades and stone flooring; it's good to see that the gay commu-nity has to suffer the same shite as the straight. There is also a...oh look, fuck this. Let's just report the trials and tribulations of our old friend Allan Weir of the excellent pubsnewcastle.co.uk site, who does this pub review lark properly instead of pissing about like we do. Even he, stout of constitution and open of mind, clearly looked at the promo flyers on the windows, peered round the door to clock the décor, and then ran like the fucking wind as far as his little legs would carry him. You bottled it too then, Al?

For: This space is intentionally blank.
Against: Why do 90% of internet forums - like the one I rifled for research for this - seem to be directed at some bloke called Lol, as in 'I shud of getting banned I was pissed and fell over, lol xxx'? Who the fuck is Lol, and why is he so interested in all that crap?

In desperation, I lifted the facts for this so-called review from a well-informed gay website called JH's Homo Pages. In it, JH gets in a tizz about the punctuation in the phrase 'Newcastles Pre-mier Gay Bar (sic)'. I know how he feels. It gets on my floppy tits the way that there are about eight people left in this country who know how to use apostrophes properly. You see when I die? Some dunce in the stonemasons will take one look at my sur-name, see there's an 's' on the end, and decide it needs an apos-trophe in there. 'Here lies Mark Jone's...' That'll be me: trapped for all eternity beneath a punctuation error. You think I should just go and shoot the fucker now?

11

The Gate

'Opened in November 2002 after three years of construction work, The Gate leisure complex has expanded rapidly, and now boasts fourteen venues, among them a cinema, a casino and numerous restaur-are you sure this isn't the last one? Are we talking about that glass monstrosity over the road from Argos here? The one that's infested with kids? The one whose beer 'gardens' are under a mall roof? Can't I just write something about the escalators? I LIKE escalators...' – Norman Undercroft, Historian.

Bar Bannatyne
The Gate, NE1 1UN
'God's gift to comedy'

I came in here with a couple of mates before the match, hoping for a perspective other than the 'this is shite' one I normally get from our lass. 'It's just like *Cheers* in here,' they said. Hmmm. Let's weigh up the evidence, shall we? How about we start with the things from the long running TV sitcom that this bar lacks? One: the stairs. Two: The warm, friendly, everyone-knows-your-name greeting. Three: the characters, unless you count a whole host of pissed-off Geordies getting angrier by the minute at the woeful, no-eye-contact service and the hundred-degree heat. Also missing: the personality, specifically the sense that a bar is part of a tradition and the fabric of a city, and not just another gap-filling exercise in some shitty leisure mall. Oh, and let's not forget the lack of that legendary *Cheers* live-before-a-studio-audience laughter, or indeed any sort of laughter at all, come to think of it. What about the similarities, I hear you ask. Well, for a kick off it did have a stump-dumb barman. In fact it had several. It had a scattering of the Kirsty Allie syndrome - lasses you might have chucked one up when they were young and slim, but would be a bit more reluctant now they're twenty bloody stone. Also in attendance: plenty examples of that fuck-awful short-arse wife with the perm, thinking she's God's gift to comedy and the scathing putdown, when it's plainly obvious most people have seen funnier jokes in a Christmas cracker. Christ, it was awful. Paddling through the internet looking for a picture of the place - my cacky digital camera doesn't work too well in the gloom of The Gate - I found one other similarity. As with the plethora of identical '*Cheers*-branded' bars springing up to cater to fuckwits the world over, it seems that Bannatyne is also part of a chain, though whether that includes the health clubs of the same name is anyone's guess. It fucking wants to, judging by the clip of the lardies in here.

For: I'm hearing that, rather than being a *Cheers* tribute, Bannatyne is actually supposed to be a Moroccan theme bar. Blimey, that was design money well spent, wasn't it? Casting my mind back, I did see some sparkly curtains and what looked like a fortuneteller's booth in the corner. 'I see your future. I see you drinking up and getting the fuck out of here.'

Against: The weakest beer pumps in the northern hemisphere. You could watch two episodes of the TV smug-fest in the time it took to pour our pints.

I will be Prime Minister one day. There's no point in arguing; the job is mine. And when I'm in power, I will outlaw the piss-dribbling beer taps that are so frustratingly commonplace in our bars, and in their place will be the Parisian rocket-powered version. Schoomf-spatula-serve, all in under ten seconds: that's how it'll be when I'm at Number 10. A nation will rejoice.

Beyond

The Gate, NE1 5RE
'Cheap'

Well, nobody can say I haven't tried to give Beyond a fair crack of the whip before I stick the boot in. I've been here on numerous occasions over the years, with different people, under different circumstances, and it's always, always been cack. Despite the change from its original virginal white to standard pub-issue purple, this place still retains, and will always have, all the cosy ambience of a chain hotel lobby, and it fair takes me back to the times I've stood in some cheap European reception area arguing the toss over the room rate in hopelessly inept French with a poor teenager on the minimum wage. Over-friendly bar staff with League Two footballer mullets serve up shockingly-priced beer to unsuspecting after-work punters whose only crime is fancying a change from their usual venue, while evenings bring in the sort of arsewits who like to give off an air of sophistication, as if getting ripped off in a leisure mall bar makes you some sort of debutante. The nipple who served me last time had an unnerving habit of winking at me; whether he was trying to communicate 'I understand your order', or 'Mmm. Good choice of terrible beer', or 'Meet me in the shitters in five, handsome' is not something I want to ponder too deeply. I wasn't going to go back for another round to find out, that's for sure. And now that the pocket-plundering restaurant to the left of the bar has been ditched and walled off, each peak time has the same number of people as before, but jammed into a smaller space, with every one of them obeying the first rule of group drinking: you always have to put up with what the biggest cunt in the group wants. And bearing in mind that even the most normal member of these groups is still a fucking mallrat, a fool who'd tolerate any number of shit bars as

251

long as they didn't get rained on going between them, then this place doesn't really strike me as somewhere I'd want to strike up a casual conversation with a stranger. Add some grinning dickhead of a toilet attendant pouncing on you and showering you with Eau de Donkey's Dong every time you go for a widdle, and you really have got an experience to rival root canal surgery. It's 'Beyond' the fucking joke.

For: I liked that strange shaped glitterball. But that was all.
Against: This is the future of the pub. All bars will be like this unless we join together and take a stand. And I mean it.

I didn't see this, but my missus tells me that when she was on her way to the bogs, she saw the lasses behind the bar were doing all that 'mwah, mwah' air kissing on shift change over. You're a barmaid in a mall in Newcastle, love. You are not Naomi Campbell. Please try to understand that.

Hide

The Gate, NE1 5RF
'A shining example'

I was once of the opinion that Hide was the only bar in The Gate leisure complex with any merit. That was based on an impromptu pint after work on a Tuesday, and bears no relation to what we found on our prime time Friday night refresher. Hide is appalling. Situated in the Dockside area of The Gate, at least a mile from the nearest waterway - unless you count Newgate Street's legendary flash flood zones in the pissing rain - Hide is a shining example of how to create a bar with no character, no depth and no pride. Run by a chain, designed with contempt and staffed with no real interest, this is a shocker even for a mall bar. And from what I can remember of the last time I was here, it looks like people have been pinching stuff since it opened, leaving only the glued-down black and white tiles and the leather pouffes, the ones nobody with a spine would ever find comfortable enough to

steal. There aren't even any real punters to discuss, just an endless parade of spotty, gum-chewing adolescents in hoop earrings
and cropped sportswear, scowling their way to the bogs and back
out again. I'm looking at their pasty faces as they pass, and suddenly I realise why the English are getting progressively uglier.
This is why: the good Lord in His wisdom has provided for the
people the miracle of public transport. In His omnipotence, He
bestowed upon mankind the intelligence to make use of the
Earth's natural resources, like oil and metals and rubber, and He
trusted us to use His gifts with care. The trouble is, by the time
the average teenager on an English estate - yours, mine, anyone's
you care to name - has realised that the big moving thing with
the wheels and windows is there to take you to other places, and
not just for hurling rocks at, they're already the proud parent of
seven puking, dribbling kids with their equally rodent-faced next-
door neighbour. Those children are outside in the mall, and their
mothers are in here, getting on my fucking tit ends. Finally, I
have to see what the hell is so fascinating back there, so I disen-
tangle my legs from the booth and hobble to the lavs. And this is
what I see while I'm splashing my wages into the trough: a huge
price comparison chart above the urinals, like a breakdown of the
weekly shop, totting up how much you'd save if you bought every
item on the drinks menu here instead of in Tiger Tiger or Mood.
Well, that's me convinced. That's the only way I could stay here
for more than a solitary jar, by working my way through the list
until the tears flowed and I no longer knew or cared about who I
used to be. What a fucking night that'd be. Is next Saturday OK
for you?

For: Why not take up their special offer and hire your own booth
for that big sporting occasion?
Against: And then sit wedged in and cramped, with your face an
inch off the TV screen, until the Deep Vein Thrombosis kicks in.

*Hoop earrings and natural resources: some thoughts. Can there
be greater evidence of the stupidity of the human race than the
concept of 'precious' metals? How can one sort of metal dug
from the ground be of more value than another? Why isn't, say,*

tin stashed away in the vaults? Yes, I understand its rarity, the nature of status symbols and 'Do you know how much this costs?' But why? How did it become so sought-after in the first place? What does it do? I'll tell you: it does nothing, except say 'I am rich and I am flaunting it,' or 'I am poor and I'm trying to look like I have something to flaunt.' And when Mammon's carefully constructed economic fabric rips at the seams, when hyperinflation hits and we're all carrying home piles of worthless currency in Netto bags, who will be the ones with the smug grins and the deluxe pizza menus? The ones with the lump of fucking yellow metal buried in the allotment, that's who.

Keel Row

The Gate, NE1 5RE
'Kids are scum, too'

The Wetherspoon chain specialising in cod-authentic traditional bars has recently branched out into catering for the more discerning, upmarket customer under their Lloyds No.1 brand. And this place, the Keel Row, is an example of how they hope to make their riches. Take one carpet off-cut from the colour-blind range, add a selection of flat-pack, self-assembly, black ash effect furniture from the Argos catalogue, circa 1985, and then turn the lights down really low and hope that people don't notice how crap everything is. Fair enough, it's nice to have a bit of gloom and atmosphere in a bar, but when you can't see where you're going, it tends to be a bit of a health hazard. Take that barely visible spindly branch thing, like an upturned witch's broom, on the wall by the quiz machine. The damn thing nearly took my fucking eye out and I'm not lying just to get the sympathy vote. Like a dying man heading for the bright light at the end of the tunnel, we made for the crappy *Saturday Night Fever* dance floor on the off chance of actually being able to see something. Oh, we saw something, alright: reams upon reams of menu pages advertising vodka-Red Bull combinations and child-sized food portions available in the - blink, blink, shit it's real - family area at the back of the bar. Look, I might as well spell this out since nobody else seems willing to do it: anyone who takes kids to the pub is obviously scum. There can be no argument about that. And their kids are scum, too. So, you turn up at the pub expecting a relaxing pint and some adult conversation, and what happens? You get irritating little bastards barging their way past you to their tables, screaming the bloody place down 'cause they can't have another Coke and their fish fingers haven't got peas for eyes like it said on the menu, and then being dragged back out by the wrist after they've shown Mummy and Daddy up. You little fuckers. I don't care if you are top of your class: you spill my pint and you get a slap in the face. Christ almighty, this bar is shite. Not even the dirt-cheap beer is enough to bring me back here again.

For: The seats outside have an unrivalled view of an escalator and a cash point.
Against: If you sniffed the contents of a vacuum cleaner bag, puked on the floor, left it to dry, hoovered it up, then sniffed it again, you still wouldn't come close to the awful smell we encountered by the tables to the right the last time we were in.

The Keel Row is the darkest bar in the darkest mall. I hate the dark. Not like Mummy-leave-the-light-on, but in that pathetic SAD way, the one that gives me carte blanche to act like an utter twat from October to March. I only mention this because I'm sitting here at work, skiving, and across the other side of the office they're covering the windows up with the panels from the air conditioning. No matter where you toil, you're subjected to a constant penny-pinching squeeze, with corners cut and luxuries slashed to make the brand lean, mean and more obscene. Bring your own coffee, I can understand. Pay for your own parking, yes. Chip in for your protective clothing, maybe. But provide your own fucking daylight? Now that's just taking the piss.

Mood

The Gate, Newgate Street, NE1 5TG
'Someone is gonna get lamped'

So, I walk through the portals and survey the decor, and I'm thinking, 'Mmm, yes. Heavy Gaudi influence, with strong elements of Gothic and Moorish, coupled with striking wrought iron and almost breathtaking use of catenary arches.' My mind races as I try to remember which of Gaudi's works this most closely resembles: is it the secular splendour of the Palau Güell, or the fairytale façade of Casa Batlló? Maybe this incredible interior is most redolent of the little-known but supremely sumptuous Puerta de la Finca Miralles. And then my learned companion captures the very essence of the building with his carefully worded summary: 'Wha-hey! It's just like Noel's House Party in here!' He's right, you know. The staircase looks just like the one the bearded goon used to bound down every week, before his wilderness years and subsequent Deal Or No Deal resurrection. On first impressions Mood is better than any bar in a shopping mall 'village' has a right to be, and scores extra points for letting in any old riff-raff, which is more than can be said for the door policy of 'Too old, too young, too pretty, too bloody ugly' Tiger Tiger out the front. The beer's cheap enough, at least in the afternoon, and there's a complete absence of the over-officious 'touch NOWT' stupidity you get in some bars. The communal bathroom area is a novelty, though how it'll pan out at pissing in the sink time when the pub turns into a club after 11 o'clock is anyone's guess. I can guarantee someone is gonna get lamped by the bog doors, though. Two floors provide plenty of space for all manner of punters, from strimmer-cut fashion victims to tanked up match goers; from office girls after work to shopping families. That gives me an idea: why not pull up a stool and listen to bag-laden pensioners trying to explain away the huge abstract images of ladies' front bottoms on all the windows to their inquisitive young charges? I can see it now: 'Well, Connor, they're just lines to try to hide the escalators outside and to make the beerbar a nicer place to sit in.' Little Connor thinks for a minute, and then pipes up: 'Cor, Grandma, you know tons! And I thought they were twenty foot high fannies, an' all...'

For: The massive screens for live sports are way, way over the head height of even the lankiest twat.
Against: The constant stench that is beyond mere vomit and into human decay.

I think I've whinged before about my problems with depth perception, and about how I have real bother walking into glass because I just can't see it. Coming out of Mood before the match, slightly the worse for wear, I see what I think are two doors and, seeing my mates go through the one on the right I look at the one on the left and think, 'Right. These bastards aren't going to get me this time. That's an open door and this is a window.' So I sidle up to it, practically checking my barnet in my reflection and, would you believe it, there's nothing there. No glass, no nothing. I'm pressing thin air like some two-bit mime artist and the bouncers are pissing themselves. What the hell is wrong with me?

Opera Piano Bar

The Gate, Newgate Street, NE1 5RE
'Tremendous'

I am in hell. I am at the bar of a pitch-black pub in the already dismal Gate complex, and I am standing underneath a mirrored ceiling, peering over at the finest quality Dralon upholstery. The barmaid is struggling vainly with the cocktail menu, and she has just told the lad being served before us that this is the bar with no beer. Not as a general policy, you understand: opening time just took them by surprise again, and the draught's off. So, I pay through the nose for our bottles of Belgian-brewed Mexican lager and, pausing only to wonder how a bar this dark can safely be strewn with nigh-on invisible glass tables, I slump down in my seat. There's a couple in the corner. They're forty-odd; he's like a whippet with a traffic cone on its muzzle, and she's like a gable end. And they're snogging. Not just a delicate peck, or a respectful loving embrace, but a full on neck-fest, like two charvers in a bus shelter, ripped to the tits on Diamond White. I think he's getting his tops, too. It's horrific, and heaven knows how I'm going to make it to the end of my overpriced Corona without fetching up my lunch. Inevitably, there's a lull in our conversation, and I realise that what I had initially taken for the hum of the air conditioning is actually the bar's choice of music. In the absence of a real piano player it's Omar, it's the Brand New Heavies, and it's ambient lounge-jazz. Tremendous. All I need now is a li'l bit of M People and blood will be shed. Outside there's a commotion. I can see they need to leave the door open to make passers-by realise that there's a bar here and not just a dark, empty retail unit, but just listen to those clowns out there in the mall. There's not one of them who wouldn't benefit from an iron bar right in the kisser. Meanwhile, back in the bar, the DVD player's showing Ocean's 11, as if the sophisticated, sharp-dressed, wealthy casino goer is the sort of market Opera are aiming for or, more worryingly, think they have. Not even close, not unless George Clooney's been shopping at TK Maxx. Staring really hard at the promotional literature I notice - among the spelling mistakes - the buzzwords for the Opera experience. Finest cocktails? Ambient atmosphere? Class? I snort, derisively and justifiably. This is the sort of place you'd struggle to find 'classy' if you'd just done a twelve-stretch at Her Majesty's pleasure, pissing in a bucket and drinking rainwater. It's awful. Christ, my eyes. Surely they could have put in something other than a wall full of illuminated bottles to lift the murk. I head to the toilets, hoping to relieve, in addition to my bladder, the tension behind my poor straining lenses. And this is when I find that Opera shares the pissers with Beyond next door. It's not even a new bar! It's clearly just the failed restaurant bit of Beyond given a coat of paint (brown, naturally) and a new sign to hoodwink the punters. What an absolute debacle. Imagine if I offered a bike rack for sale on eBay and then, when the poor sap with the winning bid paid up, said, 'Sorry, it's not technically bicycle storage: it's actually my arse.' There'd be a fucking rabbit off, wouldn't there? How come this lot can get away with it, then? C'mon, tell me. It's a gyp, a sham and an absolute fucking disgrace, and we fell for it, like the sad, grasping losers we are.

For: Go in through Opera, use the bogs out the back, and leave through Beyond. No shame, no embarrassment, no charge.
Against: Every time a new bar opens in the frigging Gate, we always think, 'Well, it can't get any worse.' Tiger Tiger, Bar Bannatyne, even the Keel Row, you have our humblest apologies. THIS bar is clearly rock bottom.

This disgusting Gate complex was built on the site of the old Mayfair Ballroom, a venue that was thriving until some cunt demolished it specifically for the purpose of building the mall. If you were to drop a plumb line from the bar in Opera, while you might not hit where the stage used to be, you'd certainly leave it hanging somewhere near the merchandise tables. The Mayfair: scene of legendary gigs and landmarks in my musical history, from the Sigue Sigue Sputnik swindle to Nirvana just as they broke. And what does the fucking Gate - and Opera in particular - have as entertainment? Sinatra tribute acts. Whoever gave the planning go-ahead should be publicly castrated.

Players

The Gate, Newgate Street, NE1 5TG
'Copyright-be-damned'

There's an old Newcastle tradition of fingering the latest craze amongst the kids, churning out cheap copies and then flogging them from a barrow or amongst the seagull shit on the Quayside market. From Rubik cubes to Sudoku; from Frankie Says T-shirts to Crazy Frog hoodies; from Tamagotchis to Roboraptors; they've all been there under a grubby tarpaulin, and they're all as tacky as fuck. One thing you can guarantee is that whatever's fashionable will be exploited for the masses, regardless of whether the original was any bloody cop, and while you or I may think, 'Eh?!

Why?', rest assured there'll be some fucking idiot along in a minute keen to part with his readies. And this bar, Players, this
shameless cash-in, is no more and no less than a piss-poor, toxic
paint, fall-apart-in-your-hands version of the already-hopeless
Sports Café on Grainger Street, together with a few copyright-be-
damned bits from other equally rank places. It truly is fucking
awful. Fair enough, they boast the biggest telly in Newcastle, but
two things marred my viewing enjoyment just a tad. One, the
pain-in-the-arse yappy - as opposed to chin-stroking - DJ shouting
endless shite about drinks promotions (Foster's is not a premium
lager, you fucking chump); and two, the antics of the Players All-
Stars dancing girls on the high podium in middle of the bar and
right in front of the bastard screen. Laugh as I might at the woefully unchoreographed dirty dancing - you could have dragged in
two lasses at gunpoint from any bus queue you care to name for a
better performance - when I'm in a sports bar I want to see
Ameobi's Greatest Hat-tricks and not some dumb bints gyrating
over-enthusiastically for a quid an hour. A bit less 'Tits oot!' and
more 'Siddoon!' wouldn't come amiss. And the dancers are the
best part of the whole sorry experience. If you're looking for
something out of the ordinary in the rest of the bar, then forget
it; it's just a big round room with two floors, the gallery above
having as little to recommend as the non-entity below. If you
want pool tables, go to a snooker hall; if you want dance floors,
go clubbing; and if you're after ever-changing lighting effects,
then drink Domestos and whack yourself with a mallet. You can
get everything you get here just by sacking off the insulting fac-
simile and going elsewhere. Believe me, you'd feel less ashamed
afterwards. There it is then; and you're welcome to every last
over-polished inch of it. You can keep the laminate flooring and
the massive padded cell effect on the TV wall. Help yourself to
the wall covering that's so godawful it's hard to tell where the
bogs end and the bar begins. Take it all and shove it. And if this
place actually is your thing, then you'd better get along sharpish,
since some other type of bar will be trendy in a few months, and
all this bandwagoning crap will be out the back in the skip. Until
then, though: Get yer white sports socks, three pairs for a pound.

For: It's impossible to come up with a 'for' when this bar aims to combine the very worst bits of Shearer's and Sam Jack's.
Against: I don't think this is the final piece in the horrifying Gate jigsaw. I'm sure there's just enough room to cram in one more terrible bar.

For all their pouting and hip-grinding, those hapless lasses on the podium reminded me of nothing so much as Boyzone's legendary non-singing debut on Irish TV's Late Late Show with Gay Byrne. Just in case you've so far had enough of a life to avoid all those Ladgeful Telly Moments rundowns, here's a brief précis of the performance. 'Ah, yer a fine lookin' bunch o' lads, so ye are. Have ye got a song for us?' No. 'What about some anecdotes?' Not really, Gay. 'Sure, what can ye do for us?' Well, Gay, we can chuck ourselves about like tits on a trampoline on live television. 'Grand. Off ye go'. Picture Ronan Keating bodypopping with his flat cap on sideways: these girls weren't far behind in the embarrassment stakes, I'll tell you now.

Sam Jack's
The Gate, Newgate Street, NE1 5TG
'Not even after thirteen Bacardi Breezers'

It's not very often I feel I have to apologise to friends for taking them to a bar, but after our pre-match pint in Sam Jack's, I had to do just that. It wasn't my round so I can't be 100% sure, but the lads swear blind that the barmaid came up to them dressed in a cowboy hat and pink gingham and drawled, 'Howdy! What can I get y'all?' and that was just for starters. Welcome, pardners, to Sam Jack's, NewcastleGateshead's second western-style saloon bar, the place they're already calling a poor man's Buffalo Joe's. Stupid hats, cowboy pictures, and a humiliating rodeo bull at the front of the pub; they're all there to make you wish you'd gone somewhere else. Like the dentist's, for example. Sam Jack's bills itself above its entrance as a 'Good Time Educator' but the only link to education I could find was the DJ, struggling against the cavernous acoustics, whose banter sounded exactly like the 'Mwah maa mwah' teacher from the old Charlie Brown cartoons. And she knew fuck all about good times, not even after thirteen Bacardi Breezers. The pub's really just a big shed with a mezzanine level, populated here and there by sporadic groups of punters who really should be old enough to know better. To liven the place up they keep getting regimented dancing girls - fully clothed, tragically - to arse about on the platforms above the bar, cavorting like Madonna in that stupid video where she pretends to be a cowgirl. If there's not someone pointing a Smith & Wesson at their heads before they get up there then I want to know why. Seriously, it was that pitiful. One pint and we were off, scratching our heads as to why the designers even bothered, crying out for a bar with just a smidgen of sanity. We were followed by the dancing girls on the way out, pompomming away the last of their self-respect in the doorway in an attempt to pull in the passers-by. Unbelievable.

For: I would have said the cheap beer, but imagining the place stuffed full of whooping arseclowns off their faces on two-for-one makes my skin crawl.

Against: They've had a refit since we wrote the review. Three things and three things only have changed: They've smashed the displays of antlers to make room for big screen tellies; the 'fully clothed, tragically' dancing girls have now given way to astonishingly inept pre-match strippers; and the bucking bronco has clearly legged it in shame. Everything else remains.

Much as it made me weep to do so, I used the appalling name NewcastleGateshead simply because Buffalo Joe's is on the other side of the river. That's the way the box-tickers in committee-land want you to refer to the two distinct places from now on: all one word with a capital G in the middle, as part of a pitiful attempt at a Budapest-style merger. Think what we'll amount to: pointlessly but inexorably linked, every mention of the proud city of Newcastle will be tarnished by what amounts to no more than the geographical Schnorbitz, with the scabby mutt dragged forlornly behind on a leash. Great.

Tiger Tiger

The Gate, Newgate Street, NE1 5RE
'Denim's fighting fabric'

One of the most prominent bars in The Gate leisure complex, Tiger Tiger boasts the very latest in up-market drinking experiences. With seven differently themed rooms, you can indulge your senses as you relax with the freshest vibes and most happening sounds. Sorry. I'm lying again. Whether you're young or old, black or white, rich or poor, you're not getting in, and that's final. Let's be honest here: I could tell you there's a frigging live unicorn roaming around the bar on the top floor, and there'd be no way on earth you could call me a liar. Everyone I've spoken to about Tiger Tiger - and every two-bit hard luck 'ruined birthday' story in the papers - has a different excuse for why the bouncers won't let you in. It could be anything: pushing or blushing, your shoes or tattoos, whatever the ballbag on the door pulls from the tombola this week. Fair enough, refuse people entry for trying to carry weapons, or for being blind drunk, but excluding the punters on the grounds of, say, the material they're wearing does seem a little bit bloody childish. 'Sorry, son: denim's fighting fabric.' Maybe they're right, though. When I'm wearing dress pants or, like, a nice fresh pair of chinos, I'm an honest and upstanding member of society, but once I pull my jeans on, I start eating babies and making replica B-52 bombers out of my own turds. Dearie, dearie me. So, the decor, like you care, is typical uninspiring, modern-bar, slap-it-up-and-paint-it-brown stuff, with a wacky touch here and an amusing gadget there. This is a pub that's so obsessed with laminate flooring, they've got it up the fucking walls an' all. And if you've managed to get as far as the bar, in addition to the insult of the scattershot dress code, you're then smacked in the mouth by the bloody prices. Once legendary for being too obtuse and too fucking incompetent to serve pints, Tiger Tiger are now slapping up posters telling you that they now do draught, as if it's something to brag about. It's like they're saying, 'Draught! Great idea, huh?! We thought of that! Aren't we fantastic?! Mind if we charge you double?!' Christ, this place really blackens my shite. I'd tell you to avoid it, but what's the bastard point? I might as well tell you to avoid winning the Lottery, for all the chance you have of actually experiencing it.

For: You can be excused for having one pint - as a souvenir to say you got in...

Against: ...but if you go back to the bar for so much as a little bendy straw, you want a bullet in the back of your skull.

A few words on their function room upstairs: Anyone who bought or moved into a house in the early '80s and had to rip out the nightmare brown and orange 'contemporary '70s' kitchen will scratch their heads in bewilderment as to why these idiots have painstakingly recreated the whole look for their sleek modern bar.

Bigg Market

'A disgusting melange of vomit, pizza boxes, and bottle tops between cobbles; a shameful display of boarded up restaurants, eight-inch stilettos and nightly carnage; a veritable blot on the landscape. This is the area that is unaware of the dividing line between tantalising midriff and fat fucking gut. This is the epicentre of Newcastle's legendary nightlife. And this is enough to make a grown man weep. Screw this: you're not paying me anywhere near enough to put up with this crap. I'm offski.' – Norman Undercroft, Historian.

Balmbra's Reflex

5 Cloth Market, NE1 1EE
'Clueless Brummie fuckers'

We haven't been to Balmbra's for ages following the embarrassing furore there a couple of years ago; embarrassing for Mitchells and Butlers, that is. It's not very often you get a motion in Parliament to stop a pub chain from pissing around with stuff - more's the pity - but the saga of this place tells where it all kicked off. And here, in lieu of a review, we're going to explain how. Once upon a time those clueless Brummie fuckers at Mitchells and Butlers decided that, to satisfy their brand value of 'social responsibility' (see their website - I'm not making this up), the former music hall concept of Balmbra's was redundant, and that the area would be better served by a shitty '80s theme bar called Reflex. And even though they obviously they hadn't been in for a while, since it already WAS a shitty '80s theme bar in all but name, this got the politicians up in arms, yelling about the 'blatant disregard for Tyneside' and about how the proposed changes were 'deeply resented by the people of the area'. M&B then stated their case, sort of along the lines of, 'Tough. The kids who pay their money don't give a fuck about history, so why should we?' And you can see their point: how could over a hundred years of North East tradition - immortalised in the song *The Blaydon Races*, sung by 52,000 every other week at St James' Park - compare with the cultural might of a hit by Birmingham's own Duran Duran? Still, anxious not to shoot themselves in the shitter, M&B hammered out a compromise of paying the sign writers a couple of hours of overtime to prefix the tacky wire puzzle-effect logo with the word 'Balmbra's'. This, apparently, meant that the whiners would be happy while the 'well-recognised and popular Reflex branding [would be] there to reassure our existing customers and to attract new ones'. Oh aye, and they agreed to keep the blue plaque in the doorway. The bottom line is, though, that they still fucking got away with it, and there it sits today, forlorn and tainted with derelict shite either side. I'm not going to claim any sort of nostalgia for what was there before. I hated it when it was still just Balmbra's, and I could list any number of complaints about unpleasantness I encountered, like the toilet troughs full of broken glass, and the pig-fucking-obstinate bar staff who seemed to think that a pub full of punters wearing Toon shirts would rather listen to Atomic Kitten than hear live reports on Sunderland getting relegated. Even before the Mitchells and Butlers debacle, the place had been wrecked, mangled, battered and desecrated beyond all hope of salvation. But it's the principle that counts, and without principles where are we? Up a lapdancer's pole with a feather up our arses, probably.

For: Old time music hall is the equivalent of the modern DJ bar, which means that, sooner or later, with the passing of time and a change in fashion, we'll be rid forever of the dicks with the decks.

Against: Could have been a legend, chose to be a fun pub. What a fucking waste.

The bar stinks like the time I drunkenly made the mistake of peering into the sanitary bins in the unisex bogs in the missus' halls of residence. I could never forget that stench. Well, that's me skipping the jam roly-poly for pudding, then.

Bar M

7 St Nicholas Street, NE1 1RE
'And, inevitably, I'm going to complain.'

We're always ranting on about refits ruining pubs and stripping out all the character. Well, I'm happy to report that, despite its last name change from Masters to Bar M, little has ever changed about this place: I hated it when I first came here in 1986 and I still hate it now. I'm fairly certain that they've been playing the same song all these years, the one that goes 'du-du-du-du', and at a volume that makes ordering anything more complicated than a pint (like, say, two pints) virtually impossible. Bar M is far and away the smelliest bar in the whole wide world. It. Stinks. From the front door to the back end, there's a different appalling stench every ten feet: sweaty pits and cheesy bots, litter trays and budgie cages, ripe gorgonzola and rotting halibut, they're all there to turn your stomach inside out. Someone - it ain't going to be me - ought to tell them that one of the big lighting panels on the ceiling at the far end seems to have a crumpled corpse above it; maybe if they shovelled that out there'd be an improvement in the aroma. This place is laid out in an L-shape, with some Hollywood illuminated stairs at the back, giving you a good view of curtain-parting g-strings and bits of stray bog roll wedged in flabby butt cracks if you stand underneath, plus a shower of tab ends kicked down from above and into your beer. Those stairs are also fucking treacherous, as reported by many a soon-to-be ex-friend who's tumbled down them after a few Cheeky Vimtos. Speaking as the Dog's resident art-critic ('Art? It's shit'), I can tell you that the design on the sticky carpet here matches the pictures on the walls, and looks suspiciously like the work of that mad Hundertwasser geezer in Vienna, the bloke who took run-down city buildings and turned them into fairytale versions of the Byker Wall. I appreciate that you might not know what the fuck I'm on about here, but I'm going to elaborate and disappear up my own arse simply because I DO NOT want to talk about Bar M for any longer than is absolutely necessary. I've seen a lot of his stuff first hand, I have, in his wonky little museum near the muddy Danube. And, inevitably, I'm going to complain. Normally, when you're feeling cultural and la-di-dah, and you go to an art gallery when it isn't even raining, you expect a bit of class. But instead of oil on canvas, or gouache on hand-made paper, with this fucking joker it was, like, felt pen on envelope. And the bastards charged us a tenner just to get in. Bloody Austrians: never trust any nation that aspires to be German.

For: City centre regeneration has reached Bar M. The grilles on the windows like those on an empty Elswick Road council flat have been removed and refitted with glass. Plenty of brick-lobbing room in the alleyway, too.
Against: The punters. Big gangs of lads, big gangs of lasses, all of them looking for love but too stupid to do anything to find it. Look, I don't want to come over all David Attenborough here, but if you want to get into the mating game you've got to, like, mix. You think someone's just gonna come and lick your lollipop while you're standing there? Actually, don't answer that.

As I'm sure I've already said, I like an early start and an early finish when I'm out on the drink. Avoiding the late-night violence is how I've managed to keep up the enthusiasm to write these idiot reviews. My bus stop is just down from Bar M, and every time I'm there on a Friday night, I see them loading up the coach to Tall Trees - or the Shagging Wagon, as it should be known - at the adjacent stop. I use the word coach in the loosest possible sense: third-world countries have better quality vehicles than that, and I'm willing to bet they aren't crammed full of desperate social retards and spattered with blood, piss, puke and semen. How fucking tragic do you have to be to go to smogland because you can't pull in Newcastle? I've started hanging around truck stops, finding the most exhausted-looking long distance drivers, and drugging their cuppas in the hope of causing a motorway pile-up between Newcastle and Yarm. I'd like to think Darwin would approve.

Beehive Hotel
2 High Bridge, NE1 1EN
'Eat, drink, sleep and shite'

If you judged the Beehive purely on its decor, you'd have a fine example of a well-kept heritage pub, with Burmantoft tiling, ornate carved ceilings and tons of authentic historical detail. You can guarantee, though, that when the man from the tourist board arrived with his clipboard he'd be told to fuck off in no uncertain terms, and his photographer would be buzzing the office for an insurance form before he'd even got his lens cap off. The Beehive is - and there's no getting away from it - a wee bit on the rough side. But don't let me put you off. After all, there's rough and there's rough, and I've never had any grief in here, despite my condescending manner and my supremely punchable face. It really depends on when you go, I'd say; for my money, as long as you arrive at a time that the price list classes as Level 1 - Monday to Thursday - then I think the emphasis tends to be on cheap beer, best of order, and very little fighting. (This might just be a load of bollocks that I've invented to fill up space; I can't imagine anyone paying a Level 2 premium to get their head stoved in.) If you're that bothered about personal safety, you can get a good idea of what to expect from the outside, through the huge windows lined constantly with haggard old bastards who look like they eat, drink, sleep and shite on their stools, although that isn't the full punter range by any means. While I can honestly say we were standing next to a honking old duffer on his own, muttering down the sleeves of his demob suit, that would be to ignore the generous helping of chatting couples, fact-packed quiz-jockeys, young lasses sipping wine and, over in the corner, Frank N Furter and Janet Weiss on their way to the Theatre Royal. You know, this place isn't all that bad, and it's a hell of a lot better than what you've been fearing in all the years you've been passing it by. Fair enough, maybe the first thing you notice is that you're knee-deep in dog-ends, and maybe it is looking a bit tatty in places, but it still remains an atmospheric little boozer serving a good pint at a sensible price, with no fucking about or inescapable beats. And if the jukebox choices are rubbish or there's sod all on telly, you can always sit and watch the blokes from the council cleaning up all the shattered glass and broken teeth in the Bigg Market from the night before.

For: A down-to-earth traditional pub. You know, the type that people - as any leisure chain will tell you - apparently don't want any more.
Against: The toilets were absolutely minging, and that was noticed from outside the bog door. Jesus, what a Judi Dench.

And speaking of lavs, there's a view from the Beehive's upper level of the Bigg Market's public toilets. These loos - according to the campaigners who want to see them afforded listed status - are some of the best still-functioning Victorian conveniences in Britain today. It's a valid point, I suppose, but I don't support their preservation as a matter of aesthetics, but as one of simple financial sense. The Bigg Market needs public pissers to stop it turning into a torrent of wee at closing time, from KFC down to the job shop, but installing the fancy new ones would just attract enraged spotty hooligans and kebab-clutching fornicators, eager to trash them on general principle. As for the ancient underground ones, well, have you been in them lately? Unwreckable doesn't even scratch the surface.

Blackie Boy

11 Groat Market, NE1 1UQ
'I simply cannot be arsed today'

In 1967, high on amphetamines and full of despair, the late Johnny Cash crawled into Nicajack Cave in Tennessee and waited to die. 'If I crawled in far enough,' he said, 'I'd never be able to find my way back out, and nobody would be able to locate me until after I was dead'. I feel like that whenever I hobble into the Blackie Boy although, admittedly, I have a fair bit in the way of creature comforts and nothing more troublesome on my mind than making it through the hangover to the three o'clock kick off. The Blackie Boy is my post-Friday night, pre-Saturday match boozer, and it's far and away the darkest, gloomiest bar the Bigg Market will ever know. I can think of no better pub opposite the back of the Pig & Whistle for when you've got a head like a Wurlitzer, a creak in your bones like a ship in a storm, and sadness in your soul that says, 'I simply cannot be arsed today.' So you slump in the armchair beside the roaring fire, stare vacantly at the stained glass fittings, and grumble yourself back to health. And as your body starts to thaw and your eyes regain focus, you might pull a weighty tome from the dusty bookshelves, before putting it straight back in disgust and reaching for a wetwipe. Your pint is soothingly poor, the atmosphere comfortingly dead, and your fellow punters want nothing more than a nod of recognition that you are brothers in pain. It's blissful. Of course, this is MY Blackie Boy I'm describing, in the way that only I see it. You, on the other hand, think I'm on about a completely different pub, don't you? The Blackie Boy you know is the heaving meat market on a Saturday night, but I'm ever so tired and I'd rather you didn't make me think too hard about that. And in my fragile state I'd prefer not to remember that everyone knows someone who's been tempted into the adjoining back lane and engaged in an impromptu act of knee-buckling love over the wheelie bins, before returning, breathless and spent, to rinse away the evidence with ice from the Smirnoff bucket. Oh, that lane! It's so romantic! Who needs oysters, champagne or springtime in Rome, when that tart, pissy aroma is the only aphrodisiac your heart could desire?

For: The signs on the toilet doors: 'Dick' and 'Fanny'.
Against: Pick the wrong chair to collapse into and you'll break your arse in three.

You're interested in the Blackie Boy's bookshelves? You like stories? Then here's an apocryphal tale you might just enjoy. Once upon a time, there was a big, bad boss who worked for the street cleaning department at the council. The big, bad boss couldn't control his big, bad bladder and, after drinking heavily in the Blackie Boy's function room one night, was nabbed urinating - some say in the street, some say down the stairs - by a handsome prince from, you've guessed it, the street cleaning department at the council. And he was bollocked and spanked and disciplined by the king, and they all lived happily ever after. Sorry, did I say this story was apocryphal? It's apocryphal in as much as the Chronicle had it splashed - huh huh huh - all over their front page, with suitably lurid headlines. Me, I'd have rubbed his fucking nose in it, too. Dirty dog.

Bzar

5-7 Groat Market, NE1 1UQ
'Eyes of a shithouse rat'

Well, what a fucking gyp this turned out to be. Fair enough we might not have scrutinised the small print on the flyers - or any of the print for that matter - but when Bzar advertised itself as a karaoke bar, then karaoke is what we expected to find, only in a less life-threatening way than you'd find in the Grainger Market hellholes. So, karaoke on Mondays only, is it? You could have fucking well told us. It'd been a while since we'd darkened the doors of Bzar, on a hungover Saturday afternoon just after it had changed from the Groat House to the predictive text-baffling Bzar, at which point the colour scheme seemed to be a heady mix of white and white with accents of white. Returning to look at it through the gimlet eyes of a shithouse rat and not the sheep's fannies we'd been cursed to squint through last time, we noticed a definite brightening up of the decor, with glitter balls, comedy art deco lamps, ghostly paintings, and exposed brick pillars. Nothing out of the ordinary there. And even though, down the far end, there's a carpet that would rival the one in your nearest Burger 'n' Bowl ten-pin delinquent magnet, there's nothing we saw here to really make anyone kick off. But what did have us cursing and scowling and vowing never to make such a dumb-assed drinking decision again was the rest of it; the piss-taking, vomit-making, chair-shaking volume from the shit-for-brains in charge of the music, the fun-fighting jack-the-lad punters, and the beer. Christ, that beer. I can't vouch for every pint ever poured in Bzar, and for libel's sake I'm going to say - through gritted teeth - that I'm sure they got it right at some point that weekend, but the stuff we got served was nowt but hot piss, or at least was warm enough to rinse your knackersack in without leaving you squealing like a piglet. Whose stupid idea was it to come here? Makes no odds, really. We left, disappointed and unserenaded, and headed for home, our night in ruins. And I remember feeling not just angry as I approached the top of the stairs, but furious enough to stot my glass, the empties of everyone who'd been at the table before us AND all those pints to hand off the nearest insolent, bobbing head. Would the fucker have noticed? I doubt it.

For: There's a door situated half way up the wall on the left hand side. Inaccessible though you or I might deem it, they've still had to visibly padlock the bloody thing to keep the drunken baboons from climbing up there for a laugh.

Against: Bouncers are supposed to be there to protect the customers. Why the hell didn't they warn us on the way in?

Ten years ago this wouldn't have bothered me. Questioning how the fucking hell people can stand this sort of experience is just one of those things you find yourself doing as you grow older, wiser and more explosively frustrated. Example? Ten years ago I wouldn't even have noticed the estate agents, never mind pondered why their letterboxes are never at trouser fly height. Good job I always carry a funnel and a length of rubber tubing.

City Vaults

13-15 Bigg Market, NE1 1UN
'I just miss the seediness'

I'm not really sure what the owners' plan was for this place when they did the refit: they spent billions doing it up, making it into a swish, modern, chilled lounge bar, and then ruined it all by letting the usual Bigg Market riff-raff back in. Like something out of London's Covent Garden, the City Vaults has been brought up to date with space enhancing mirrors, and stylish-yet-functional decking, and then wrecked by grunting morons dressed head-to-toe in snidey Rockport gear. What they've done here - if you remember the old Vault - is glass in the piss-stinking alleyway at the side, and make the whole thing into one big bar. There's a big drop-down screen in the old ramp bit, most likely there to give a central focus to people watching the match on Sky. I take it that idea was meant for evening kick-offs, since you can see bugger all on it during the day, the light shining through from behind giving an effect not entirely unlike watching a pair of beige curtains for ninety minutes. Or Sunderland. Ho ho ho. Carried forward from the old bar's previous lifetime are the 'shock' DJ, looking like he'd rather be anywhere than shouting the same nonsense to the same losers week after week, and the legendary topless totty, giving a half-hearted frug and a quick flash of the norks to whatever's clogging up the charts this week. They've moved the stage to one side instead of at the end of the pub, but it's still a bastard to see what's going on unless you're in the front row. No, wait a minute, I've just remembered that the stage bit goes up behind the bar, to a hidden walkway with holes cut in, so at least you can avoid seeing that fucking idiot Geordie Dancer, if the stupid twat is still making an arse of himself every weekend. It's been a while since I've been in, like. So why do I keep avoiding the place, then? Maybe I just miss the seediness of what was the stickiest floor in the city. Or maybe I just can't bear to admit that - what with the Toon being so bleedin' awful to watch nowadays - that seeing some bored girl take her top off to a Britney Spears 'classic' is the highlight of a match day. Terrible state of affairs either way.

For: The old Vault really was an absolute shitehole.
Against: Have I sworn about that Geordie Dancer yet? Have I sworn enough?

The extended layout has done away with the Ram Jam Inn downstairs, so we'll never have to worry ourselves about reviewing that. Apparently there was some other bar called Steam down there at some point, too. It never even made our 'to do' list, which just goes to show how fucking useless we are.

Fizz Fun Bar

24 Cloth Market, NE1 1EE
'Anorexic poledancers'

Taking over the shit-smeared baton from the Cage Bar - closed down by the filth for drug offences, violence and general mayhem, remember - the very name of Fizz Fun Bar tempted me to not even bother going, and to just sit in the house on my smug, fat arse writing the usual twisted bollocks about people younger and happier than me. But fuck, morbid curiosity and a misplaced sense of duty dragged us in for a couple of quick jars on a cold Saturday night, and left us looking as out of place and unwelcome as a couple of turds on a birthday cake. The bar being mercifully empty at eight bells, we were free to have a good gawp round without some pilled-up juvenile imagining that I was looking for a kicking, so we got to see what looks like contemporary flock wallpaper - if you can imagine anyone being insane enough to make it - mirrors, chairs even, all the stuff the Cage Bar didn't bother with since they knew it'd just get wrecked anyway.

THE BURGLAR'S DOG

There's a podium next to the DJ booth, with a row of poles about a foot apart across the front; I hope to sweet baby Jesus it's a low-budget take on the humiliating cages in the likes of Buffalo Joe's, and not a showcase for some worryingly anorexic pole-dancers. Not even the Bigg Market could be that sick, could it? It's comforting to report in an ever-changing world that, not only were the floors at the mandatory level of stickiness, but the fucking chairs were covered in a film of gloop. It just wouldn't be the same without that traditional clag. I'm not going to pretend we stuck around to see this place in full swing: it's a bloody Bigg Market bar, so it's hardly likely to have poetry recitals and even-song; it's going to have execrable thumping music and epilepsy-bothering lighting displays. It's going to be terrible, but is it really worth getting riled about? Let's be honest: nobody with an ounce of gumption is going to drink here. It's clearly a junior starter bar, catering for kids who want to fuck, fight and fall over. Griping about what goes on here is like bellyaching about not getting much in the way of rational debate from a toddler. So aye, it's absolutely, utterly, irredeemably shite, but what the fuck did I expect? It says 'Fun Bar' on the sign outside: that's the price on the ticket, as that tit Souness used to say after each spirit crushing defeat to lowly opposition. It's designed to be awful, and as long as the kids are learning how to handle their drink in here and not under my bloody feet, I wouldn't have it any other way.

For: Shite though it may be, even a miserable, jaundiced old cunt like me can see that it's still a vast improvement on the bloody Cage Bar.

Against: The place doesn't open until half seven. In at 7.35, served by 7.40, review mentally composed by 7.50, and pint supped up by 8pm at the latest. That only leaves us a maximum of five hours to wash away the shame in decent bars elsewhere.

I'm sticking this bit at the end so I can Tippex it out later without having to butcher the main review. We might be wrong (we usually are), but it looked on our cursory visit as if the new owners are Chinese, so hopefully a bit of fearful stereotyping and lazy prejudice by the shit-thick punters about Triads and the Chinese Mafia might mean a bit less bother and fewer stabbings. Here's to shoddy education and straight-to-DVD Asian cinema.

Flares

31-33 Mosley Street, NE1 1YF
'The staff canteen on Monday lunchtime'

Look, I might as well come clean here. I've been in Flares once, whilst very, very drunk, and even though I'm normally a stone-faced snob, I think I enjoyed it. Ah, here, if you're not going to take me seriously... I also think that I may have pre-empted Ricky Gervais' terrible dancing from *The Office* by a good eighteen months, so it must have been a while ago, but that hardly excuses my actions, does it? Still, it's out in the open now, anyway. The shame of it: I think I'd be less embarrassed telling my folks I'd fallen in love with a goat than owning up to having a half-way decent time in Flares. I don't know what the fuck we were thinking even stepping through the doors, to tell the truth. Let's look at the evidence: it's part of a chain, it's a '70s-themed, groovey (Flares website's own spelling) fun pub, and it was absolutely rotten when it used to be Circus Circus. What on earth possessed us? I obviously don't remember much of what was there or what went where, but that really doesn't matter in a bar like this; what does matter is how fucking mental the overall atmosphere is, especially to sneering, broom-up-the-arse miseries like us. So aye, the '70s theme: the headfuck lights, the Don't Walk: Boogie signs, the mirror balls, the platform heels, the wigs and the glitter. It's all there. I seem to recall you can even buy tons of costume stuff from behind the bar to make your night go with a real swing, but I'll fight to the death anyone who says I even considered putting my hand in my pocket for anything other than the beer. You get the staff dancing all over the place, in the windows and that; you get really cheesy DJs, and I'm talking about mobile disco standard and not the git-beard elitists from your average lounge bar; and you get all the annoyingly infectious tunes you thought you'd purged from your mind. And the punters: hen nights with their amusing pseudonyms – Anal Angie? Blowjob Barbara? Oh, my sides - and stag parties with their attendant violence-for-dignity trade-ins, plus the usual after office forty-something crowd for whom self-esteem is but a distant memory. Ain't gonna bump no more (with no big fat woman), especially not if she's gonna be in the staff canteen on Monday lunchtime. It is, to all intents and purposes, hell on toast. So, did I and would I ever go back after the review visit all those years ago? No. Did I really, unapologetically, enjoy it? Yeah, I suppose so. Maybe that's where we've been going wrong all these years. Maybe we should just put our sad little notebooks away and start strutting our collective stuff. Maybe. More like maybe not.

For: As Thomas Beecham once famously wrote, you should 'Try everything once except folk dancing and incest.' Can't argue with that.
Against: Why does seeing the word 'fun' in print or on the screen make me want to weep?

Right, this is the last time I'm going to try to get this through your thick skull. Flares used to be Circus Circus, but when the Flares that was up the road changed to Reflex, the concept was shipped down here. The place that was Reflex then became Boom! when the people behind Reflex tried to muscle in on the Balmbra's legend, shortly before being told to fuck off in no uncertain terms, hence the appallingly named Balmbra's Reflex just up the hill. What a fucking carry on, and what a fucking waste of time and energy. All of those bars are shite.

Kiss
18 Cloth Market, NE1 1EE
'Includes major surgery'

In the heart of Newcastle's legendary Bigg Market, [insert name of bar here] has been happily serving gassy swill to problem drinkers and borderline psychotics for a good while now. Under-dressed teens and their shame-free mothers shimmy on down to endlessly pounding holiday disco music, while hollering morons whip up a storm behind the turntables. An abandoned wreck of overstuffed wheelie bins by day, [insert name of bar here] comes alive after 8pm, the times when only a lunatic with a death wish would set foot in the Bigg Market without a Kalashnikov. Gangs of brainless turds pile in, squeal and rage over their cut-price alco-pops, and flood back out again, pausing only to make obnoxious eye contact with their prospective sparring partner come the chucking-out time free-for-all. It's hideous, it's embarrassing and it's very, very worrying. Welcome to Faliraki on Tyne. I can honestly say the review visit was one of the worst experiences of my life - and that includes major surgery - and it'll be a long time before I darken the doors of [insert name of bar here] again. Dump.

For: Ample opportunity for Mr Plod to wade in and crack some skulls.
Against: Fuck me, why didn't I think of this one-size-fits-all re-viewing technique before we suffered the rest of the Bigg Market hovels?

My dictionary clearly states that 'Party' is a noun and not a verb. Party is something you have, and not something you do, trust me. The disgraceful appropriation of the American usage by the crème-de-la-shite of our once-proud nation - we invented the fucking English language after all - breaks my fucking heart, it really does.

Liquid
32-36 Cloth Market, NE1 1EE
'Exposure to blinding lights lowers the sperm count'

If they stuck you in Liquid and faced you away from the beer pumps, you'd be hard pushed to recognise this as a bar. You would, I'm certain of it, make the mistake of thinking that this stinking, echoing shed was some sort of slaughterhouse, half-heartedly hosed down for the next truckload of wide-eyed ruminants. You won't be far off, though. Liquid is a horrible single-room bar, devoid of anything whatsoever except walls, floor, pillars and ceiling. I'm not even going to try to describe the paintjob, since it seems to defy classification; I can't see a colour, only shadows, as if Dulux have brought out a range off the edges of the visible spectrum. The last time I came in here - young, foolish and irresistibly handsome - I remember they had some bubble lamps scattered around, as a sop to the 'liquid' theme. Returning now, saggier round the cheeks, eyes and buttocks, and with a hint of an arthritic limp, I find those lamps are nowhere to be seen. They're gone, smashed, and drained, and the only liquid that decorates the place these days is the sloshed beer and the sticky globules of fuck knows what, both inevitable when you allow dangerously stupid people to move about un-cuffed and unmanacled. For such a notoriously raucous bar - you can hear it from the other side of the globe, never mind across the road - I have to admit I'm shocked to see miserable fuckers sitting around at the back of the room, like reluctant greyhounds in the traps. I needn't have worried, because soon it all kicks off, and people start hurling themselves around to what passes for tunes in bars of this terrible ilk. Stick on any late-night schedule-filling TV show, then wait for the adverts, and you will hear what I am hearing now, only at a less lethal volume. Watch in be-musement as yet another compilation of 'darnce anthems' and 'classics from the cluuuubs' is paraded for your indifference by the horrible yappy voice that is mandatory for that type of crap. At least on the adverts the fools shimmying on down are reasonably good looking; in here you just get a parody of Ibiza glamour, with spelk-thin boys circling dirigible-fat girls in an interminable hobble of lust. His weedy biceps display - in footballer-aping Olde English script - tattoos reading Mam & Dad, while sticking out over her see-through white pants is not so much a muffin top as a whole fucking patisserie. And, looking at the blossoming of their courtship, I'm praying that exposure to blinding lights lowers the sperm count. Fucking hell man: how is this volume legal? Why are the Old Bill not outside waiting for the signal to charge in and break it up? I know I'm cracking on a bit, but I've had my fair share of racket. I've been in the front row at a Metallica gig - twice - God damn it. But this is just ridiculous. Why do I put myself through this? I don't stay to finish the pint, never mind long enough to write a thesis, but just have one last peer through the glare to confirm my prejudices, then scarper before the windows finally blow out. Incredible. And I mean that literally.

For: I now don't have to pay to go on that sign language course.
Against: That's offset against the bribes I had to offer my mates to even cross the doors.

If you're on the dancefloor in some £100-in Ibiza superclub, pilled up or on one or whatever the fuck they call it, you're doing your 'thing', and out of the corner of your eye you see someone else doing your thing, what do you do? Do you challenge them for stealing your moves, or do you inch over to them and gimp in their ear, 'Do you want to be my frieeeend?' Freaks on pharmaceuticals; the only chemicals they deserve are ones given American style, intravenously, while strapped to a bed in the presence of the warders, the doctor and the priest with his last rites fact sheet. See what sort of a fucking buzz they get off that.

Pig & Whistle
Cloth Market, NE1 1EE
'A gift-wrapped body bag with a broken zip'

Resurrected in summer 2005 after the three-week spell when it was known as just plain Whistle, the Pig & Whistle has always been one of the shoddiest bars in Newcastle. And guess what? Now it's worse than ever. In addition to being host to the dregs of both ends of the drinking age spectrum - from fresh-faced felons to pensionable pissheads - they're now promoting 'For Your Eyes Only dancers and bikini barmaids before every Newcastle home game!' Go on, go in. Watch indifferently as a parade of desperately unhappy exotic dancers whip their knockers out and climb shiny poles like drunken monkeys up the rigging. Stand astonished as your bottle of expensive-yet-piss-weak lager turns out to be plastic, and think what that says about their trust of their customers. And punch yourself, repeatedly, in the face, genitals and solar plexus, for being dim enough to enter, let alone hand over your entire soul in the search for entertainment. You want me to elaborate on those punters - and why not, since there's absolutely fuck all in the way of decor or anything else to discuss? Fair enough. Look at the junior end of the scale for starters. See the Toon's great white hope, young Steven Taylor, all innocent charm and low-budget haircut? And see the look on his face when he realised his sniper attack routine was fooling nobody in THAT 3-0 defeat to Villa, the Bowyer and Dyer one? Imagine a bar full of identical copies of him at that moment, and that's your match day punters. And while I swear to you now that I will never, ever go in after dark to see the night-time clientele, I've seen what traipses up and down the Bigg Market and into places like this; it's that whooping, saggy-titted, fight-starting, overpainted dog mess that we all know and avoid like the chlamydia. For the love of God, when these women are getting ready and they say to their mates or their husband or whoever, 'How do I look?' why, instead of saying, 'You look nice, dear,' can someone not say, 'Christ; sort yourself out. You look like Eddie Izzard'? It's like; you get Daytime TV fashion spots where they wheel out some old trout for a makeover, slap too much blusher on her mush, spruce up the beans-on-toast perm, and stuff her into some horrendously inappropriate black and gold dress. 'Eeeh!' they say, 'I might get a (giggle) Toy Boy! I look a million dollars!' No, love; you look like a gift-wrapped body bag with a broken zip. And you're making me feel sick. Now stamp your feet, pull your knickers up, pick up your tabs, and fuck off.

For: The advert that I got handed on the way out has a convenient pocket-sized fixture list on the back.
Against: Ah, man. Where do you start?

There's a Pig & Whistle in Stockholm. There is: I saw it with my own eyes. I would have nipped in for a Spendrups or a Pripps, but with even Swedish cooking lager heading for four and a half quid a pint, the name alone was enough to put me off. I'm obviously aware that the whole fucking world has already seen it, but if you search one more time on Google for 'sthlmvip' and 'pig & whistle' you will come across the pictures that show the contrast between Sweden and here, all nicely packaged in a PowerPoint presentation. And while I know the Stockholm pics weren't taken in their Pig & Whistle, there's no harm in having one more chuckle at the expense of the typical Bigg Market punter.

Popworld

14 Bigg Market, NE1 1UW
'The stylish café-bar with pavement terrace'

A few years ago a bunch of bright sparks made a big hoo-hah about smartening up the Bigg Market. Was it the council, or was it private investment? I dunno, but some flaming half-a-job outfit gave the area a much-needed facelift, improved the quality of life by putting in new seats, restored the fountain, and tried to bring it more into line with the Grainger Town regeneration around the corner, only to then wreck it all by allowing this place to open up slap-bang in the middle. Maybe it was lack of funding, maybe it was internal politics, or maybe some lazy get just pissed off early on a Friday night before the paperwork was finished, but somehow the stylish café-bar with pavement terrace from the original blueprint failed to appear, and instead there's now a loathsome pop nostalgia pub. From the outside Popworld is an insult to the building that houses it, and from the inside it's an affront to everything I've ever held dear. Here we are having a shocking time, wondering exactly why we've just been charged festival prices for standard lager in a shit-tip like this. These punters are really annoying me tonight, pillocking about to some minor chart entry from yesteryear, one that was abysmal when it first went down and tastes no better now it's being burped back up. And they're staring at us - not glancing but glaring outright - with expressions that quiz, Why are you so miserable? Why are you not having fun? Whoo! C'mon! Why? I'll tell you. I'm here because I have to be, because I need to cross this fucker off my list. I'm surrounded by some of the most appalling disco decor I've ever seen, with terrible pop star cartoons and a whole gallery of glitter wigs and those frigging cowboy hats. This being the Bigg Market's closest thing to a gay bar, there is a fifteen stone mohicaned lesbian rampaging about, knocking people flying; none of them seem to mind, though, because it's a FUN pub and accidents will happen, even if they require surgery to put right. I'm propping up this padded rail because I'm knackered, and because there are no chairs of any description. And I'm miserable because I'm being danced at by a mother-and-daughter team, who I can just smell are looking for love and are clearly not fussed who gets the beef and who gets the dripping. What the fucking HELL was that? That gimpy twat DJ - him, over there on the dancefloor in that ball that looks like an oversized Christmas ornament from the saddest tree in the street - has just upped the bass on his system and literally bounced me off the rail and up against the claggy table. I've taken all I can stand of this. There is no need for this enforced jollity when I could be more happily occupied being tortured in a third world death camp somewhere. Here, mate: do you want this pint? I've barely touched it, swear down. You can have it. We're fucking out of here.

For: Nothing.
Against: The cocktails are so knowingly dire that the menu's admission of 'comes with a straw' is seen as a major selling point.

Dancing is a bloody ridiculous pastime. If we're such intelligent creatures, then how come evolution hasn't stamped it out yet? I know it's a throwback to the dawn of time when we were just another species struggling for survival and maybe a bit of domination as a bonus. I know it's a prelude to mating, that it's supposed to be erotic, and that the attraction of drumbeats is that they replicate the increased heart rate of the sexual act. I know all that, but I'm still having trouble tying it in with the vision before me, galumphing about with her elbows wedged into her waist and her wrists hanging limply in front. I can't decide which she more closely resembles: is it a Tyrannosaurus Rex, or is it Tommy Cooper in drag? Either way, I have no desire to breed with the pedal-pushered troll.

Pumphreys

44 Cloth Market, NE1 5UF
'Cheapskates and bandit-slaves'

For all our incessant and frankly tedious carping about how bars should be left alone, looking at the state of Pumphreys these days, it appears we might have to have a rethink. Because this pub, this grubby, neglected, stinking hovel of decay, is what Balmbra's down the street might have been like if it had been left untouched by the soft, healing hands of those loveable pub chains. With a carpet that leaves sticky standing at the bus stop and is roaring off towards sodden, everywhere you look the bog-standard - for 1918 - English pub decor is starting to look more than just a bit tatty. And while I'm never going to appear on Life of Grime tsk-tsking about the squalor of the nation's cities, I always worry when the wallpaper on the sloped ceiling directly beneath the toilets is peeling off and sliding down the necks of the punters below. Who is responsible for this? And which idiot designed those toilets? Wee Jimmy Krankie? Seriously, if you're over four feet tall you'd be better off running up the street to the Beehive or the public bogs, because if you unleash the beast in these pissers, you'll splash your bloody chin never mind your trousers. Look, I know I'm basing this on a selective viewpoint; I'm clearly not fucking mad enough to go at night when the rest of the Bigg Market piles in and starts setting about the fixtures and fittings. But every time I've been in here before the match, dragged in against my will by cheapskates and bandit-slaves, there's always been an unbroken line of watery-eyed old wheezers, clinging onto the bar for dear life like it's some sort of Touch The Truck competition. What the fuck are you so scared of,

Grandpa? The man on the other side of the room wearing your jacket and your greasy flat cap? It's a mirror, you silly old fool. Jesus, what the hell is that smell? I'm sure I know it from somewhere. It's... it's... it's like I've been scratching my nadbag on a hot summer's day, fresh from a three mile run in my nylon shorts. That's what it is. And it ain't pleasant.

For: I came in here the day Shearer broke Milburn's record. Abysmal though it is, Pumphreys will always be a part of my mental image of that day.
Against: Has anyone got the number for Mitchells & Butlers? I think I might have a suggestion for their next compulsory purchase.

Pumphreys used to have a bloke behind the bar who bore - if you'd just spent an hour staring at the sun - a faint resemblance to Chris 'fucking' Moyles. It's a shame he doesn't work there anymore, because it robs us of the opportunity to set down in print our opinions about the self-appointed saviour of Radio One. Actually, bollocks to that. We will not be denied by the turnover of bar staff. We'd like to state this here, clearly, both on and off the record. Moyles: cunt. His toadying hangers-on: bigger cunts. And anyone who's put up with any of his prattle and thereby kept him in a job all these years: the biggest cunts of all.

Rewind
31 Groat Market, NE1 1RE
'By kids for kids'

Now on its fourth incarnation, Rewind is aiming to succeed where Macey's, Lord Chancellor's and Pop! at this site have all obviously failed. Once again we have to haul our sorry arse down the Groat Market to try to spot the tiny changes. And you know what? We can't even be bothered to get annoyed about it. Instead, there's just a bored indifference, like some poor bloke stuck outside the changing rooms in Top Shop, witnessing an endless parade of interchangeable yet wholly unsuitable jeans emerging from behind the curtain. What about these, he's forced to consider. Yeah, whatever, is the half-hearted reply, knowing fine well that there'll only be three months' wear in the bloody things anyway. Look, there's just no point in raging about this place any more. It's clearly not meant for the likes of us. It's a bar run by kids for kids. Simple as that. They say your heart beats more slowly as you grow older, and your perception of time changes accordingly; that an hour to a child seems like forever, but to a bitter, thirty-summat, hacked-off pub reviewer, it's only the time it takes to mix a cocktail in some pompous, gloomy wankbar near the station. And that must be the reason why this bar sees no problem with the idea of Rewind-ing all the way back to the golden age of Girls Aloud six months previously and making a fucking theme out of it. That's the only logical explanation I can find. Like I said, I'm not in the mood to take the piss, so the sub-Mondrian geometric patterns and the bad black paintings of the likes of Wham and Grace Jones on the horrible purple walls will have to go un-ridiculed. Likewise the bulbous orange lights and the white daubs on the walls outlining the silhouettes of people dancing and livin' it up. Actually, scrap that. They're not slipping that one past me. Those white lines would have been ones of chalk, marking where the fuckers had been put against the wall and pumped full of lead, if this was my bar. Dancing? In the sodding pub? Summary execution's what they really want.

For: Decent pint, strangely enough.
Against: '...plus drinks, sweets and games to bring back those fond memories.'

We're not saying it's been done on the cheap or anything, but after going to the expense of putting in some new sinks in the gents, they clearly didn't feel like putting their hands in their pockets for a new bench to fit them into. Don't be taking off your rings when you wash your hands, or they'll be straight down the penny-pinching four-inch gap in the fittings. Hang on? Wash your hands in a bar like this? Who the hell are we trying to kid?

Yel

Centro House, Bigg Market, NE1 1EE
'With horseradish and chunky fries'

I would like to use the review of Yel to express my feelings to anyone who has ever contacted or spoken to us about The Burglar's Dog in a positive manner. Thanks to your encouragement and your desires to see this project followed through to its logical A-Z conclusion, reaching the letter Y has left me with a sense of bitter resentment about ever starting the stupid project in the first place. Yel is, simply put, unfathomably bad. One of Ultimate Leisure's travesties, Yel heaps further shame on the already tarnished Bigg Market and underlines why only complete demolition could ever save this entire area from eternal damnation. Like the wifey in the gypsy caravan parked at the other end of the street claiming SHE is the real Rose Lee and all the others are liars and fakes, Yel tugs on your sleeve and insists that IT is the original home of good times. I can tell you without fear of contradiction that it is no such fucking thing. I should have known that I was in for a spectacularly miserable time when I saw all the framed photos of Yel's gurning punters on the stairwell down to the bar. Look at the bloody plight of those idiots. And look at the captions they've got for each snap of insensible, lobotomised juveniles; how in the hell does droppin' your Gs mean you're havin' fun? They want shootin', every single one of them. Pushing open the doors to this, possibly the worst bar we have ever been in, we come across a tepid Frankenstein theme, with reanimation equipment and various bzzz things stuck wherever they couldn't fit a plasma screen. There's a cheap stained-glass effect on just about every surface, and pathetic sub-Hammer House lights in the gaps in between. We'd done some prior research on Yel - mainly in the hope of finding that it had been shut down - and had been assured by their website that we would be served by a 'tasty barmaid'. I can only assume they meant in the culinary sense, maybe with horseradish and chunky fries, because our wet-permed button pusher has a face like the man in the moon hit with a frying pan. And I don't know what the fuck she's done to to our drinks, but there are poisonous frogs in the Amazonian rain forests that are far more appetising than the so-called beer we've been lumbered with. We have a choice here: should we stand on one of the galleries overlooking the dancefloor, or would it be better to loiter by the pole-skewered stage at the far end to watch the 'legendary' degrading party games? In the end we decide on neither and head for the quiz machine in the corner, turning our backs on the horror behind us. And, in the time it takes us to force down no more than an inch of our frothing lager-style slop, we've cleaned the cunt out, winning enough to not only refund our stake and our drinks bill, but ample cash for a maxi bottle of Listerine and a taxi to hospital. They tell our lass that the blindness is only temporary.

For: There can be no 'For' for a place this poor. It defies positivity.

Against: Dodging the hole in the floor of the stinking, mouldy bogs, I see the machine on the wall vending vibrators, tickling sticks and other battery-operated gadgets. Why? This is a bar for adolescents, recklessly wasting the prime of their lives. What's the world coming to if Yel's kids, blessed with hormones, agility and enthusiasm, are still in need of sex 'aids'? Wait until you get to my age, son.

The quiz we shafted? The one based on Nuts magazine, the mag for inadequate onanists too scared of mummy's knowledge of the internet cache and too damned stumpy to reach the top shelf in the paper shop. Our gruelling mental challenge went something like this: Q1 - Are you a virgin? Q2 - You really think Nikki, 19, from Crawley gets a sog-on when she's hoovering, don't you? Q3 - Your pink T-shirt is an hour out of date. Will you spend £55 on another pink T-shirt on our say-so? Q4 - Rank these football-related items in order of importance: Haircuts, wives, close-ups of injuries, her off Soccer AM's arse. Bonus round: Touch this picture of tits. Q5 - Have you just lost your mess in the coin slot? Jackpot.

For more of this vituperative cage-rattling, plus monthly updates of knee-jerk spite on the topics of the day, visit

www.theburglarsdog.co.uk

Go on, man.

Index

Read more from Tonto Press:

Wor Al

A Fans' Tribute To Alan Shearer
Edited by Paul Brown and Stuart Wheatman
Tonto Press 2006
ISBN 0955218330, paperback, 192 pages, £7.99

Shear class: 206 goals for Newcastle, 173 more for Southampton and Blackburn, plus 30 for England. A total of 409 goals in 733 top-level games - Alan Shearer's record speaks for itself. But what do Alan's many fans have to say about their hero?

This unique tribute to the England hero and Geordie legend looks at Alan's brilliant career through the eyes of fanzine, website and terrace writers. Crammed with goals, games and wonderful memories, it is a fantastic celebration of a true football great - Our Alan, Wor Al.

The book contains more than 30 features written by some of Shearer's biggest fans, plus illustration sketches by *Football Weekly* artist, Tony O'Donnell.

The publisher will donate 50p from each copy sold to the Alan Shearer Testimonial Fund, benefiting the NSPCC.

Available from bookshops and www.tontopress.com

Read more from Tonto Press:

The Unofficial Football World Championships:

An Alternative Soccer History
by Paul Brown
Tonto Sport 2006
ISBN 0955218314, paperback, 184pp, £9.99

We all love the official World Cup, but it only comes around every four years... Welcome to the unofficial alternative.

What if football's world championships pitched teams into a continuous series of boxing-style title matches running way back to the very first international game in 1872? That's the idea behind the Unofficial Football World Championships (UFWC) - probably the least-known but most exciting football competition on Earth.

The UFWC title has been contested by almost 100 nations at more than 800 matches spanning over 130 years. Its amazing story involves legendary teams and footballing minnows, classic finals and forgotten friendlies, and celebrated players and unsung heroes.

This official guide to the UFWC is packed full of classic matches, key players, and fascinating statistics. Irreverent and entertaining, it adds up to an alternative soccer history - and represents a fresh perspective on the most beloved sport in the world.

Available from bookshops and www.tontopress.com

Read more from Tonto Press:

Dial M For Monkey

by Adam Maxwell
Tonto Press 2006
ISBN 0955218322, paperback, 124 pp, £7.99

Adam Maxwell's first collection of short stories is inventive, funny, dark, and hugely entertaining. The twenty stories included here range from a bizarre quest to find a dead rockstar's limb (Jim Morrison's Leg) to a memorable warning about the hidden dangers of building sites (the acclaimed Shooting Jelly With A Shotgun). Effortlessly fusing pop culture, gunplay, and simians, Dial M For Monkey contains a vibrant mixture of short stories.

Tonto Short Stories

Edited by Paul Brown and Stuart Wheatman
Tonto Press 2006
ISBN 0955218306, paperback, 224 pp, £9.99

Tonto Press launches its search for new writing talent with an anthology of twenty fresh stories by twenty exciting writers. Eclectic, absorbing, affecting, and memorable, this page-turning collection represents the very best of short but sweet original fiction. 'Book of the Month' – The Crack. 'To say that English writers don't take risks is stuff and nonsense, as this collection proves' – San Diego Union-Tribune.

Available from bookshops and www.tontopress.com